Chaucer's
Troilus and Criseyde

TITLES OF RELATED INTEREST

from the Unwin Critical Library

The Canterbury Tales
Derek Pearsall

The Faerie Queene
Humphrey Tonkin

Chaucer's
Troilus and Criseyde

C. David Benson

London
UNWIN HYMAN
Boston   Sydney   Wellington

Published by the Academic Division of

Unwin Hyman Ltd
15/17 Broadwick Street, London W1V 1FP, UK

Unwin Hyman Inc.,
955 Massachusetts Avenue, Cambridge, Mass, 02139, USA

Allen & Unwin (Australia) Ltd,
8 Napier Street, North Sydney, NSW 2060, Australia

Allen & Unwin (New Zealand) Ltd in association with the
Port Nicholson Press Ltd,
Compusales Building, 75 Ghuznee Street, Wellington 1, New Zealand

First published in 1990

British Library Cataloguing in Publication Data
Benson, C. David
    Chaucer's Troilus and Criseyde
    1. Poetry in English. Chaucer, Geoffrey 1340?–1400
    I. Title
    821.1

    ISBN 0-04-800085-X

Library of Congress Cataloging in Publication Data
Benson, C. David.
        Chaucer's Troilus and Criseyde / C. David Benson
        p.   cm.
        Includes bibliographical reference and index.
        ISBN 0-04-800085-X (HB)
        1. Chaucer, Geoffrey, d. 1400.   Troilus and Criseyde.   1.   Title.
    PR1896.B46   1990   90-39824
    821′.1–dc20   71492   CIP

Typeset in 10/11.5 Plantin
Printed in Great Britain by Billing and Sons Ltd., London and Worcester

Contents

FOR MY PARENTS
AND BERNICE

Acknowledgements

I wish to thank the John Simon Guggenheim Memorial Foundation for a fellowship during 1989 that gave me the time to complete this work. I also wish to thank the Research Foundation of the University of Connecticut and its director Thomas Giolas for their generous support over the years.

My debt to students at the University of Connecticut with whom I have read Chaucer is great, and I am under a special obligation to a wonderful graduate seminar on *Troilus* at the University of Virginia during the spring of 1987. They know how much I have learned from them.

I am grateful to a number of academic friends here at Connecticut and throughout the country, who generously read and commented on individual chapters: Stephen Barney, Piero Boitani, Frederick Biggs, Wendy Clein, Nina Dorrance, Leah Freiwald, Charlotte Gross, Linda Georgianna, Warren Ginsberg, Barbara Nolan, Sarah Stanbury, and David Wallace. I have tried to profit from their advice, though there are limits to what even such a distinguished group could accomplish. I am especially grateful to Howell Chickering and Derek Pearsall, who were generous enough to read the entire manuscript and who commented on it with their usual good judgement. They have repeatedly saved me from myself, though many obscurities and errors remain irredeemable. My research assistant Tamarah Kohanksi has heroically corrected faults both small and profound. Once again my deepest gratitude is for the learning and editorial skills of my wife, Pamela J. Benson – my first and last reader and always the most sympathetic.

A Note on the Text

All quotations in the text from the works of Chaucer are taken from the *Riverside Chaucer*, ed. Larry D. Benson *et al.* (Boston, Mass.: Houghton Mifflin, 1987). Citations of *Troilus* are by book (roman numerals) and lines (arabic numerals).

All quotations in the text from Boccaccio's *Filostrato* are taken from the edition of Vittore Branca in *Tutte le Opere di Giovanni Boccaccio*, general editor Vittore Branca, Vol. 2 (Milan: Mondadori, 1964). The poetry of *Filostrato* is cited by book and stanza (in arabic numerals); the prose prologue is cited by page numbers. The prose translations, though indebted to previous translations, are my own.

1
Introduction

Despite its widely acknowledged greatness, Geoffrey Chaucer's *Troilus and Criseyde* is today too often neglected even by highly educated readers. The story itself has receded from the collective memory of our culture. The love between Troilus, prince of Troy, and Criseyde, daughter of the seer and traitor Calchas, was once a familiar literary motif in English, but their affair has become so obscure that a Japanese car company can name its most expensive model the 'Cressida' and, without irony or fear of customer scepticism, advertise it as trouble-free. Troilus' passion for Criseyde and her betrayal of him near the end of the siege of Troy appear frequently in fifteenth-century English literature (several times in the works of John Lydgate) and are found throughout the lyric poetry of the sixteenth and seventeenth centuries – in the works of such as George Gascoigne and in collections like *Tottel's Miscellany* (Rollins; Benson, 'True Troilus'). The love-story is also told at length by some of Britain's major poets. In addition to Chaucer's *Troilus*, the great Scots poet Robert Henryson gives a harrowing account of Criseyde's later life in his *Testament of Cresseid*, Shakespeare makes the affair the centre of his corrosive 'problem play' *Troilus and Cressida*, and John Dryden, in his sentimental tragedy of the same name (significantly subtitled *Truth Found Too Late*), reveals that Criseyde's supposed betrayal was all a terrible misunderstanding, for she was always true to Troilus and wanted nothing more than to return from the Greek camp.

The affair of Troilus and Criseyde came to be accepted in English literature as a classical love-story like those of Jason and Medea or Ulysses and Penelope, but the ancient world knew nothing of their passion. Although the events of the Trojan War form the oldest secular narrative in the West, the love between Troilus and Criseyde is a purely medieval creation. The names of the principal figures in the story (Troilus, Calchas, Pandarus and, of course, Diomede, Hector, Sarpedon and Cassandra) go back to Homer's *Iliad* (even Criseyde can be recognized in Criseis), but the affair itself is found nowhere in classical literature. Nor does it appear in those influential medieval pseudo-histories, the *De Excidio Troiae Historia* (attributed to Dares the Phrygian) and the *Ephemeridos de Historia Belli Troiani* (attributed to Dictys the Cretan), two brief prose works dating from the early centuries of the Christian era, which the Middle Ages believed contained the true eyewitness record of the Trojan War in contrast to the poetic fancies of Homer and Virgil.

The love-story first appears in Benoît de Sainte-Maure's long French poem *Roman de Troie* (*c.*1160), which transformed the meagre details of Dares and Dictys into a lavish romance of the pagan world with a distinctly pro-Trojan bias. In addition to long battle-accounts and exotic architectural marvels such as Hector's tomb, Benoît, who has a special interest in human psychology, includes accounts of several love-stories in his narrative: the fatal passion of Paris for Helen and of Achilles for Polyxena are retold along with the entirely original affair of Troilus and Briseida (as Benoît calls the character who was later known as Criseyde). The account of these new Trojan lovers occurs in episodes interspersed throughout the narrative and serves an important structural function (Lumiansky). In contrast to Chaucer's version of the affair, Benoît tells us nothing about Briseida's life with Troilus before her father requests that she be returned to him in the Greek camp. The French poet begins his version only with the parting of the lovers, and he then goes on to tell of Troilus' growing despair after being separated from his beloved and of Briseida's decision, not without regret and hesitation, to accept Diomede as her new lover. Although he sympathetically represents the thoughts and feelings of Briseida, Benoît draws a conventional lesson from the affair about the untrustworthiness of women.

In the next century Benoît's romance was translated with significant modifications by Guido delle Colonne as the *Historia Destructionis Troiae* (1287). The earnest seriousness of the *Historia* (Benoît's pagan marvels are much reduced, for instance), as well as its increased learning and composition in sober Latin prose, ensured its acceptance throughout Europe until well after the Renaissance as the standard history of the Trojan War. Guido retains all the details of Benoît's numerous accounts of battle, but he is much less interested than his predecessor in affairs of the heart. The episode of Troilus and Briseida, in particular, is briefer and cruder in the *Historia* than in the *Roman*. Guido has little sympathy for either lover, but his particular contribution to the tradition is to lengthen and intensify Benoît's anti-feminist passages, as in the following example: 'Accordingly, what is to be said about the constancy of women, whose sex has as its property to dissolve its plans with sudden frailty and to change and be fickle in the shortest time? For it does not fall to a man to be able to describe their ficklenesses and wiles, since their flighty intentions are more wicked than it is possible to say' (Guido, 166; trans. Meek, 160).

The first full version of the love-story that is not merely one episode among many in the history of the Trojan War but an independent text of its own is Giovanni Boccaccio's fourteenth-century Italian poem *Il Filostrato*. *Filostrato* is the principal source for Chaucer's *Troilus and Criseyde* and establishes the shape of the story that would be followed by all later writers: Boccaccio adds a long account of how the couple fall in love, introduces the character of Pandarus as friend and go-between, and first calls the heroine by the name Criseida. Although Boccaccio draws no overt moral lessons during the course of the narrative and generally treats the affair with interest and apparent admiration (he claims it reflects his own amorous history), *Filostrato* does contain a brief formal *moralitas* near its end that insists, as do the versions of Benoît and Guido, on the guilt of Criseida and on such behaviour as representative of the general unreliability of her kind: 'Giovane donna, e mobile e vogliosa/è negli amanti molti' ('a young woman is fickle and desirous of many lovers', 8.30). Boccaccio's lesson is addressed exclusively to men, and the values it promotes are secular rather than Christian. It tells men to beware of women's faithlessness in love without addressing either male fidelity or the general sinfulness of illicit sexual passion itself.

Despite differences of intensity and expression by individual writers, the same lesson appears in all examples of the medieval story of Troilus and Criseyde known to Chaucer (Mieszkowski): Criseyde's betrayal of Troilus illustrates the fickleness and deceit of womankind. Although he is fully aware of this traditional conclusion, Chaucer deliberately does not repeat such condemnations in *Troilus and Criseyde*, as we shall see, but instead repeatedly attempts to mitigate his heroine's guilt. The need for such an explicit anti-feminist lesson was strongly felt by some of the earliest readers of Chaucer's poem, however. The beautiful final lines of *Troilus*, which recommend the love of Christ instead of the vagaries of human affection, seem not to have been thought a sufficiently clear moral to the story, and several attempts were made to remedy the perceived defect.

The conclusions that were appended to Chaucer's poem are far from unexpected and tend to repeat the familiar anti-feminist lesson of earlier versions of the story. The second printed edition of Chaucer's *Troilus* (1517) by Wynkyn de Worde, for instance, ends with three new and rather inept rhyme-royal stanzas, under the impudent title 'The Auctour', that denounce Criseyde as 'woman most vnkynde' while making the general statement that 'There is no woman I thynke heuen vnder/That can be trewe' (Benson and Rollman). Wynkyn's stanzas had limited influence on later readers; but, beginning with Thynne's standard edition of 1532, another, more significant ending was attached to *Troilus* and generally accepted as Chaucer's own: Robert Henryson's short but brilliant *Testament of Cresseid*, which tells of Cresseid's life in the Greek camp.

Henryson plays on the fact that Chaucer (like Boccaccio) does not tell us what happens to the heroine after she has rejected Troilus for Diomede, forcing the Scots narrator, as he claims at the beginning of the *Testament*, to turn to another book to supplement the information in *Troilus*. Moreover, even though Henryson treats Cresseid's guilt, punishment and possible redemption with great moral sophistication (and I believe sympathy), the startling new information he provides about her life in the Greek camp (that she became a common prostitute after being rejected by Diomede and died a grotesque leper) quickly became absorbed into the received story and gave later, less subtle English poets even more ammunition for facile moralizing and anti-feminist attacks. To give just one example of many, Thomas Howell in his short poem 'The Britlenesse of Thinges Mortal' (*c.*1570) dwells on the leprous decay invented by Henryson ('Her comely corpes that Troylus did delight/All pust with plages full lothsomly there lay') and accepts Criseyde's miserable death with smug satisfaction: 'Lo here the end of wanton wicked life.' Even Shakespeare's *Troilus and Cressida*, especially through the figure of Thersites, expresses the standard censorious attitude towards Criseyde and towards women as a whole.

Chaucer's *Troilus and Criseyde* is unique in its time and remained exceptional thereafter in refusing to make Criseyde an *exemplum* of feminine wickedness. The narrator is quick to defend his heroine even against an imagined attack by 'som envious' persons that she falls in love with Troilus too quickly (II.666–79). Later his advocacy is more severely tested, though never found wanting. The proem to book IV regretfully announces that the subject of the poem must now be 'how Criseyde Troilus forsook', but that accusation is instantly softened: 'Or at the leeste, how that she was unkynde' (IV.15–16). As he relates Criseyde's hesitant acceptance of Diomede's entreaties, the narrator continues to find extenuating excuses. He is certainly critical when Criseyde gives Diomede a gift that she had received from Troilus ('that was litel nede', V.1040), but he refuses to confirm that she ever really loved the Greek and instead pleads ignorance: 'Men seyn – I not [know not] – that she yaf hym hire herte' (V.1050). As Criseyde irrevocably gives up Troilus for Diomede, the narrator insists on her grief (V.1052–3), and he repeatedly expresses his own sympathy for her plight: 'And if I myghte excuse hire any wise,/For she so sory was for hire untrouthe,/Iwis, I wolde excuse hire yet for routhe' (V.1097–9). *Troilus* even anticipates Dryden in briefly entertaining the possibility that the accusations against his heroine might be nothing but malicious lies (IV.19–21). Although some have argued that the effect of the narrator's extreme solicitude is to arouse our suspicion against Criseyde, it nevertheless remains true that the text of *Troilus and Criseyde* repeatedly expresses compassion for its heroine and never draws the anti-feminist moral found in all previous versions of the story. In fact, near the end of the poem women are specifically addressed and told that if the narrative teaches anything it is exactly the opposite of the usual warning: 'Beth war of men, and herkneth what I seye!' (V.1785).

This surprising lesson against men, even if its primary effect is thought to be comic, alerts us to the striking moral openness of *Troilus*. Chaucer is the first writer who does not attach to this tale of Trojan love a condemnation of its heroine and with her all womankind.[1] The refusal of Chaucer's narrator to endorse the usual anti-feminist lesson reveals a general reluctance in the poem to draw moral conclusions about any of its characters or about the love-affair itself. The story of Troilus and Criseyde that Chaucer inherited and introduced into English literature was strongly and conventionally moralistic, but his poem instead asks readers to defer judgement and to consider alternative interpretations (such as the untrustworthiness of men). We may detect in *Troilus* something of the dialectic method of contemporary scholastic thought or the deliberate irresolution of the medieval debate poems, which deal with the sort of questions (which is better water or wine? summer or winter?) that can never have a final answer.

The lack of moral closure in *Troilus*, especially in respect to Criseyde, has some precedence in both Benoît's *Roman de Troie* and Boccaccio's *Filostrato*, despite the anti-feminist lessons each offers. Benoît gives his heroine a long final speech whose many inner contradictions (at one point she represents herself as a selfish opportunist, at another point as a pitiful victim and so on) suggest the radically different ways in which she might be interpreted. The openness of *Filostrato*, by contrast, is largely the result of silence, for even though Boccaccio concludes his work with the usual censure of women he allows the body of the narrative itself to unfold with little explicit authorial comment. Although Chaucer develops his *Troilus* with many narrative statements, it has its own kind of reticence, such as the deliberate opaqueness of the characterization of Criseyde, as we shall see in later chapters, but the primary way in which the English poem achieves openness is through multiplicity. Chaucer follows the general narrative structure of *Filostrato*, but he continually alters and supplements it with a range of different kinds of material.

What follows in this book is a study of the profound and often contradictory ways in which Chaucer transforms his source. No argument for the death of the author will be offered here. *Troilus* is the conscious product of a long series of specific decisions, which are available to our scrutiny, undertaken as Chaucer reshapes Boccaccio's *Filostrato*. But, if the text of *Troilus* is a deliberate creation of its author, the result is anything but simple. Chaucer's changes do not alter his source in any one direction, nor do they produce an organic whole. Instead *Troilus* contains something like the many roads to Rome mentioned in the proem to book II. Chaucer has transformed Boccaccio's contained if elegant romance garden into a much more spacious, dense and challenging landscape. On any one journey through *Troilus*, individual readers will necessarily look closely at some things and not at others, but such readers should always be aware of the alternative sights and routes, perhaps even the forking paths, that are also available, both to other readers and to themselves on different occasions.

Although *Troilus* is a poem I have read many times, probably more often than any other single literary work, whenever I pick it up I feel that I am experiencing it for the first time. It is not just that I find new ways of interpreting familiar episodes, for that is common enough with any piece of great literature; rather, with each reading there are passages, even scenes, that I seem to be encountering for the first time, as though I were walking through a familiar neighbourhood and came upon an interesting old building that I could not remember ever seeing before. For a long time I was embarrassed by my inability to master the poem, assuming that it was a clear sign of mental deficiency or decay, but when I finally dared to mention the phenomenon to others who knew the poem well I discovered to my surprise and delight that they, too, had similar experiences. I think this says something significant about the multiplicity of *Troilus*. Perhaps it is the very simplicity of the plot, whose main action can be summarized in a few sentences, that allows Chaucer's development in over 8,000 lines to be so intricate and diverse.

Of course I am far from the first to announce the multiplicity of *Troilus*. As Derek Brewer has recently written, Chaucer's poem contains 'no single dominant point of view, no single perspective' ('Comedy', 106). In a felicitous image, Miskimin compares the complex overlapping layers of *Troilus* (which 'yields evidence to reading after reading, few of which can be called false, and many true') to the archaeological site of 'Schliemann's multi-leveled Troy' (196). Yet, even though many critics have recognized the variety of Chaucer's poem, their actual analyses tend to limit the work rather than acknowledge its full plurality. Whatever they say, in practice they usually discuss only a few aspects of *Troilus* as though they were the whole poem.

In one of the most influential articles ever written on *Troilus*, C. S. Lewis noted four ways in which the English poem was different from *Filostrato*: Chaucer, unlike Boccaccio, approached his work as a poet of *history*, *rhetoric*, *doctrine* and *courtly love* ('What Chaucer'). Lewis's detailed analysis of the ways in which Chaucer transformed *Filostrato* is persuasive, but it does not go far enough. The four identified qualities make too neat and coherent a pattern, which Lewis sees as a general 'process of medievalization' that

Filostrato underwent at Chaucer's hands (56). True as this may be, it is not the whole truth, for it fails to account for the full spectrum of different materials that Chaucer has added to *Troilus*. One could easily demonstrate that Chaucer has also transformed *Filostrato* with elements that are precisely opposite to the four named by Lewis. In addition to history, Chaucer also supplements *Filostrato* with myth and psychology; in addition to rhetoric (by which Lewis means high rhetoric), he also supplements it with colloquialism and naturalism; in addition to doctrine, he also supplements it with broad comedy and practical human inventiveness; in addition to courtly love, he also supplements it with ideas and images that allow us to criticize such amorous devotion. Moreover, as well as medievalizing *Filostrato*, Chaucer also gives it a profound sense of the ancient past. My purpose here is not to refute Lewis, only to show that he has not said the last word. *Troilus* is more various, with many more competing layers and aspects, than most discussions of it recognize.

Literary criticism often reduces the complexity of *Troilus* to a fundamental duality, as in Charles Muscatine's famous contrast between courtly and bourgeois elements, E. Talbot Donaldson's contrast between what the narrator says in defence of Criseyde and what the text implies, or D. W. Robertson's contrast between what the text seems to say in favour of sexual love and the condemnation demanded by Christian doctrine. It is perhaps understandable that so many books and articles on *Troilus* use the concept of doubleness and contrariness in their titles or subtitles. The poem itself introduces the idea in its first line ('The double sorwe of Troilus to tellen'); and, indeed, human thought seems to fall naturally into binary patterns, as some modern philosophers argue and anyone who has tried to write at length about more than two things at once soon discovers. In the pages that follow, I shall also frequently approach some aspect of *Troilus* by presenting two contrary critical interpretations, each of which, despite their disagreements, will be shown to describe elements actually in the text. But recognition of the validity of opposite readings is just the first step in appreciating the multiplicity of *Troilus*. Medieval religious and political thought often organized the world by threes rather than by twos (as in the three orders of society: those who fight, those who pray, and those who work), and the most revealing figure in *Troilus* may not be the doubleness mentioned at the beginning of the poem but the mysterious Trinity cited at the end, whose unity and plurality contains and transcends the opposition of the human and the divine.

In my discussion I will attempt to get beyond simple dualities in order to explore the extraordinary complexity of *Troilus* that previous critics have frequently noted if not always completely demonstrated in their analyses. Too much criticism of the poem is a matter of individual assertion. Critic A tries to prove that Chaucer is a fatalist, critic B to prove that he affirms freedom of the will. Critic C believes that Criseyde is cleverly in control of events, critic D believes that she is a victim of others. Instead of adding one more vote to this scholarly poll, I want to stress how many of these apparently contrasting views have textual validity because of the many possibilities that Chaucer has allowed in *Troilus*. I am less interested in resolving the contradictions produced by the poem than in exploring their extent and diversity.

Rather than attacking previous criticism of *Troilus*, I want to show its achievements, though I am not undertaking a full summary of past scholarship. To the new student of Chaucer today the volume of published critical writing on the poet, which has dramatically increased in the last few decades, may seem to produce only an incomprehensible Babel, but the variety of these voices can help us to see the genuine multiplicity of *Troilus*. Almost all schools have something to contribute to our understanding of the poem, for criticism has been wrong less often than it has been limited. Even views that are deeply antagonistic to one another have much to teach us, if we will only listen. Exegetical critics, for instance, have exposed a strong vein of moralism in the poem that questions the value of human love, just as others have noted its celebration of human sexuality. Both groups have understood something important about the poem; their only fault is to mistake the part for the whole. *Troilus* is never only one thing, and the most satisfying readings are those that make us aware of its various possibilities.

My ambition here is not so much to offer another reading of Chaucer's *Troilus and Criseyde* as to encourage and support the readings of others. Although the following pages contain my personal biases and interpretations (how could it be otherwise?), I have tried throughout to stress the literary and moral multiplicity of *Troilus*. I have pointed out the many different layers that

Chaucer has added to his poem as well as the tensions that can be found within those layers without attempting any final resolution of this extraordinary literary diversity. Obviously, I have not been able to treat all the complexities of *Troilus*, but I hope that my discussion will help others understand the variety of this great poem and that they will continue to pursue the riches it contains. *Troilus* has much to offer modern readers, if only they will respond to its challenges. I have tried always to remain alert to the historical context in which Chaucer wrote, but I am also particularly interested in the qualities that make the poem live today.

Although I follow no particular school, in the course of writing this book I have certainly been influenced, however indirectly and superficially, by recent trends in critical theory. It might be more accurate to say that I have overheard theory rather than studied it, and my disagreements with particular theorists are fundamental as well as local: I accept the metaphysical, recognize authors as real, and value an accessible writing style. Nevertheless, recent critical thinking has forced me to ask new and unexpected questions. I have certainly learned from the widespread contemporary attack on organic unity and agree with the desire of Roland Barthes, maddening as his playfulness can be at times, to find pleasure in the multiplicity of texts. My interest in literary variety has also attracted me to the work of Mikel Bahktin, even though *dialogic* must be one of the most over-used critical terms in the last few years. One of the things I shall attempt to demonstrate in the following pages is that several recent critical concepts, startling as they may be to students of nineteenth-century literature, have been anticipated to varying degrees by traditional Chaucer criticism. I have also taken courage from the attempt of some new theorists (certainly not all) to question their own authority and to insist that they are asking questions rather than supplying answers.

If this study assumes the importance of individual poets (we shall watch Chaucer as he deliberately transforms Boccaccio's *Filostrato*), it also values the reader. Along with the general field of narratology, the recent critical approach that I have found most useful is the modern emphasis on the role of the reader. Chaucer encourages the creativity of his readers and forces them to be his collaborators. The openness and multiplicity of *Troilus* do not mean that it, like so many modern works, is morally nihilistic or even relativistic, only that interpretation is left to us. As I shall argue in chapter 3, Chaucer seems to imagine a division of labour: his job is to produce an exciting literary experience, whereas the meaning of that experience is the job of individual readers. Reader-response criticism sometimes assumes one true interpretation of a text by an ideal or super reader, but *Troilus* is always redefining itself and demanding that we respond to it as different kinds of reader (readers of romance, comedy or philosophy, for example). Any single meaning or even series of meanings claimed by the author would only limit the usefulness of *Troilus*. Chaucer trusts his audience to interpret what he has written in appropriate ways because of their shared cultural and religious values, but the openness created for the original audience of *Troilus* remains available to readers of all beliefs today.

In the chapters that follow I have somewhat resisted the appeal of narrative, though it is often strong in *Troilus*. Rather than discuss the story chronologically, which is the usual approach of previous critical studies, I have organized my discussion around several of the central topics in the poem, though these chapters generally follow the progress of the story. In this way I shall be able to look at some passages from different perspectives. I hope this book will be of special interest to those who are reading *Troilus* for the first time, but that it will not be without use for those who know it well. I begin with a discussion of Boccaccio's *Filostrato* because we can only understand what Chaucer has done in *Troilus* by understanding the source he so radically and variously transformed.

Notes

1   We have already seen this lesson in the works of Benoît, Guido, and Boccaccio, despite Benoît's sympathetic treatment of his heroine's final speech and Boccaccio's evident pleasure in retelling the affair. Although the same lesson is usual in English versions of the story after Chaucer, there are limited exceptions, some undoubtedly influenced by *Troilus* itself: a few poets present Criseyde as an ideal mistress, and fewer still, like Henryson's fellow Scotsman Henry Fowler, share the compassion of Chaucer's narrator for her plight (Benson, 'True Troilus'). Most writers, however, before

and after Chaucer, are content to repeat the standard anti-feminist conclusion. Henryson's *Testament* also uses the story to offer moral instruction, though it is moral instruction of a superior and challenging kind. Even Dryden's vindication of Criseyde is not an exception to the moralism so firmly associated with the affair, it merely reverses the usual verdict: innocent as opposed to guilty.

2

Boccaccio

The true source of Chaucer's *Troilus and Criseyde* only became known with the rise of modern scholarship. Early readers accepted Chaucer's claim that the poem was a close translation of the work of a certain Lollius (I.394). In the introduction to his 1679 play *Troilus and Cressida*, John Dryden asserted that 'the original story was written by one Lollius, a Lombard, in Latin verse, and translated by Chaucer into English' (Spurgeon, 1.254). Chaucer may have believed that Lollius was a genuine historian (as suggested by his inclusion with other writers on Troy at line 1468 of *The House of Fame*) or the poet may be indulging in a deliberate playful fiction. Whichever is true (possibly they both are), it was left for Chaucer's great eighteenth-century editor Thomas Tyrwhitt first to announce that the actual source of *Troilus and Criseyde* was in fact Giovanni Boccaccio's Italian poem in ottava rima *Il Filostrato* (Tyrwhitt 4.85–86).

Detailed accounts of Chaucer's specific borrowings from Boccaccio were undertaken in the early part of this century by Karl Young (*Origin*) and Hubertis Cummings, whereas Lewis ('What Chaucer') and Meech produced more imaginative explorations of what the English poet really owed to his Italian model. After mid-century, unfortunately, this kind of close, comparative work all but stopped when Robert Pratt announced and seemed to prove that Chaucer was probably not working directly from Boccaccio at all. Citing a long series of generally similar brief passages, none of which is itself definitive, Pratt argued that Chaucer was at least equally (and perhaps mainly) indebted to a French prose translation of *Filostrato*, the *Le Roman de Troyle et de Criseida*, attributed to a certain Beauvau, seneschal of Anjou.[1] For a generation Pratt's conclusion was widely accepted, if rarely tested, with the result that anything more than general comparisons between *Troilus* and *Filostrato* were considered futile.

Only recently has the work of Barry Windeatt ('Chaucer and *Filostrato*' and *Troilus* edition) and David Wallace ('Chaucer and Boccaccio' and *Early Writings*) restored *Filostrato* to its rightful place as the immediate and principal source of *Troilus and Criseyde*. Both critics demonstrate the English poet's sophisticated understanding of Italian and show how subtly he responded to Boccaccio's poem. They make it clear that Chaucer had read *Filostrato* closely and well. Windeatt argues that Beauvau's pedestrian prose translation had little to offer, even if (as seems unlikely) it was written before *Troilus*, and both he and Wallace justify a central assumption behind the present study: Boccaccio's *Filostrato* provides Chaucer with the fundamental matter of *Troilus and Criseyde*, the story and often the style that the English poet transforms but never ignores. As we read Chaucer in the following pages, we shall watch as he reads and rewrites Boccaccio.

Troilus and Criseyde is apparently the first narrative poem in which Chaucer depends primarily on a single source. His previous works – the *Book of the Duchess*, *The House of Fame* and *The Parliament of Foules* – owe much to French, Latin and Italian predecessors, but each is a complex mix of various influences and quite original in structure. In *Troilus and Criseyde* Chaucer is content to retell another's story. During long stretches *Troilus* matches *Filostrato* stanza for stanza, but its debt is greater even than the number of lines actually imitated.[2] Each time that Chaucer abandons *Filostrato* (to add the scene at Deiphebus' house, for example, or Troilus' long speech on predestination from Boethius), he always returns to the Italian narrative. As well as providing the outlines of the love-story, *Filostrato* also suggested to Chaucer some of the ways by which he might go about transforming that story. As we shall see, much of what seems most powerful and original in the English poem, from its rhetorical sophistication to its pathos, has its origin, in some form or other, in Boccaccio.

Chaucerians usually cite *Filostrato* only to measure the more brilliant achievement of *Troilus and Criseyde*. In later chapters we, too, shall look back to Boccaccio and see how often Chaucer transmuted dross (and sometimes silver) into literary gold, but first it seems appropriate to try to discover those virtues in the Italian poem that first attracted the English poet. For the moment, let us speculate about the reasons that Chaucer might have thought *Filostrato* worthy to be the foundation for his greatest finished work. We shall try to view the poem from Chaucer's perspective and imagine what he liked about it. In this chapter, *Filostrato* will be treated not as an ugly Italian duckling that was metamorphosed into a lovely English swan, but as a valuable and innovative work in its own right. We must come to know *Filostrato* and appreciate its achievement before we can understand that of *Troilus and Criseyde*.

The Art of 'Filostrato'

Boccaccio is largely responsible for the shape of the story of Troilus and Criseyde as we know it today. In Benoît and Guido the tale is only one event, beginning *in medias res* with the departure of Briseida from Troy and told intermittently, among the larger ruin of the Trojan War. Boccaccio detaches the story from the rest of the history of Troy, expands its particulars, and adds three long opening parts that tell how the lovers meet, fall in love, and consummate their passion. While rarely contradicting the particulars in Benoît, Boccaccio also seems to have drawn on material from a wide variety of medieval retellings of the Trojan story, none of which can be considered his primary source (Gozzi; Wallace, *Early Writings*, 74). What had been before only a relatively brief example of female faithlessness becomes in his hands a fully developed narrative of the rise and fall of a passionate love-affair.

After a prose prologue in which the narrator declares that he has chosen to tell this story because it mirrors his own troubles in love, part 1 of *Filostrato* relates how Criseida (as she is now called instead of Benoît's Briseida) is left behind in Troy when her father, the seer Calchas, deserts to the Greeks. At the first sight of the young widow during a spring religious festival, the Trojan prince Troiolo falls instantly in love. *Filostrato* then describes at length Troiolo's solitary love-pangs, which are somewhat similar to those of Benoît's Diomede, before introducing an original character, Criseida's cousin Pandaro. By means of his friend Pandaro, Troiolo woos the cautious but not unwilling Criseida, until she welcomes him into her bed in part 3. Only in part 4, when Calchas asks that Criseida be returned to him, does Boccaccio pick up the story as it is found in Benoît and Guido.

Filostrato is the work of a young man and was apparently composed in 1335 when Boccaccio was in his early twenties.[3] It has a clear, energetic narrative line (the gift for story-telling fully realized in *Decameron* is already evident here) and follows no single source and no single style. The Trojan poem lacks the extensive classical learning of *Teseida* and the complex structure of *Filocolo*, two other narratives from approximately the same period in Boccaccio's career; instead it offers a relatively direct story that explores at length the private emotions of a small group of characters. *Filostrato* is a unique work in Boccaccio's canon and in many ways, despite its vaguely Ovidian tone, it is unlike any other literary work that would have been known to Chaucer. His encounter with it would make him a very different poet.

One aspect of *Filostrato* that must have attracted Chaucer is its rich mixture of learned and popular literary traditions. Boccaccio's variety of styles and skill at combining high and low literary genres provided a powerful model for Chaucer's own practice in *Troilus and Criseyde*. Boccaccio's imitation of high poetic style is clear as early as the elaborate opening invocation to his 'bella donna' (1.1–6), which cites Jove, Apollo and the Muses. The formal division of *Filostrato* into parts in the manner of epic also signals a bid for literary distinction. Although the poem contains little of the learning that marks the Italian trecento as a whole and much of Boccaccio's other work, it occasionally echoes a moment from classical poetry, such as the account of 'la fama velocissima' ('most swift fame' 4.78) from 4.174 *Aeneid*. Boccaccio also gives Troiolo a long speech in praise of love with several classical references derived from Boethius's *Consolation of Philosophy* (3.74–80), a work that Chaucer himself translated and that would become his second most important source for *Troilus*. In addition, *Filostrato* contains such sophisticated rhetorical elements as the long letters exchanged between the lovers and their speeches to each other, to Pandaro, and to themselves when alone.[4] Wallace notes the limitations of Boccaccio's literary skills – for example, his attempt to imitate an epic simile from *Aeneid* (9.435–7) at 4.18 ends in 'disarray' (*Early Writings*, 134) – but the effort itself reveals the young poet's ambition to follow the greatest authors of the past.

In addition to its attempts to imitate classical poetry *Filostrato* also contains much that is popular. Ever since Branca's pioneering study, *Il Cantare Trecentesco*, it has been generally accepted that Boccaccio was powerfully influenced by the Italian *cantare*. These unsophisticated poems, which flourished especially in the fourteenth century and were usually designed for recitation in the piazza, turned common romance plots and other traditional stories into lively, often extravagant verse narratives. Mixing naïve piety with cheerful sensuality, and crude comedy with an interest in mystery and magic, the *cantari* have been persuasively compared to Middle English metrical romances, especially those in tail-rhyme (Havely, 7; and especially Wallace, *Early Writings*). Like their English counterparts, the *cantari* were designed for a general audience, and, as a result, their plots tend to be clear, fast-moving and continually exciting. Story and audience involvement are paramount.

According to Wallace, Boccaccio was apparently 'the first major author to involve himself with the *cantare*' (*Early Writings*, 90). *Filostrato* is composed in a similar metre (stanzas of eight hendecasyllabic lines rhyming abababcc) and contains other specific elements of the genre, including the use of simple epithets and formulas (such as 'cuor del mio corpo' – 'heart of my body' – at 3.50, 4.90, 4.145, 5.59), and proverbial phrases and homely similes, such as comparing the fire of love to a blacksmith's fire (3.68) or saying that the ladies who come to comfort Criseida are 'scratching her heels when her head itched', 4.85). *Filostrato* shares even more fundamental similarities with the *cantari*. Their frank sensuality and attempts to invoke an idyllic courtly world are also found in Boccaccio's poem, as is their love of extreme, even melodramatic gestures. Examples of the latter are Troiolo's public swoon during a Trojan council when he hears that Criseida will be handed over to the Greeks and his attempted suicide after he dreams that Criseida has been unfaithful.

Although it has long been assumed that Boccaccio was influenced by the *cantari*, the late date of the surviving examples of the latter make it also possible that it was Boccaccio who inspired them. If this is true, then the colloquial elements in *Filostrato* must derive instead from other popular writings, such as chronicles and classical vulgarizations. Whether Boccaccio's Trojan poem was influenced by or itself influenced the *cantari*, the crucial point for our purposes is their undeniable similarities. Although the action of *Filostrato* is more psychologically intimate and less full of battle and adventure than that of most of these romances,

Boccaccio equals the vigour and drive of their story-telling. Whatever its other qualities and higher ambitions, *Filostrato* is a fast-moving narrative that aims to keep the attention of its readers. Within seven stanzas of Pandaro's entrance in part 2, Troiolo declares that he is in love, within fifteen he announces that his beloved is Pandaro's relative, and within twenty he admits that she is Criseida (it takes Chaucer's Troilus forty-seven stanzas to name Criseyde). As Branca speculated, Boccaccio may well have deliberately set out to adapt the robust narrative virtues of this popular form to more courtly and fashionable tastes and thus become 'il canterino della societá galante' (*Cantare*, 57).

If Boccaccio shares much with the *cantare*, he was also deeply influenced by a very different contemporary literary form: the *dolce stil novo*, which first proved that Italian poetry could equal the elegance and delicate emotion of French and even Latin verse (for a recent account, see Natali, 62–5). The most explicit borrowing from the *stil novo* here is a close imitation of a famous *canzone* by Cino da Pistoia in part 5 (62–5). In addition, stilnovistic phrases and images appear regularly throughout *Filostrato*, as Boccaccio's editors have noted. The description of Criseida's weeping eyes surrounded by a purple ring (4.100) is probably a remembrance of Dante's *Vita Nuova* (XXXIX), and countless other echoes from this central work of the *stil novo* have been identified, as well as many borrowings from Dante's *Commedia*. *Filostrato* imitates not only the stylistic habits, but also some of the central themes of such poetry. We find the same profound emotional response, similar to a religious experience, when Troiolo first sees his lady and the same close analysis of the lover's suffering and hopes. The *cantare*, with its enthusiasm for action and the marvellous, has no time to explore such inner experience in detail. Although Boccaccio does not here equal the sensitivity or literary virtuosity of the greatest *stilnovisti*, their lyricism and psychological insight had a profound influence on his more expository narrative.

Boccaccio's choice of a Trojan story to represent his own amorous adventures is not surprising given his deep interest in the classical past, but in contrast to the poet's other early works, like *Teseida*, which contain learned accounts of ancient history and practices, *Filostrato* provides its readers with only a minimal sense of the Trojan setting and the pagan customs of the city. Apollo is mentioned in the opening invocation (1.1) and occasionally thereafter (for instance, 1.8 and 7.90), just as Jove's name occurs several times (for instance, 1.24, 3.67, 4.97, 4.121, 5.6), but there is no serious attempt to make the ancient religion of Troy particularly convincing. Despite a vague mention of 'sacrificii' (1.17) early in the poem, a specific god is only rarely addressed by the characters (as in Troiolo's praise of Venus at 2.80 or Pandaro's oath to Pallas at 5.30), and the most intensely pagan passage in the poem, which alludes to Venus, Jove, Mars, Cupid and Hercules, is borrowed from Boethius (3.74–80). These brief references give a light classical flavouring to *Filostrato*, but they contribute little more.

In the prose proem to *Filostrato*, Boccaccio describes his story as a convenient vehicle for his own experiences in love, and the reader has little reason to doubt that he is reading about fourteenth-century Italy rather than about prehistoric Ilium. The Trojan War is mentioned only briefly and distantly at the beginning and end of the poem, and so this seminal historical conflict achieves little narrative believability. Too much is familiar and almost nothing is strange about the locales in *Filostrato*. Pandaro's reference to Mount Etna ('Mongibello', 7.10) and Troiolo's lament that the absent Criseida is hidden by mountains (7.64) have less to do with the traditional geography of Troy than with the author's statement in the proem that his beloved has left Naples for the mountainous region of Sannio (p. 18). Without ignoring the sense of immediacy created in *Filostrato*, Chaucer will take the nominal Trojan setting and develop it into a profound exploration of the pagan past.

Characterization in 'Filostrato'

Boccaccio's characterization offered Chaucer a naturalistic model of human description. *Filostrato* is nothing like the dream visions that had been the inspiration of the English poet's early work; instead it is a story set in the real world that explores the intimate personal relations of a small number of characters. Troiolo, Criseida, Pandaro and Diomede are strong, lively, if not especially complex figures. Although their thoughts and feelings are fully accessible to the reader, they contain little depth or shadow. None of the characters is given a truly individual personality, for their actions and attitudes are essentially a result of their narrative roles. They are types and therefore a function of their actions. Troiolo is the true lover, Pandaro the faithful friend, and Criseida the passionate unfaithful beloved. Boccaccio does not reveal any substantial depth in the psyches of his characters; instead he is content to describe their dramatic amatory adventures and obvious emotional displays.

Troiolo is the hero of *Filostrato*, the experienced, active, faithful lover through whom the story is told. He has been in love before (1.23) and, though he suffers and feels self-pity after seeing Criseida, he is also capable of immediate practical action in his own cause, unlike Chaucer's Troilus. He relies on Pandaro for companionship, but not for courage or incentive in wooing. When Criseida at last summons him to her house, he leaves his friend outside and takes his beloved into his arms as soon as they meet. Troiolo's only timidity is in response to the Greek request that Criseida be given over to her father. Torn between his passion for Criseida and his desire not to compromise her honour, he is paralysed by indecision, though after the event he wishes that he had carried her off whatever the consequences. Despite his sufferings after Criseida leaves Troy, Troiolo remains an active protagonist. He himself interprets the fateful dream of Criseida and the boar (7.27) and, from his sickbed, eloquently defends his lover against Cassandra's attack (7.89–101). Although Troiolo at one point momentarily weakens and attempts to kill himself, he quickly accepts that this act is foolish and agrees with Pandaro's advice that they should instead die like men in defence of the city (7.47–8). Most of all, Troiolo is faithful and unwavering in his devotion to Criseida.

Pandaro is a much simpler and more youthful character than he would become in later versions of the story. Introduced as a 'young Trojan of high lineage and great spirit' (2.1), there is no reason to doubt that his motive is simply to help his best friend win his cousin Criseida. Pandaro is a secondary figure in *Filostrato*. He is active on Troiolo's behalf, but displays no real ingenuity or personality. Soon after his entrance, Pandaro tells Troiolo, 'you can talk to me as though to yourself' (2.14); and, indeed, Pandaro is little more than an extension of the prince – his double. Pandaro sometimes makes proposals, but it is always Troiolo himself who decides whether or not to take action. Pandaro is friendly enough with his cousin Criseida (she welcomes him happily to her house, and they laugh and joke 'in the way relatives often do', 2.35), but they share no special intimacy beyond the ties of age and family. Although he is the loyal go-between and comforter of the lovers, Pandaro is kept distant from the affair itself and is never present when Troiolo and Criseida are alone together.

Diomede is another double of Troiolo. Both are honourable sons of kings who are smitten with Criseida's beauty and act courteously in pursuit of a sexual relationship. Like Troiolo, Diomede falls in love with Criseida at first sight (5.13), and his passion is equally sincere and deep, the latter seen in his declaration that he, too, would rather serve Criseida than be king of his native land (6.22). Diomede never tricks or manipulates his beloved, but, like his predecessor, he is an attractive, well-mannered prince who truly cares for her. Given all this, we are hardly surprised when her thoughts in the enemy camp begin to cool towards the Trojan and warm towards the Greek; Diomede seems to have all Troiolo's virtues as a lover and one more – he is available.

Boccaccio's Criseida is not very different from the male characters, though she must act more cautiously because she is a woman. She is as active and assured as Troiolo, if less loyal and less central to the narrative. Criseida impresses Troiolo from the first with her lofty self-possession (1.27–8), and her self-confidence is apparent throughout the story: she quickly decides to accept Troiolo as a lover, after making sure that her reputation is safe, arranges their first assignation herself, and goes to embrace him without hesitation. Criseida even asserts herself as she is handed over to the Greeks, disdainfully ('disdegnosamente') telling Diomede that it is time to go and spurring her horse away without listening to more farewells (5.8–9).

Although he avoids the constant anti-feminism of predecessors such as Benoît and especially Guido, Boccaccio gives less attention to Criseida than to Troiolo, whose experiences supposedly mirror his own. Her entire story after she leaves Troy is narrated in the thirty-four stanzas of part 6. In contrast to Troiolo's much more extensively detailed sufferings, her anguish at being separated from the prince, though sincere, occupies a scant seven stanzas (6.1–7), and by the eighth stanza we learn that 'soon she was turned from this high and great purpose [returning to Troiolo regardless of the risks] by a new lover' (6.8). Perhaps because she is less well born than Troiolo (4.69), such high and great purposes are not thought to become Criseida (the worst thing that Boccaccio says about his heroine is to accuse her of being base – 'villana', 8.28). Her interest in Diomede is presented as consistent with her practical self-reliant character (Bergin calls her a 'pragmatic hedonist', 108), for this new affection is as much the result of hope ('speranza') as of fear (6.33–4). Her new lover is as courtly and passionate as Troiolo, and Criseida suffers no special regret over the second alliance. But her role in *Filostrato* is now over, and she appears in the rest of the poem only in letters and in the thoughts and dreams of Troiolo. At the conclusion of a valuable discussion, Warren Ginsberg describes Criseida as, in many respects, 'the most interesting and complete woman Boccaccio ever drew' (107). The parallel he notes with Virgil's Dido is particularly apt, though I would deny that Criseida, any more than the Carthaginian queen, ever degenerates into a 'simple harlot' (106). Yet, for all the undeniable fascination of Boccaccio's Criseida, Chaucer will do much more with her, transforming an interesting character into a great one.

The strength of Boccaccio's human portraits is their clarity and directness, which produce natural figures not found in the more allegorical literature on which Chaucer had modelled his early poetry. The characters in *Filostrato* are fully accessible – even Criseida, who will become so mysterious in *Troilus and Criseyde*, is open to the reader. After she has decided that she will accept Troiolo's love, Criseida for a while preserves a certain modesty in speaking with Pandaro and in writing to Troiolo, but both we and they understand exactly how she feels. When she is ready, Criseida shows no reluctance in informing Troiolo that he may spend the night at her house. She later responds to Diomede with similar directness. Throughout *Filostrato* we are left in no doubt about what the characters are doing or why. Their desires and motives are never very complex and always available to view.

Rather than subtlety of characterization or an intricate plot, Boccaccio offers intensity of emotion – the joy and especially the grief experienced by the lovers. His narrative is drenched in tears. The human pathos of *Filostrato* would have had a special appeal to Chaucer, who explores human loss and suffering from the early *Book of the Duchess* to the religious works of *The Canterbury Tales*, though this important element of his poetry has often been overlooked by modern critics in their headlong pursuit of Chaucerian irony. None of the other great fourteenth-century

English poets – not Gower, Langland or the *Gawain*-poet –
begins to match Chaucer's interest in the pathetic.

Boccaccio's characters experience deep emotions, the manifestations of which are frequently as simple as they are extravagant. Howard Schless detects 'an either/or world of adolescent
responses' (214), and Wallace sees the continuing influence of
the 'staginess and exaggeration' (*Early Writings*, 93) of the *cantari*
in such grotesque episodes as Troiolo's attempt to stab himself to
death with a knife in the presence of Pandaro (7.33–6). Troiolo
goes from great suffering, associated with images of death, when
he first falls in love, to great joy when his love is consummated,
to even greater suffering when Criseida leaves. The psychology
of *Troilus and Criseyde* is much more sophisticated than that
of *Filostrato*, but Chaucer retains the structure of extremes of
emotional intensity, which he explicitly outlines at the beginning
of the poem: 'Fro wo to wele, and after out of joie' (I.4).

The emotions of Boccaccio's characters, which are at the centre
of *Filostrato*, are most commonly expressed in formal speech.
Bergin notes that of the 700 octaves in the poem 'more than half
are *spoken* by the various actors' (110). Except for a few exceptional passages in which action or speech is reported secondhand
(for instance, 6.12–13 and 8.1–7), we are not told what happens in
Filostrato but are instead allowed to observe it happen – or, rather,
we hear it happen through the words of the characters themselves.
But, if *Filostrato* often reminds us of a play, Boccaccio is no simple
realistic dramatist. His people only rarely talk colloquially (an
unusual example is the quick dialogue at 2.118–20); instead,
as Howard Schless has pointed out, they utter 'long, almost
set pieces of rhetorical elaboration' (209). Pandaro's triumphant
announcement that he has succeeded in winning Criseida's pre-
liminary consent and Troiolo's joyful response are not expressed
in rapid idiomatic speech, as we might expect, but in two quite
long and rather stiff addresses (3.5–10 and 3.13–19). Similarly,
Troiolo and Criseida greet each other with great ceremony when
they are first alone together (3.28–9). Although the lovers manage
briefer and more spontaneous dialogue once in bed (3.32–5), they
revert to lofty rhetoric in their parting speeches the next morning
(3.43–50).

The most wrenching emotional moments of *Filostrato* occur
in part 4, the longest section of the poem, when Troiolo and
Criseida learn that they must separate. The crisis in their love

is told through a series of passionate speeches, from Calchas's fervent demand for the return of his daughter (4.5–11) to the piteous dialogues in which Pandaro attempts to advise and console both Troiolo and Criseida in turn (4.46–77 and 4.97–107). The most moving statements, of course, belong to the lovers themselves, including Troiolo's operatic complaint 'O misera Fortuna' (4.30–40) and Criseida's wretched lament in response to the fatuous comments of the Trojan ladies about her departure (4.88–94). In a final statement to the absent Criseida, which is actually spoken to Pandaro, Troiolo laments his beloved's faithlessness in characteristically formal rhetoric and declares his wish to die in battle (8.12–21). With the admission that he is now a warrior and not a lover, Troiolo's sufferings and voice are finally stilled. Speech is infinitely more various in *Troilus and Criseyde* than in *Filostrato*, but Chaucer maintains Boccaccio's reliance on the spoken word to narrate his story and express the powerful emotions of its characters.

Love in Boccaccio's 'Filostrato'

Filostrato seems to have taught Chaucer how to write about love in a new way. Nothing like its sensuality appears in *The Book of the Duchess* or *The House of Fame*; indeed, the only Chaucerian passage before *Troilus* that begins to approach such eroticism is the brief picture of Venus naked on her bed in *The Parliament of Fowls* (260–73). Boccaccio provided Chaucer with a narrative of sexual love that he probably could not have found elsewhere. The French antecedents that most resemble *Filostrato* in this respect, the romances of Lancelot and Guinevere and Tristan and Isolde, were apparently unknown to Chaucer or unappreciated by him.[5] The story of Troiolo and Criseida was also unprecedented in the Italian literature available to the English poet. Although Boccaccio's lovers occasionally echo the refined sentiments of the *stil novo*, sexual consummation and the pleasures of the body are central in *Filostrato* as they are not, for example, in Dante's *Vita Nuova* or in Petrarch's poems to Laura. The attraction between Troiolo and Criseida – their 'cheerful sensual abandon' (Wallace, 'Chaucer and Boccaccio', 157) – is always essentially physical. Troiolo is first attracted by Criseida's beauty (1.27–9), and his immediate and urgent passion, which is compared to a flame that grows the more that it is fed (1.40–41), is alternately called *disio*, *ardore* or *appetito* (all three occur at 2.87). Troiolo himself recognizes that such intense love makes its own rules and may even lead to incest (2.19–20).

Although careful of her reputation, the young widow Criseida is as sensual as her lover. She is initially described as 'amorosa' (1.3), and later admits to having also been struck by arrows of love (4.146). Pandaro declares that, though restrained by fear of shame, 'every woman lives amorously in her wishes' and that he would not believe his cousin if she claimed to feel otherwise (2.27). Criseida soon justifies Pandaro's view of female sexuality when she expresses the thought that 'stolen water is much sweeter than wine in abundance', by which she means that the joys of illicit love are far greater than any available in the ordinary marriage-bed (2.74). Later, after reading Troiolo's first letter, she becomes so full of desire (though the two have still only exchanged distant glances) that she wishes she were already in Troiolo's arms pressed face to face ('stretta e faccia a faccia', 2.117).

There is no hesitation when the lovers are first alone together at Criseida's house. They quickly embrace, kiss passionately and often, and proceed directly to bed (3.28–30). For much of this first night, the little that the couple has to say keeps being interrupted by kisses, and when they do talk at length, as dawn approaches, it is about their anguish at being separated. The bond between them is deeply physical. When Criseida asserts her devotion to Troiolo, it is in terms of violent possession: she says that whenever Love takes something he holds it firmly in his claws and that she has been so seized that she can do nothing about it (3.48–9). After the lovers part, Criseida dreams about Troiolo holding and kissing her again (3.55), just as the prince himself wishes to return to Criseida's 'amorose braccia' ('loving arms', 3.62).

The love of Troiolo and Criseida continues to be presented as sensual throughout the rest of *Filostrato*. When Criseida must depart, Troiolo rejects Pandaro's suggestion that he find a new woman (4.50–62), but his loyalty has nothing of the transcendence of the speaker in Donne's 'A Valediction: forbidding Mourning', who assures his beloved that they need not fear separation because they share a love 'so much refin'd' that they have less need for 'eyes, lips, and hands'. On the contrary, Troiolo is one of Donne's

'Dull sublunary lovers' whose 'soule is sense'. We can see this in the physical way he describes his passion: he says that from Criseida's eyes have come the sparks that have inflamed him and insists that the fire burns so powerfully in him that he could not extinguish it even if he so desired (4.51–2). Significantly, Troiolo can imagine his materialistic love coming to an end only as a result of stronger physical forces, such as death, poverty or the absence of his lady (4.59).

The bodily death of Beatrice does not end Dante's devotion in *Vita Nuova*, but separation in *Filostrato* undermines the lovers' passion, as Troiolo had feared. Because their relationship is essentially carnal, it cannot survive when they are no longer together. The sensuality seen from the first in Criseida, which Pandaro had identified as natural in women, explains the transference of her affections to Diomede. Her new lover desires her with no less sincerity, and no less appetite, than Troiolo, and she responds in kind (6.33–4). The noble Troiolo neither finds nor desires another Criseida, though he also has no interest in a spiritual union with his beloved after she leaves. All he wants is her physical presence back in Troy so that their pleasures may continue. When the dream of the boar tells him that Criseida has accepted another man (7.23–6), Troiolo seems less bothered by the infidelity itself than by her continued absence. He would gladly have her back in his arms regardless of her having embraced Diomede (7.69–71). When he finally accepts that Criseida will not return and that he has no hope of further sensual pleasure, the prince can only seek its opposite: physical dissolution, first in attempted suicide and then in battle.

Boccaccio provided Chaucer with a narrative of sensual love from which the judgements of religion and ethics are excluded. Any objections to sexual pleasure in *Filostrato* are wholly pragmatic and worldly. Troiolo's initial criticism of love is simply that its admitted pleasures are not worth the resulting suffering (1.23–4). As soon as he sees Criseida, however, he disregards such calculation and accepts the pain of loving, even unto death. Not once, however, whether in or out of love, does Troiolo consider the morality, Christian or pagan, of sexual passion. For his part, Pandaro promises not to rebuke Troiolo, citing the saying of wise men that love alone can set the heart free of itself (2.12).

Criseida's shocked response when Pandaro first recommends Troiolo as a lover would seem virtuous enough to satisfy the strictest medieval cleric. Insisting that, had *she* desired Troiolo, she would have expected her cousin to beat her for such folly, she declares that she has had no thoughts of love since the death of her husband (2.48–9). In the next stanza, however, she admits that Troiolo would be the first to have her love if only she did not suspect that his interest was just a passing fancy (2.50). In short, she is not rejecting the proposed affair on moral or religious grounds – her only concern is about its durability.

The argument that first convinces Criseida to agree to love is purely pragmatic: Pandaro insists that she should lose no time because 'old age or death will take away your beauty' (2.54). Far from recoiling from such worldly advice, Criseida immediately wonders whether she might indeed experience the 'pleasure and joy of love' (2.55). In her subsequent inner debate, Criseida's objections to love, like Troiolo's before, are exclusively practical: she notes its uncertainty, the difference in rank between herself and Troiolo, and the possible risk to her reputation (2.75–8). More profound scruples are simply not present. That her conception of evil is purely social is revealed by a remarkable statement during the same inner debate: 'come gli altri far non è peccato' ('it is not a sin to do as others do', 2.70). On the one occasion in *Filostrato* when religious sanctions against sexual love are cited, they are ridiculed as hypocritically self-serving. Pandaro says that priests praise chastity in women only if they have not been able to violate it themselves (2.135).

Boccaccio's Criseida never has to be convinced that love is to be desired, only that it is safe. The 'onor' (honour) that she constantly talks about, especially in the first two parts of the poem, refers to little more than her social reputation. Boccaccio's characters operate in a world of shame rather than of guilt, and they fear not private remorse but only the public judgement of others.[6] In her first letter to Troiolo, Criseida declares that she cannot satisfy his desire because she would thereby lose that which is most valuable in the world: to live and die in 'onesta' (2.123) – a complex concept, which translates as honour or decency or sometimes specifically chastity. But 'onesta', like 'onor', has little in common with deep moral principles of right and wrong. Criseida's letter makes it clear that she herself does not object to returning Troiolo's love: it is only the opinion of the world that makes her hesitate (2.124–5). Her 'onesta' depends not on whether she actually sleeps with Troiolo, but on whether it is known that she does.[7]

References to Criseida's loss of honour or to the shame of Pandaro's arranging a love affair for his cousin (3.6–10) concern potential damage to public reputation rather than any sense of personal guilt. The remedy is always more secrecy, never reformation, because neither the characters themselves nor the narrative voice ever suggest that correction is needed. Whatever judgement an individual reader may make, the only actions explicitly labelled as sins in the poem are public breaches of social obligations, like Calchas's betrayal of Troy, which he himself calls a 'peccato' ('sin' or 'fault', 4.94). Likewise, it is not Criseida's affair with Troiolo, but her desertion of him for Diomede that is described as a moral failure ('fallo' and 'fallire', 7.23, 8.22, 8.23, 8.24) and earns her the title 'Criseida villana' (8.28).

If love in *Filostrato* is worldly, it is nevertheless elegant. In addition to her angelic beauty, Criseida is a proud lady valued for her manners, delicacy and other refined social virtues, just as she admires Troiolo's high birth and discretion. The love that Troiolo and Criseida share is indeed appetite but one that is described, in Pandaro's phrase, as a high or noble appetite ('alto appetito', 2.26).[8] This love is not the simple rutting of a medieval fabliau, but resembles the operatic passion found in Verdi's *La Traviata*. When Pandaro describes his cousin Criseida, he mentions her manners, greatness of soul, and worth, before her beauty ('di costumi, o di grandezza/d'animo, o di valore o di bellezza', 2.21), and then compares her nobility of action to that of a king (2.22).

Although her virtues are entirely worldly, with none of the spirituality of Dante's Beatrice or Petrarch's Laura, Criseida is presented as a courtly lady of great style. At the end of their last night together, Troiolo insists that he did not come to love her because of her beauty, birth or riches, but because of qualities that fortune cannot take away, such as her noble acts, chivalric worth and speech, and gentle manners that make her scorn vulgar desires and works (4.164–5). Unfortunately for Troiolo, fortune can, and soon will, snatch away Criseida and all her virtues, but this does not deny the nobility of their love and the elegant secret world they have created to enjoy it.

Chaucer may not have known another romance, domestic or Continental, whose narrative so thoroughly ignores public life to chronicle the private feelings of two lovers. Once Troiolo sees Criseida, 'every other thought of the great war and his own well-being fled', and he concerns himself only with how he might cure his amatory wounds (1.44). We usually see the lovers only when they are alone together, alone thinking about one another, or, less frequently, alone with Pandaro. For most of *Filostrato*, the concerns of the rest of Trojan society hardly exist. Yet the secret world of the lovers is hardly natural, as Criseida notes when she tells Troiolo that their sexual pleasure has lasted only because they have met rarely and 'furtivamente', for the torch of passion would go out if they had enjoyed each other freely and openly (4.153).

The demands of the larger society finally destroy the private happiness of Troiolo and Criseida. Criseida is returned to her father in the Greek camp, where she gradually comes under the sway of Diomede. Troiolo is reclaimed by the royal family of Troy, who have barely been mentioned before: his brothers and father are concerned when he collapses after hearing of Criseida's promised return in part 4, and his sisters go to console him while his brothers and father again worry about him in part 7. Finally, Troiolo takes Pandaro's advice to die like a man on the battlefield in defence of the city (7.45). This is no heroic ending, of course, but the prince's recognition that the elegant worldly love he has secretly shared with Criseida is gone forever.

The passion of Troiolo and Criseida, which older critics sometimes attributed to Boccaccio's Italian temperament (Lewis, 'What Chaucer', 75), has been interpreted by recent critics in two opposite ways that have had a direct influence on readings of Chaucer's *Troilus*. In 1972, Robert apRoberts defended Criseida's libidinousness by asserting that the purpose of *Filostrato* was precisely to praise the powerful sexuality of both lovers: 'Boccaccio, in my opinion, presents what he regards as a perfect affair, and its salient feature is that very sensuousness which love *paramours* affords and marriage cannot. The immorality of clandestine love is what marks such love as an *alto appetito* (high desire).'[9] In apRoberts's view, Criseida's sexual appetite is not a blemish, but what distinguishes her as an ideal courtly mistress – her only fault is her unfaithfulness ('Love', 23). In fact, the pleasure of the affair, as she had stated, is a direct result of its illicit secrecy: 'Love *paramours* is to be preferred to marital love because, being proscribed by society, it can be engaged in only by stealth and hence, because the desire it arouses cannot be satisfied freely, it maintains an intensity which desire cannot maintain under the free access of marriage' ('Love', 7).

More recently *Filostrato* has been read in an entirely different, Christian way by Robert Hollander, by Janet Smarr and, in most detail, by Chauncey Wood. These studies, which follow the moralistic approach to medieval literature of D. W. Robertson, Jr, agree with apRoberts's view that love in the poem is sensual but, instead of imagining that Boccaccio approves of such love, they argue that he is deeply critical. Both approaches agree on what is depicted in the poem, but not on how it should be interpreted. For Hollander, Smarr and Wood, the suffering produced by the love of Troiolo and Criseida, even to the point of making them both desire death, is not a sign of its noble intensity, but proof of its foolishness and moral error. According to Hollander, *Filostrato* 'is not a celebration of love, but an analysis of its terrible power' (52). Physical love brings little lasting pleasure and instead robs humans of their freedom. Wood argues that careful attention to the strategies of the poem shows that 'Boccaccio takes a clearly disapproving attitude toward illicit passion. His use of scripture, of Dante, his imagery, the narrative framework – all these debase rather than exalt the seduction of Criseida' (*Elements*, 30). The 'alto appetito' praised by Pandaro (and apRoberts) is seen as nothing more than base carnality.

Both interpretations of the meaning of love in *Filostrato*, despite their fundamental disagreement, are coherent, skilled, plausible analyses, yet objections can be found to each and neither is definitive. For instance, apRoberts's untroubled faith in the surface meaning of almost everything said in *Filostrato* will seem naïve to many. He has no doubt that Boccaccio is, in fact, describing his own personal experiences in love through the story of Troiolo, though, as we shall see below, there is little evidence for reading the poem as genuine autobiography. Along with the prose prologue, the final moral against women (or at least against certain young women) is also taken at face value. Indeed, apRoberts generally regards the narrator as the unmediated voice of the poet ('Love', 8–9, 23–4). Even the thoughts of the characters are accepted as authorial; we are told Boccaccio means us to see Criseida as almost perfect because 'her beauty, her exquisite manners, her superior bearing, her good reputation, and her superior virtue are insisted upon over and over again in tributes by the narrator, Pandaro, Troiolo, and Diomede' ('Love', 23). As apRoberts himself indicates in the first statement quoted above from his essay, the view that Boccaccio means to celebrate the sensual love of Troiolo and Criseida is finally little more than his 'opinion'. In a recent restatement of his position against the attacks of Hollander and Wood, apRoberts appeals, somewhat desperately, to the 'normal reader, medieval or modern' (apRoberts and Seldis, xlvi), though it is hard to imagine who exactly such a creature might be. *Normal* is a famously slippery term (which often means little more than the opinion of the writer), and we would certainly expect there to be a significant difference between what is normal for modern and medieval readers.

If apRoberts too readily trusts what appears to be the obvious sensible meaning of the text, Hollander, Smarr and Wood do not trust it at all. Although their arguments may keep us from any easy idealization of the passion of Troiolo and Criseida, the severe Christian irony they claim for *Filostrato* (and every other medieval work) is clearly the result of prior conviction: they know even before reading a work that all praise of human sexual love actually means its opposite, whereas every criticism is to be taken literally. This is not the place for a detailed critique of the Robertsonian position, but we might briefly look at its claims for the use of Dante in *Filostrato*. Scholars have long recognized that Boccaccio borrows a number of phrases from the *Vita Nuova* and *Commedia*, and that he sometimes uses them in seemingly inappropriate contexts. Nicholas Havely, for instance, recognizes the possible ironic effect of passages that make Criseida appear 'at times as a rather reluctant Beatrice, and Pandaro as a somewhat disingenuous Virgil', whereas Troiolo is a pilgrim who goes from Hell to Paradise and then back again (8). Hollander, Smarr and Wood go further in their argument, however, for they assert that Boccaccio's brief and scattered borrowings from Dante produce a clear ideological pattern that utterly condemns the love of Troiolo and Criseida. Hollander finds the Dantean echoes parodic (175–6), a view that Wood supports in his more detailed investigation of their satiric intent. Yet even the latter recognizes the limits of the evidence: he concludes that he can offer no more than a 'tentative' analysis (*Elements*, 21) and admits that the 'vast majority of the parallels' are probably 'accidental, coincidental, or stemming from a common source' (*Elements*, 17).

If nothing else, the context of the borrowed passages in *Filostrato* is radically different. Dante clearly condemns illicit love in the famous Paolo and Francesca episode of canto 5, but he needs the theological framework of *Inferno* to make the moralistic point clear. Even so, the swooning of the pilgrim as he hears the lovers' story acknowledges a natural human sympathy for their plight. Boccaccio imitates some of Francesca's words at 2.7 of *Filostrato* and he adapts phrases elsewhere from the episode (for example, at 4.56 and 4.59), but without the explicitly Christian context supplied by the *Commedia* the lines in *Filostrato* do not necessarily demand a Christian judgement. Robertsonian critics claim that every medieval reader would automatically supply such a context, but this is to deny the complexity of medieval views about love and to ignore the care Dante obviously feels he must take to show why the passion of Paolo and Francesca, for all its superficial attractiveness and warrant in Arthurian literature, is sinful.[10]

Hollander, Smarr and Wood assume a consistent uniform attitude towards sexual love in the Middle Ages that cannot be justified historically. The moral danger and sufferings of amorous passion are well recognized during the period (from the work of the troubadours to Guido Cavalcanti's famous 'Donna me prega'), but so are its pleasures and delights. The varied imitations of, modifications of, and attacks upon the *Roman de la Rose* suggest something of the complexity of the topic of love. Medieval people knew the Church's official opposition to sexual pleasure and most probably accepted it intellectually, but similar ecclesiastical disapproval of wealth did not prevent poets from extolling material luxury or individuals (including churchmen) from enjoying it. The popular Italian *cantari* frankly celebrate the joys of sensuality, as do some of the generally more proper English romances, a conspicuous example being the tail-rhyme *Sir Launfal*. More elevated writers, such as Dante or Petrarch, often sublimate, but do not ignore, the claims of carnal love. The lyric poetry of Petrarch, who was later a good friend to Boccaccio, is a particularly revealing example. Petrarch may say he wants wholeheartedly to choose philosophy over sensuality, but much of the force of his poetry depends on the powerful tension between the two. Debate about the nature and role of love, especially the relationship between divine and earthly love, is at the very centre of the greatest poetry of the Italian trecento.

If apRoberts's interpretation of Boccaccio's attitude towards love in *Filostrato* is finally his 'opinion', the conclusions of the other Robertsonians, despite their historicist claims, are equally subjective, as their own language suggests. For instance, Hollander begins his argument by saying that the 'praise of love which we find in the *Filostrato* should *probably* be understood as being the praise offered by fools and knaves' (50, my emphasis), and Smarr similarly signals a tentativeness in her claims about Boccaccio's view of Pallas: 'He is *probably* considering her . . . the goddess of wisdom and reason' (16, my emphasis).[11] Indeed, despite the apparently irreconcilable gulf that separates the two positions, which each school insists upon, their two interpretations of *Filostrato* actually share a number of basic similarities in addition to their subjectivity. Both judge the love in *Filostrato* to be illicitly sensual, both think marriage would solve none of the problems, and both are relatively uninterested in Criseida's infidelity (apRoberts because he considers it her only flaw; the moralistic critics because it is only a small part of the larger carnality), though this is the main focus of the story both before and after Boccaccio. Most important of all, both insist that Boccaccio intends to persuade us of a specific attitude towards sexual love, whether positive or negative. These similarities suggest that there is room for other approaches to the poem, especially those whose principal interest is not in identifying the author's final lesson. What if Boccaccio had no strong didactic purpose in mind when writing *Filostrato*?

The Openness of Boccaccio's 'Filostrato'

A way to get beyond the two opposing critical arguments just discussed is suggested by Warren Ginsberg's observation that throughout his career 'each of Boccaccio's books simultaneously propounds the virtues and the defects of love', although none 'offers a final judgment' (101). We might go even further than the duality proposed by Ginsberg and see *Filostrato* as remarkably open on the question of love. Instead of offering a single or even double position on human sexuality, the poem presents no view that has any claim to authority. Boccaccio is a storyteller not a moralist; he provides his readers with an exciting narrative rather than an interpretation of its events. Individual readers may find evidence in *Filostrato* for the conclusions of either apRoberts or the Robertsonians, but also for a number of other, different conclusions.[12] Unlike Dante's *Commedia*, *Filostrato* offers no ideological context to guide the reader. Although various lessons are occasionally suggested in the poem, especially at the beginning and the end, all such clues turn out to be more playful than definitive.

Filostrato does contain a formal frame structure that comments on the story – a frame that includes a prologue, an address to young lovers at the end of part 8, and a farewell to the book in part 9. Yet, instead of answering the problems of interpretation, the different elements of the frame war against themselves and undermine one another. The long prose prologue, for instance, explains that the poet chose the story of Troiolo as the one closest to his own sufferings in love. Although the preface used to be considered an account of Boccaccio's supposed affair with Maria d'Aquino, the natural daughter of Robert, King of Naples, recent scholarship has cast serious doubt on any such clear autobiographical claims.[13]

Whatever the actual facts, the prologue is so designed that it raises as many questions as it answers. Although the author says that he hopes *Filostrato* will persuade his lady to return and think kindly of him (p. 23), it is difficult to imagine any woman being flattered by a tale with such a faithless heroine. The story of Troiolo and Criseida actually has very little similarity to what Boccaccio tells us about his own claimed affair. His *donna* has neither loved nor betrayed him, and there is no mention of a contemporary Diomede. Boccaccio also does not clearly explain why he adds the first three books about the lovers' consummated bliss to the traditional story, a bliss that he confesses he never enjoyed. I raise these contradictions not to show that Boccaccio is inept or has failed in the prologue, but to suggest the nature of his achievement. He provides a witty if slippery introduction to *Filostrato* (anticipating the clever words to women readers at the beginning and end of the *Decameron*) whose gaps, inconsistencies and silences call into question any simple interpretation of what is to follow. Boccaccio blandly admits that the lady will have to discover for herself the personal application of the story (pp. 22–3). The obvious corollary is that each reader must likewise interpret the narrative. If the prologue was present in Chaucer's copy of *Filostrato* (it does not exist in all surviving manuscripts), the English poet must have been delighted with its elusive wit, which so resembles his own practice.

Boccaccio provides almost no guidance about how we should read *Filostrato* during the story itself. The narrative is allowed to unfold with remarkable objectivity, with little authorial intervention or didacticism. Very occasionally the narrator will inform us of what is to come, as when he notes in passing that Criseida will soon betray Troiolo (5.14), or will allow himself a brief comment on events, as when he declares that Criseida's letter to Troiolo has many false excuses (7.105), but such comments are unusual. Equally rare is any direct expression of personal involvement in the story despite the autobiographical claims of the proem. The small number of exceptions include the poet's address to his lady in the middle of the story (4.23–5), a few conventional formulas that announce his inability to express some deep emotion (3.31, 3.33, and 4.95), and his denunciation of misers for their criticism of love (3.38–9).

Contrasting interpretations of the love-affair are provided late in the story by the characters themselves. During a family visit to Troiolo, who is grieving over the departure of his lady, Cassandra spitefully criticizes the 'maladetto amor' ('accursed love', 7.86) her brother has shared with the low-born daughter of a wicked priest. In reply to his sister, Troiolo praises Criseida, whom he denies is his lover, as an ideal of gentility because of her chastity, discretion and modesty (7.86–101). Despite its energy and complete silencing of Cassandra, Troiolo's long defence of Criseida is clearly no more definitive than Cassandra's snobbish attack. We have already been shown Criseida's betrayal in part 6, and Troiolo himself has begun to suspect the truth.

The concluding frame of *Filostrato* offers two additional views of the love-affair that further complicate our response. Both are conventional. After the story ends, the reticent narrative voice reappears to speak in disapproving tones not heard before of Troiolo's 'ill-conceived love' ('il mal concetto amore') and of Criseida as base ('villana', 8.28). In these lines a purely practical lesson is drawn: young men are urged not to choose lovers who are too young and flighty or who are too stuck-up, but instead to choose those rare women who are eager to love and to keep their promises (8.29–33). Such anti-feminism, which echoes the harsher strictures of earlier versions of the story, offers utilitarian (if fanciful) advice that is obviously inadequate as the lesson of *Filostrato* and completely ignores (if it does not insult) the absent lady for whom the poem is supposedly written. Immediately following the advice to young men, Boccaccio changes tone and theme once again with eight elaborately rhetorical stanzas of formal leave-taking. Envying his book because it will see his lady, the poet hopes that it may persuade her to return to him (9.1–8). By offering two such radically different interpretations of the love story in the concluding frame – the practical lesson to young men and the rhetorical address to his book and lady, not to mention Cassandra's earlier attack on Criseida and Troiolo's courtly defence – Boccaccio manages to prevent any simple closure of his text, which is kept open to a variety of readings. Chaucer may have been especially attracted to *Filostrato* because it offers no single view of love, positive or negative; instead its playful frame and series of pseudo-lessons permit a wide spectrum of possible meanings. Chaucer's own conclusion to *Troilus and Criseyde* will allow a similar, if more complex, freedom for the reader.

Despite the many qualities that Chaucer obviously admired in *Filostrato*, he may have been particularly attracted by the poem's potential. Like an imaginative buyer shown a small if well-made house, he saw how much more might be made from what was already there and the ways in which he could extend the basic structure. For all its ambition and energy, *Filostrato* indeed lacks 'allusion and implication' (Windeatt, *Troilus* edition, 5), but the very directness of its telling gave Chaucer a strong framework on which to build. Moreover, Boccaccio himself had already indicated possible areas that might be developed. His mixture of literary traditions, for instance, though sometimes awkward, points the way to the greater and more various stylistic experiments of *Troilus and Criseyde*. Any number of Chaucer's most brilliant moments in *Troilus*, from characterization to setting, have their origins in *Filostrato*. Most of all, Chaucer must have responded to the openness of Boccaccio's poem. The freedom of interpretation produced by the self-contradictory frame structure and objective narrative not only allowed Chaucer to take the story in new directions, but also encouraged his own tendency against poetic closure. The various, often contradictory layers of allusion and implication that Chaucer added to *Troilus and Criseyde* produce a richer work than its source, but one that nevertheless follows Boccaccio in allowing individual readers to discover a wide range of literary experiences.

Notes

1 Pratt, '*Roman*'; the only printed edition of the *Roman*, by Moland and d'Héricault, is not trustworthy, but a new edition has been promised by the Chaucer Library.

2 Payne's statement (*Key*, 176), which follows Rossetti's claim in his parallel text (iii), that only 2,580 lines of *Troilus*, or less than a third, are directly dependent on the *Filostrato* is therefore misleading.

3 Branca, *Boccaccio*, 42. However, Havely (5) and Bergin (106) think that it may have been written somewhat later. For an account of recent discussions of the date, see Natali, 51n6.

4 Troiolo's very first letter to Criseida (2.96–106), which is answered by her equally polished reply (2.121–7), shows the association in *Filostrato* of strong emotion and elaborate rhetoric. Troiolo's epistle is eleven stanzas long, begins with a quibble over greeting and health ('salute'), seems to echo both Ovid (2.96) and Dante's *Inferno* (2.104, 2.105), and describes in detail both Criseida's beauty and the prince's own burning passion. Havely, citing Marti, notes that the description of Troiolo as writing the letter 'come saggio' (2.95) is a reference to a rhetorically trained poet (199n14). Troiolo's letter to Criseida begging her to return is even longer and more ornamented (7.52–75).

5 Brewer, 'Chaucer and Chrétien'. No firm evidence exists that Chaucer was aware of the works of the greatest writer of French romance, Chrétien de Troyes; even if he had been, Chrétien's marvels and fancies, not to mention the frequency of battle in even his most amatory works, such as *Lancelot*, are very different from Boccaccio's realistic and intimate account of the growth and destruction of a 'modern' sexual relationship.

6 Honour is a difficult concept for most modern readers, but see the article by Burrow, and also Brewer, *Morte*, 23–35.

7 Pandaro had previously told Troiolo that for Criseida to love him would not be proper and might produce shame, but he then continues that any shame will be avoided as long as dicretion keeps anyone from knowing (2.25–6). Thus Pandaro from the first concludes that the affair can proceed, provided that Troiolo is 'wise' ('saggio') and keeps his actions 'occulto' ('hidden') from others (2.28).

8 Similarly Troiolo's first sight of Criseida is described as 'alto disire' (1.30), and her lofty disdain as well as her beauty appeals to the prince (1.28).

9   apRoberts, 'Love', 1; see also Walker, who speaks of *Filostrato* as a 'simple story of voluptuous love' (324).

10   Chaucer's *Troilus and Criseyde* will provide at least some of the necessary interpretive context, as we shall see, and by so doing it legitimizes moral questions that are irrelevant to the *Filostrato*. A serious limitation in the criticism of Wood and Hollander is that they see almost no difference between the meaning of *Filostrato* and *Troilus* despite the radical literary and thematic changes in the English poem.

11   This last example reveals something of the flexible looseness of the moralistic template. Why would a goddess in a historically pagan setting (as opposed to an allegory) be assumed to represent Christian virtues? Similarly Smarr seems to read Dante's *Vita Nuovo* as a straightforward Christian work (21), whereas others of the same general school take it as ironic (see Musa, 168–74).

12   Boccaccio might even have produced such a moralistic commentary to *Filostrato* himself, though he did not; he knew the form as he later proves in the glosses to the description of the temple of Venus in the *Teseida*, which distinguish between good and bad love. Similarly, a range of arguments about love is also found in his *Filocolo*. But no single commentary, even one that is contemporary or written by the poet himself, can absolutely limit the meaning of a poem, anymore than the *Ovide moralisé* limits the meaning of Ovid, even the meaning of Ovid for a medieval reader.

13   For the older view, see, for example, Griffin, 2–24; for the recent rejection of the supposed liaison with Maria (who is never explicitly named by Boccaccio), see Wood, *Elements*, 5; Bergin, 34–7; and Branca, *Boccaccio*, 43. These latter scholars note, among other things, how much of the action and expression in *Filostrato* (the meeting in church, the emphasis on the beloved's eyes, the imagery of fire and death) is conventional in love-poetry from Ovid and the troubadours through the Italian *stil novo*, the *cantari*, and Petrarch and his followers. Of course, this does not mean that the Italian poet's account of Criseida does not draw on his own experiences in love.

3

Readers

Style, Genre and the Reader

If we would understand Chaucer's complex transformation of *Filostrato*, there is no better place to begin than with the several distinct styles and genres that compose *Troilus and Criseyde*. As we have just seen, Boccaccio mixes high and low literary traditions throughout *Filostrato*, but stylistic diversity in the Italian poem remains subordinate to an emphasis on clear efficient narration. Chaucer, however, greatly develops the potential of this aspect of his source. He not only does more with the literary registers already present in *Filostrato* (his highs are higher and his lows lower than Boccaccio's) but he also supplements his source with many additional contrasting styles and genres, none of which dominates his poem. As Dorothy Everett has noted, *Troilus* follows no single line of development but 'reaches out in all directions from Boccaccio's'; for instance, whereas conversation in *Troilus* is 'more natural, and more colloquially expressed' than in *Filostrato*, the English poem also, at the other extreme, includes many 'highly rhetorical passages' (131). The multiple styles of *Troilus* resist unity and invite readers of the poem themselves to become creators of meaning.

As his early followers well recognized, Chaucer brought a new stylistic magnificence to Middle English literature. Within a generation after the poet's death, John Lydgate, in his own version of the Troy story and with specific reference to *Troilus*, hailed his master as 'Noble Galfride, poete of Breteyne,/Amonge oure englisch that made first to reyne/ The gold dewe-dropis of rethorik so fyne,/Oure rude langage only tenlwmyne' (Brewer, *Critical* 1.47). To the plain vigour of native English verse, Chaucer added the rhetorical sophistication of classical and Continental poetry. Golden rhetoric is immediately obvious at the very beginning of *Troilus* where Chaucer not only imitates but also extends the already elevated formal invocation in *Filostrato* (1.1–6). In place of Boccaccio's conventional citations of Jove and Apollo, for example, Chaucer calls on the more unusual Thesiphone, perhaps in imitation of Statius' *Thebaïd* (Root, *Troilus* edition, 408nI.6–9), just as his complex syntax and rhetorical figures have reminded some of Virgil's *Aeneid* (Everett, 115). In a further development of *Filostrato*, which contains only one other brief invocation (at the beginning of part 3), Chaucer introduces each of his subsequent books, except the last, with even more elaborate proems to Cleo, Venus and Fortune.[1] Such increased poetic grandeur is only one of the ways in which the literary texture of the story is transformed by Chaucer. Although imitators like Lydgate were most impressed by the noble eloquence of *Troilus*, Chaucer exploited the full range of styles already suggested (but only fitfully developed) in *Filostrato*. The opening proem in *Troilus*, for example, contains, along with soaring rhetoric and greater learning, moments that are more casual and even lighthearted than Boccaccio's original (Windeatt, *Troilus* edition, 85nI.5), including the familiar tone adopted by the narrator towards his audience and his self-portrait as a hopeless outsider in love. From the beginning, the poem addresses its readers in different voices.

The stylistic multiplicity found throughout *Troilus* is striking whether analysed in medieval or modern terms. The Middle Ages inherited from classical rhetorical theory a conception of three levels of literary style: an ornate high style, an idiomatic low style, and a middle style somewhere between these two extremes. The influential pseudo-Ciceronian *Ad Herennium* labels these three styles as grand (*gravis*), middle (*mediocris*) and simple (*adtenuata*): 'The Grand type consists of a smooth and ornate arrangement of impressive words. The Middle type consists of words of a lower, yet not of the lowest and most colloquial, class of words. The Simple type is brought down even to the most current idiom of standard speech' (252–3).[2] *Troilus and Criseyde* contains all three styles.

The grand style is found in the proems (especially those to books II and III) and also in other additions to *Filostrato*, including lyric moments like Antigone's song about refined love (II.827–75), formal narrative addresses like the criticism of the Trojans' wisdom in trading Criseyde for Antenor ('O Juvenal, lord, trewe is thy sentence,/That litel wyten folk what is to yerne . . .', IV.197–210), and four passages of 'heightened time description' (II.50–6, II. 64–70, V.8–11, V.274–9) borrowed from the epic-like *Teseida* (Pratt, 'Use'). The low style, which is more prominent and idiomatic in *Troilus* than in *Filostrato*, appears especially in the characters' speech. The many joking exchanges between Pandarus and Criseyde are particularly collo- quial (for example, II.85–98), but even the more sober exchanges between Pandarus and Troilus sometimes break into convincing dialogue (I.770–7).[3] Like high and low style, middle style is also frequent in *Troilus*. Although the usual medieval definition of middle style as a mean between the two extremes of high and low makes it hard to identify precisely, much of the poem, from the opening description of the Trojan War to the many careful transitions from one scene to another, is straightforward exposition that is neither high nor low.

Twentieth-century Chaucerians have recognized the presence of different levels of style in *Troilus and Criseyde*. In a pioneering and still authoritative study, Charles Muscatine speaks of the 'broad range of style' in the poem (*French*, 130), and he argues, in particular, that Chaucer makes his poem both more courtly *and* more realistic by exploiting the contrasting styles characteristic of the two parts of the French *Roman de la Rose* (124–65). For example, Troilus expresses a 'courtly, idealistic' view of the world (133), in contrast to the 'naturalistic style' of Pandarus (139). Although such a binary division into courtliness and naturalism does not account for other literary registers and tensions in *Troilus*, Muscatine's brilliant argument for the generic roots of the two styles points the way towards a full appreciation of the literary diversity of the poem.[4]

The protean styles of *Troilus* reveal its self-conscious artistry. As A. C. Spearing notes: 'The coexistence within the poem of many different styles, often sharply differentiated and not merging one into another, has the effect of making us aware of styles as conventions, alternative artistic choices, rather than as mere reflections of an unquestionable reality' (*Troilus*, 16–17). These stylistic choices are largely the result of the wide spectrum of genres upon which Chaucer drew to construct his poem. The variety of literary forms that make up the plenitude of *The Canterbury Tales* is here present in a single work. We can quickly identify substantial elements from a half-dozen genres in the poem and that number is far from exhaustive.

Troilus and Criseyde is usually called a *romance* by modern critics, though the poem's focus on the emotional adventures of two lovers has more in common with Continental examples of this amorphous genre, especially the stories of Lancelot and Guinevere and Tristan and Isolde (which Chaucer may not have known), than with the more moral and political native English romance tradition. Yet *Troilus* explicitly calls itself, if only at the end, a *tragedy* (V.1786), a generic label that is reinforced by the high social status of the characters, the use of rhyme-royal, and the allusions to figures like Oedipus from classical tragedy and Oënone from love tragedy. *Troilus* as tragedy will be discussed at greater length in Chapter 7. Other genres also make significant contributions to *Troilus*. Chaucer borrows information at the beginning and end of the poem from what was considered in the Middle Ages to be the authentic *history* of the Trojan War derived from eyewitness accounts of Dares and Dictys, and he makes substantial reference to the legendary history of Thebes in books II and V. Several episodes of *comedy*, some reminiscent of the fabliaux, are also added to Boccaccio's more straightforward narration, including witty exchanges between Pandarus and Criseyde and the near-slapstick scenes of Troilus' ineptitude as a lover. The second most important source of *Troilus*, after *Filostrato*, is Boethius' *Consolation of Philosophy*, and Chaucer adds many passages of *philosophy* from Boethius, especially Troilus' long soliloquy on predestination in book IV, and his interest in questions of fate and free will remains strong throughout. Previous critics have found elements in the poem of *epic* 'grandeur', which in the Middle Ages was often associated with tragedy (Boughner; Muscatine, *Poetry*, 123–5), but equally persuasive are arguments for the structural importance in the poem of *lyric* passages, such as the sonnet from Petrarch added to book I and Antigone's song in book II (Payne, *Key*). Beginning with a version of the 'bidding prayer' adapted from the liturgy of the mass in the opening proem to the prayer to the Trinity at the end of the poem, Chaucer greatly supplements Boccaccio with the language of *religious discourse*, especially in his extensive use of Christian terminology to describe romantic love.

The effect of these different genres in *Troilus*, which like the poem's various styles usually remain distinct from one another, is to challenge our notion of any single reading of the poem. Each genre presupposes its own ideal reader with a particular set of expectations, values and capacities, or what Jauss has discussed as the reader's 'horizons of expectation'. The great diversity of genres in *Troilus* complicates and multiplies the ways in which it may be read. We are constantly uncertain how to approach the poem because the generic signals, which tell us what to expect in a work of literature, are forever shifting. Do we laugh at Troilus' love-pangs as we would in a comedy, or do we sympathize with them as we would in a courtly romance, or do we condemn them as we would in a Christian allegory? We are never sure at any particular moment whether to read the poem with the generic assumptions appropriate for tragedy, epic, history, romance, philosophy or lyric. The variety of styles and genres in *Troilus* permits readers to respond in individual ways that are justified by the text. Although recent reports from Paris of the 'death of the author' are clearly exaggerated, as I noted in the opening chapter, *Troilus* is not entirely hostile to such views. Chaucer carefully does not present himself in the role that modern theorists like Barthes find so objectionable: he is no godlike author or dictator of meaning. Instead, more modestly, he appears as a craftsman, a 'maker' as he would have said; rather than being a grand *auctorite* or a Romantic poet pouring out his soul, he appeals to us for help in producing his poem. The sophisticated literary multiplicity of *Troilus and Criseyde* is created by an author, but for the use of its readers.

The Reader in 'Troilus'

Barthes's hope was that the death of the author would stimulate a new birth of the reader, and so it has come to pass. Although the 'affective fallacy' was one of many heresies condemned by the old New Criticism, in recent years the role of the reader has become increasingly important for both American and Continental theory and practice.[5] Reader-response criticism stresses textual discontinuity and variety in contrast to unity and has developed many useful terms and concepts to analyse the ways in which readers relate to texts. Two especially influential critics in this field are German scholars from the so-called Constance School: Hans Robert Jauss, who explores the historical reception of literary works, and Wolfgang Iser, who argues that the inevitable 'gaps' or 'indeterminacies' in literary texts are filled by readers who thus become co-creators in the actualization of a literary work.[6]

Troilus and Criseyde repeatedly insists on the importance of the reader. In contrast to the narrator of *Filostrato*, who writes as a passionate lover addressing his absent mistress, the narrator of *Troilus* does not claim to be telling his own personal story nor does he rely on the experiential truth of a dream vision as in the earlier works of Chaucer. It is as a consumer of old stories that the poet presents himself throughout *Troilus*. His stance towards the story is quite similar to ours, for 'his intense involvement is that of the fascinated reader or hearer' (Bethurum, 517). The events of the story of Troilus and Criseyde are impossible to apprehend directly, but are always mediated through texts: for the Chaucerian narrator that means reading and attempting to understand his sources; for us it means reading and attempting to understand *Troilus* itself.

The role of the reader is stressed throughout *Troilus and Criseyde*. In a way that Barthes himself might have approved, Chaucer consistently undermines his own authority as author while urging the audience to be his collaborator. In the proem to book I the poet/narrator portrays himself as an ignorant outsider. Although his subject is the experiences of Troilus in love (I.1–7), he admits that he is only the 'instrument' (I.10) or servant of lovers (I.15), one who dares not pray to the God of Love for help because of 'myn unliklynesse' (I.16). In the proem to book II he further deprecates himself by asserting that he is a drudge who mechanically follows his source: 'For as myn auctour seyde, so sey I' (II.18). Yet however modest this literary ambition may be, it turns out not to be easy to fulfil. The narrator later admits that the text that he is attempting to reproduce faithfully is elusive: it contains inexpressible emotions, is silent about what really happened at crucial points, and, most disturbing of all, is not a unitary source but instead multiple ('bokes olde', III.91) and therefore potentially contradictory. One of the central dramas of *Troilus* is the narrator's struggle to make sense out of the old books that tell of the romance of his Trojan lovers.

The doubts raised in *Troilus* about the reliability of the poet and of his materials have the effect of empowering readers. Each of us is put on notice not to accept uncritically what we find in the poem; instead we must carefully judge its various elements and contribute to its realization. Robert Henryson, Chaucer's greatest disciple, seems to have understood the freedom and responsibility thus granted when in his fifteenth-century *Testament of Cresseid* he asks this daring question about *Troilus*: 'Quha wait gif all that Chauceir wrait was trew?' (64). It is a question that the author himself demands we answer. Chaucer does not wait for the deconstructing angels of modern criticism to discover gaps, indeterminacies and fractures in *Troilus and Criseyde*; he announces them himself through the voice of the narrator – and most are his own invention. For instance, in contrast to the clear statement in *Filostrato* that Criseida was incapable of having children (1.15), the narrator of *Troilus* states: 'But wheither that she children hadde or noon,/I rede it naught, therfore I late it goon' (I.132–3). In a more significant admission of ignorance, Chaucer's narrator insists that the author he is following does not declare (and therefore he himself cannot know) if Criseyde believed Pandarus when he told her that Troilus would be out of town when she came for dinner (III.575–8). In fact, the entire scene is original with Chaucer.

The teller also frequently draws specific attention to his limits as a literary craftsman, as on the many occasions when he claims to be merely a translator or when he announces his inability to describe a particular moment in the narrative, such as Troilus' sorrow after Criseyde has gone over to the Greek camp:

> Who koude telle aright or ful discryve
> His wo, his pleynt, his langour, and his pyne?
> Naught alle the men that han or ben on lyve.
> Thow, redere, maist thiself ful wel devyne
> That swich a wo my wit kan nat diffyne;
> On ydel for to write it sholde I swynke,
> Whan that my wit is wery it to thynke.
>
> (V.267–73)

In contrast to the narrator's distance from love announced in the opening proem, the plea of inadequacy here is a fairly conventional example of the familiar modesty topos. The narrator insists that no one could have done any better, and his plea to the reader, who is rarely forgotten for long, is only for tolerance. Elsewhere in *Troilus*, however, the reader is more actively solicited to be the poet's collaborator.

Chaucer's most famous request for his readers to help him in the telling of the poem occurs at the very centre of the narrative as Troilus and Criseyde finally consummate their love:

> But sooth is, though I kan nat tellen al,
> As kan myn auctour, of his excellence,
> Yet have I seyd, and God toforn, and shal
> In every thyng, al holly his sentence;
> And if that ich, at Loves reverence,
> Have any word in eched for the beste,
> Doth therwithal right as youreselven leste.
>
> For myne wordes, heere and every part,
> I speke hem alle under correccioun
> Of yow that felyng han in loves art,
> And putte it al in youre discrecioun
> To encresse or maken dymynucioun
> Of my langage, and that I yow biseche.
>   (III.1324–36).

The act of creation imagiined here is at least tripartite. An auuthor, 'of his excellence', is said to have told the original story (perhaps in Latin as suggested at I.395 and II.14), but even the English poet, whose characteristically humble claim is only to have followed the essence or 'sentence' of his source, admits to having 'in eched for the beste' at least a few words. Both thus contribute to the final result, but the ultimate (at least in time) power to shape the text seems to lie with the reader, who 'heere and every part' is told 'to encresse or maken dymynucioun' of the received matter. Chaucer's special adaptation of the modesty convention here, which will itself be mechanically echoed by such as Lydgate, makes an important statement about the complex relationship between *Troilus*, its sources and the audience. The insistence that the poet speaks 'alle under correccioun' of his readers grants them something like the active involvement with the text that modern theorists advocate. Yet, if the readers of *Troilus* are allowed their place in the process of creation, their labour is part of a extended process. As he rewrites Boccaccio and the others, Chaucer asks us to rewrite him. The original author does not dominate, nor does Chaucer himself nor even the reader, but each of the three has his part to play in producing the romance of Troilus and Criseyde.

In addition to its insistence that the reader be the author's collaborator, *Troilus* contains other passages that generally suggest modern ideas about language and literary reception. The much-discussed proem to book II, for instance, which directly and repeatedly addresses its readers, confronts the cultural and temporal relativity of language and human custom as well as announcing the inevitability of different readings of the poem based on individual experience. After again apologizing for his lack of amorous knowledge, which causes him to write 'of no sentement' (II.13) and 'of love unfelyngly' (II.19), the narrator reminds his audience that language can change within a thousand years so that words that once 'hadden pris' and were effective now seem 'wonder nyce and straunge' (II.24). This statement about the arbitrariness of human language (perhaps the most fundamental insight of post-Saussurian critical thought) is followed by a longer discussion of the contingency of human social behaviour: 'Ek for to wynnen love in sondry ages,/In sondry londes, sondry ben usages' (II.27–8).

The narrator then addresses particular persons in his audience, replacing the second person plural pronoun with the second person singular:

> Ek scarsly ben ther in this place thre
> That have in love seid lik, and don, in al;
> For to thi purpos this may liken the,
> And the right nought; yet al is seid or schal.
>
> (II.43–6)

We are told that what pleases one will be displeasing to another because language and action are so radically individual: scarcely three among those in the audience will have said or done the same things in love (and some like the narrator have not loved at all). Given the poet's awareness of the diversity of human language and experience, we can understand why he would not expect a uniform response to *Troilus*.[7] His appeal to Gower and Strode at the end of the poem to 'correcte' what he has written (V.1856–9), which I shall discuss in more detail in the final chapter, again argues for on the malleability of the text and the need for each reader to be responsible for his own form of the story.

In arguing for the importance of the reader in the interpretation of *Troilus and Criseyde*, I am following not only recent critical fashion but also a significant tradition in Chaucer studies, though one that may sometimes be overlooked today because its ideas tend to be expressed in the course of practical analysis rather than theoretically. In 1963, for instance, more than ten years before

Father Ong's famous *PMLA* article 'The writer's audience is always a fiction', which argued that the reader has 'to play the role in which the author has cast him' and thus take on a *persona* as surely as the narrator, Robert Payne observed in his valuable discussion of *Troilus* that 'the kinds of roles Chaucer creates for his narrators almost necessarily imply complementary roles for an audience which is nearly as much a created fiction within or around the poem as the narrator is' (*Key*, 228). Other Chaucerians have gone even further than the concept of an author-created audience to discuss the reader's active role in helping to realize *Troilus*. Robert Hanning cites the lines from book III just quoted above in arguing that the narrator proposes 'a partnership' with the audience (19), and A. C. Spearing observes the ways in which the narrator of *Troilus* works 'to draw the audience into the poem, to share in the work of creation and judgment he seems so inadequate to perform' (*Troilus*, 10). One of the most convincing accounts of the reader's participation in *Troilus and Criseyde* is by Dieter Mehl. Citing Jauss and Saussure, Mehl examines the many different audiences implied by the poem and thus finds an intricate dialogue in the poem between text and reader ('Audience').

The reader is central to the interpretations of *Troilus* by major critics as different as E. T. Donaldson and D. W. Robertson. In two important articles, 'Criseyde and her narrator' and 'The ending of "Troilus" ', Donaldson looks at a number of specific passages in which the reader's natural expectations are deliberately undermined in order to create complex and ironic effects. For example, the stout but naïve defences of Criseyde's behaviour by the narrator (such as II.666–72) are said to raise a number of disturbing questions about the heroine's character, just as our desire for resolution at the end of the poem is repeatedly frustrated as one false ending succeeds another and we are made to understand the difficulties of literary and moral closure. If Donaldson's work seems to anticipate the 'self-consuming artifacts' of Stanley Fish's early reader-response criticism, Robertson's exegetical approach has strong similarities with Fish's later idea of 'interpretive communities'. In contrast to Donaldson's account of how a sophisticated modern reader responds to individual moments in the poem, Robertson posits a medieval reader using contemporary strategies based on St Augustine and biblical exegesis. Such a reader knows that *Troilus and Criseyde* is a poem about illicit lust

not because that is what the text 'says', but because that is what
the beliefs and assumptions of his medieval Christian interpretive
community permit him to see. Despite their different conclusions
about the poem, both Donaldson and Robertson privilege the
reader's role, although the control of meaning remains elsewhere
for both: in the author for Donaldson and in the culture for
Robertson.

The analyses by both Donaldson and Robertson are based on
the assumption that there is an ideal reader for *Troilus*. Each
posits a highly skilled interpreter who is suspicious of the surface
narrative, but whereas Donaldson's ideal is a modern formalist
Robertson's is a medieval moralist. The strong disagreement
between these two influential critics about who is the correct
reader for the poem suggests that no such person exists. Instead
Troilus accommodates, even encourages, many different readers as
well as different readings by the same person. David Lawton notes
that 'not a specific audience but every imaginable type of public
is incorporated into the process of the written performance' of
Troilus (*Narrators*, 84), and Salter agrees that the 'many different
modes of address in *Troilus and Criseyde*' suggest 'that Chaucer
anticipated many different readings of his poem' ('Poet', 283).

Critics often assume that the primary audience of *Troilus and
Criseyde* is meant to be lovers; and, indeed, such are frequently
addressed in the poem: 'ye loveres, that bathen in gladnesse'
(I.22) or 'ye loveres that ben here' (II.1751). But, even though
the narrator sometimes acts as the partisan of lovers and directly
appeals to their expertise (III.1312–13), they seem at most to
constitute only one part of his audience. Often they are viewed
from afar in the poem as a somewhat alien group ('as thise lovers
don', V.1572), and the existence of non-lovers is also explicitly
recognized: for instance, 'Ye wise, proude, and worthi folkes alle'
are warned not to scorn love (I.232–8), and envious 'janglers'
listening to the poem who might accuse Criseyde of loving too
quickly are directly answered (II.666–9). *Troilus* is not written for
only one audience (to use other terms, it does not address only
one implied reader or contain only one narratee within the text);
rather, it appeals to a whole spectrum of readers in the course
of the narrative, some of whom are addressed more explicitly
than others.

The various reading roles suggested in *Troilus*, which may
be adopted by a range of different readers or by the same

reader in different moods, presume contradictory sets of values and thereby promote multiple interpretation of the text. To read a romance as a lover will produce a different result from reading it as a wise proud non-lover, yet *Troilus* encourages us to approach its narrative from either perspective (or from both). Nor do readers who are lovers or non-lovers begin to exhaust the possibilities of *Troilus*, for the poem explicitly addresses other audiences as well. For example, learned readers are assumed throughout – those able to understand casual references to classical myth, such as the story of Proigne at II.64–9, and who can be humorously imagined to resort to their libraries to decide how long it took Criseyde to betray Troilus: 'Take every man now to his bokes heede' (V.1089). A courtly reader is implied by the description of Criseyde and her nieces playing in their beautiful garden ('it joye was to see', II.817) and by the account of Troilus riding from battle on his horse ('God woot wher he was lik a manly knyght!', II.1263). The audience urged to lament Hector is explictly defined as warriors: 'For which me thynketh every manere wight/That haunteth armes oughte to biwaille/The deth of hym that was so noble a knyght' (V.1555–7). Elsewhere, the reader is imagined to be strongly moralistic, one who will join in damning Calchas's treachery ('this false and wikked dede', I.93), view with weary scorn ('O nyce world') the Trojan folly in exchanging Criseyde for Antenor (IV.197–210), and at the end reject utterly both Troilus' chivalric accomplishments (V.1828–32) and the pagan world (V.1849–55).

The different readers implied throughout *Troilus and Criseyde* need not be different persons, of course, but may be the same person reading at different times or with different interests. In addition we must be aware of highly sophisticated readers (like ourselves) who are capable of simultaneously appreciating a variety of contradictory interpretations. At the very end of the poem a series of individual readers, who need not be mutually exclusive and will be discussed in more detail in the final chapter, are implied in rapid succession. These include moralists (V.1748–50), those interested in military history (V.1751–71), women (V.1772–85), classicists (V.1786–92), students of language (V.1793–9), moralists again (V.1828–34), young people (V.1835–48), Christians (V.1849–55), Gower and Strode (V.1856-9), and finally Christ and the Trinity (V.1863–9). One of the groups directly addressed, women, is of special use in helping us to understand Chaucer's sophisticated awareness of the possibilities and problematics of multiple readings.

After explaining once again that his subject is love rather than warfare, the narrator suddenly turns to the ladies in his audience and begs them not to be angry with him even though he has described Criseyde's unfaithfulness. He asserts that he would rather have written the stories of good women and concludes with the surprising lesson that women should beware of the treachery of men:

> Bysechyng every lady bright of hewe,
> And every gentil womman, what she be,
> That al be that Criseyde was untrewe,
> That for that gilt she be nat wroth with me.
> Ye may hire gilt in other bokes se;
> And gladlier I wol write, yif yow leste,
> Penolopeës trouthe and good Alceste.
>
> N'y sey nat this al oonly for thise men,
> But moost for wommen that bitraised be
> Thorugh false folk – God yeve hem sorwe, amen! –
> That with hire grete wit and subtilte
> Bytraise yow. And this commeveth me
> To speke, and in effect yow alle I preye,
> Beth war of men, and herkneth what I seye!
>
> (V.1772–85).

Donaldson is surely justified in saying that such an absolute overturning of the traditional anti-feminist moral of the story is an 'excursion into farce' ('Ending', 95). Yet, if the passage may be seen as comic (which it certainly is), the lines also suggest a number of serious points about how one reads literary texts. At the very least, the assertion that Criseyde's infidelity is a warning against *men* must raise questions about exactly what moral meanings can legitimately be drawn from any particular story. We are asked to consider what the relationship is or should be between narrative and lesson. Is the proposed lesson here any more unreasonable than some of the neat and improbable morals traditionally drawn from complex texts or than the chaste Christian lessons the Middle Ages found in apparently shocking pagan stories?

More to the point, the passage makes us confront the effects of different classes of reader in producing literary meaning. In his address to a female audience, Chaucer asks us to imagine what it might mean to read *Troilus* as a woman.[8] The lesson that we might expect the usual medieval male reader to draw at the end of the poem (avoid unworthy women lovers), which is found in every version of the story known to Chaucer, would obviously have had little relevance to most medieval women. But that does not mean that the poem has nothing to say to them. A female reader might easily take the more general lesson (avoid treachery in love) and, adapting it to her own circumstance, conclude that *Troilus* shows, among other things, that woman should beware of untrustworthy men. Of course this is only one of the ways a woman might read *Troilus*. Even more shocking to conventional (male) expectation in the Middle Ages, she might conclude, as have many recent critics, that *Troilus* makes a profound statement about the evils of patriarchal society by repeatedly showing the betrayal of Criseyde by various men, including her father, her uncle, the Trojan parliament and Diomede. Chaucer's specific evocation of a female audience at the end of *Troilus* carries a general lesson for critics, be they male or female, which is reinforced by modern critical thought: literary meaning is never absolute or objective, but is always a function of particular readers and readings.

Medieval and Modern Readers

The multiplicity of *Troilus and Criseyde*, which the text itself announces and Chaucerians have long affirmed, is an authentic medieval quality. Although much writing in the Middle Ages is what Umberto Eco would call closed because like modern comic books or detective stories it narrowly predetermines the reader's response (obvious examples of this are sermons or simple moral tales like the *Gesta Romanorum*), major literary works, including the *Roman de la Rose* or the *Divina Commedia*, were far from univocal even to their original audiences, as the long and complex history of their reception and annotation testifies. The ideological dominance of Christianity in medieval Europe seems, paradoxically, to have allowed sophisticated writers a great deal of freedom. Because medieval authors and their audiences shared a single faith, the former could expect that literary interpretation by the latter, however diverse or unexpected, would fall within their common system of belief. *Troilus and Criseyde* testifies to Chaucer's trust in his audience. He feels free to wander far afield and into profane and pagan subjects because he assumes his readers always know where home is. Overt didacticism is unnecessary in *Troilus* and would only limit its usefulness to readers who are encouraged to discover what is most meaningful for themselves in the experience of the poem. Although the openness of *Troilus* is the result of its medieval Christian context, that openness cannot be cancelled retroactively but remains available to modern secular readers.

My argument that interpretation in *Troilus* is not only multiple but also a function of its individual readers has some precedent in the literary thought of Chaucer's day. In his famous 'defence of poetry' in the fourteenth book of the *Genealogia Deorum Gentilium*, Boccaccio makes a traditional argument about the effort an audience must undertake to recover the moral truths hidden in literature by poets, but in support he cites potentially more radical views of the reader's role from St Augustine (14.12). Quoting from the eleventh book of the *City of God*, Boccaccio presents Augustine's recognition of the openness of Scripture and welcome of individual interpretation: 'The obscurity of the divine word has certainly this advantage, that it causes *many opinions about the truth* to be started and discussed, *each reader seeing some fresh meaning in it*' (Boccaccio, *Poetry*, 60, my emphasis). Boccaccio then cites Augustine's words on Psalm 126, which note the profit of such multiple responses: 'For perhaps the words are rather obscurely expressed for this reason, *that they may call forth many understandings*, and that men may go away the richer, because they have found that closed *which might be opened in many ways*, than if they could open and discover it by one interpretation' (60, my emphasis). For Augustine, texts (at least, divine texts) do not necessarily contain hidden nuggets of authorial meaning to be extracted by great labour, as Boccaccio's general argument implies. Instead, the saint approves of a fruitful textual obscurity or openness that encourages many different interpretations by readers for their own individual benefit.

At the end of the *Decameron* Boccaccio himself seems to come even closer to the openness of the Augustinian position. Defending his work against charges of impropriety, Boccaccio argues that 'these tales, like all other things, may be harmful or useful depending on who the listener is' (686). He thus places the responsibility for interpretation and use squarely on the reader, though he also suggests that there is a right way intended by the author: 'Whoever wishes to derive evil counsel from them or use them for wicked ends will not be prohibited from doing so by the tales themselves if, by chance, they contain such things and are twisted and distorted in order to achieve this end; and whoever wishes to derive useful advice and profit from them will not be prevented from doing do, nor will these stories ever be described or regarded as anything but useful and proper if they are read at those times and to those people for whom they have been written' (686–7).

Of course, Boccaccio is having fun here (he warns away the potential woman reader who is forever praying or baking cakes for her confessor and insists his stories run after no one begging to be read), but his assumption that the reader is a crucial source for the meaning and use of stories (because any text can be adapted to beneficial or wicked ends) is widespread in the Middle Ages. Medieval historians such as Bede, Matthew Paris and Henry of Huntington, for instance, declare that their works contain examples both to imitate and to avoid, but they leave the actual discrimination between the two (and thus the moral instruction) to their readers (Benson, *History*, 11–12). In the preface to his *Ecclesiastical History* Bede announces that 'should history tell of good men and their good estate, the thoughtful listener is spurred on to imitate the good; should it record the evil ends of wicked men, no less effectively the devout and earnest listener or reader is kindled to eschew what is harmful and perverse, and himself with greater care pursue those things which he has learned to be good and pleasing in the sight of God' (2–3). There is a division of labour here between acts of composition and acts of interpretation. The historian provides the text, but the reader must identify in it examples of good rewarded and evil punished and then act to imitate or avoid them. Bede can depend on his readers (at least, the 'thoughtful' or 'devout and earnest reader') to use the text properly because of their shared faith: the responses of such readers may be various but they will not be indiscriminate; they will be in accord with 'those things which [the readers have] learned to be good and pleasing in the sight of God'.

Even more than such works of medieval history, *Troilus and Criseyde* demands the collaboration of its audience. Chaucer's poem is not a nut to be cracked in order to discover a sweet moralistic centre placed there by the author or a puzzle with a single correct answer; instead, it is an intense literary and human experience whose meanings will necessarily vary with different readers. Chaucer, along with Augustine and the medieval historians, trusts his readers and expects them to interpret his poem as befits their particular situations without explicit authorial direction. In fact, only individual readers are in a position to know what in the poem will be specifically relevant to them. The poet is unable to proclaim the meaning of his poem for the simple reason that he cannot anticipate the use his readers will make of it.

At the end of 'The Nun's Priest's Tale', Chaucer makes a statement about both the openness of his poetry and the central role of the reader:

> But ye that holden this tale a folye,
> As of a fox, or of a cok and hen,
> Taketh the moralite, goode men,
> For Seint Paul seith that al that writen is,
> To oure doctrine it is ywrite, ywis;
> Taketh the fruyt, and lat the chaf be stille.
> (VII.3438–43)

Previous critics have correctly noted the sly humour here at the expense of over-earnest contemporary moralists, but Chaucer, like Boccaccio, is often at his most serious when he is making us laugh. In addition to the comedy, the poet seems to be explaining how all his writing, including *Troilus*, ought to be approached. The responsibility of the writer is to produce a text, whether it be about a cock and a fox or two Trojan lovers, but the responsibility for finding meaning in that text, its 'fruit,' is left to the reader. We, as 'goode men' (and women), are to take whatever fruit we find relevant, even from a beast fable. Chaucer is content to allow his readers such extraordinary freedom in deciding what his poem means to them because he assumes that, whatever their individual interpretations, they all share with him a common search for truth within the Christian tradition – 'oure doctrine'.

The passage at the end of 'The Nun's Priest's Tale' defines the separate roles of poet and reader. The poet does not instruct directly, he does not hide an explicit moral within his fictions that we must extract like a plum from a pie; instead, he delights us so that we may instruct ourselves. His job is to attract our interest in his texts and involve us in his stories, but it is our job to create meaning from them. The author does not have to die to permit the birth of the reader – both are alive in their separate functions. Despite the best efforts of some modern critics to make him one, Chaucer is not a moral relativist; the openness of his texts is the result of trusting his readers and is his acknowledgement that they know best how to use what he has written. Of course Chaucer understands that not all his readers will achieve the thoughtfulness and devout earnestness expected by Bede. He can imagine a reading in bad faith, especially of a poem set in pagan times that lacks explicit moral teaching. This may be part of his motive for the 'retraction' of *Troilus* at the end of the *Canterbury Tales* along with other 'translacions and enditynges of worldly vanitees' (X.1084). In practice, however, Chaucer seems to agree with Boccaccio's argument at the end of *Decameron* that literature should not be limited to the narrowly didactic just because any work may be used for wicked ends. He seems to have had confidence in his readers and to accept the futility of attempting to control the variety of responses that will be provoked by his poem.

Records of the late-medieval and early-Renaissance reception of *Troilus* demonstrate that different audiences did read it differently. Whereas Troilus' fidelity to his mistress is extravagantly praised in courtly terms at the end of Wynkyn de Worde's 1517 edition of *Troilus* (Benson and Rollman), Lee Patterson has shown how a fifteenth-century pious tract is able to use lines from the poem in the service of a thoroughly orthodox Christian analysis of human love. The 'fruit' of *Troilus* for some of Chaucer's early readers might have been nothing more than the pleasure of an entertaining romance, for the therapeutic power of literature as recreation was well recognized in the Middle Ages (Olson). Other early readers found other fruits. Thomas Usk regarded *Troilus* as a repository of philosophical wisdom; a fifteenth-century prose summary of the siege of Troy drew on it for historical information (Benson, 'Prose "Sege" '); and Lydgate, as we saw at the beginning of this chapter, found it an exemplar of rhetorical splendour.

Even the fruit that will be gathered by those readers primarily concerned with moral instruction cannot be anticipated or controlled by Chaucer. Depending on their situation and particular needs, individual readers might draw various lessons from the text. To adapt Bede's terms, an infinite number of good and evil examples to imitate or avoid can be discovered in *Troilus*. To choose just a few obvious illustrations, Troilus may represent heroic loyalty or weak irresolution, Criseyde may earn our sympathy or our contempt, and Pandarus may seem a scheming devil, a fast friend or, to go beyond simple dualities, a model of an effective speaker and thus worthy of imitation, like the literary achievements of pagan literature.

A central debate in recent reader-response criticism has been about the relationship between the reader's subjectivity and the text. Some argue that the text does (or should) fully determine the response of its readers, others that readers are completely free, others that there is interaction between the two, and still others that meaning is wholly determined by interpretive conventions. Chaucer's practice in *Troilus and Criseyde* suggests a somewhat different approach. Although the poem is open to many different interpretations, the Christian world in which it was written and whose values are made explicit at the end creates the specific cultural context in which the work was first read. The original Christian reader of *Troilus* is allowed such wide freedom of interpretation because Chaucer can, quite literally, assume his or her good faith. A variety of responses appropriate to individual readers is encouraged in the confidence that they will fall within a shared system of belief.

But, if the openness of *Troilus* comes from its particular historical situation in a cohesive Catholic culture, where does that leave modern readers? Our world is secular and pluralist, and it accepts few of the common assumptions and practices of the Middle Ages. Yet the openness of *Troilus* must be available to us as surely as it was to the medieval reader, even though we are not the audience for whom the poem was written. A house that is left unlocked by its owners because they trust their neighbours is also open to unanticipated strangers. *Troilus* cannot be bolted and closed up retrospectively, even if modern readers may be thought to abuse the freedom of interpretation that they have inherited along with the poem itself. In the following chapters we shall investigate some of the many ways that Chaucer has transformed and complicated Boccaccio' *Filostrato* by the addition of original and diverse materials that have incited a variety of contradictory critical interpretations. Perhaps the greatest value of this approach for us as skilled twentieth-century readers is that it may help us to avoid reductive response and better appreciate the multiple literary pleasures available in the experience of Chaucer's masterpiece.

Notes

1   The structure of *Troilus* is also much more sophisticated than that of *Filostrato*. In contrast to the nine parts of the Italian work, which vary widely in length, Chaucer reshapes his poem into five books, all of them roughly the same length except for the first. This five-book structure, which may have been influenced by Boethius's *Consolation of Philosophy* (McCall, 'Five-Book') or Roman tragedy (Norton-Smith), imitates the progress of the narrative: two books of rising action, the happiness of lovers in the central book, and two books of falling action.

2   Medieval discussion of the three styles rarely becomes more precise than this. Along with Pandarus, who in his advice on letter-writing echoes Horace (II.1030–6), *Ad Herennium* recognizes that speakers, like writers or harpists, must play more than one note to keep the interest of an audience: 'But in speaking we should vary the type of style, so that the middle succeeds the grand and the simple the middle, and then again interchange them, and yet again. Thus, by means of the variation, satiety is easily avoided' (268–9). Similarly, Augustine in the fourth book of *On Christian Doctrine* declares that all three styles can be found in the Bible as well as in the writings of such as Ambrose and Cyprian, and he insists on the efficacy of this variety: 'But no one should think that it is contrary to theory to mix these three manners; rather, speech should be varied with all types of style in so far as this may be done appropriately. For when one style is maintained too long, it loses the listener' (158). The most impressive analysis of medieval rhetorical devices in *Troilus* is by Payne (*Key*).

3   Such vivacity is generally praised by modern critics, but in the early nineteenth century William Godwin's narrow view of stylistic decorum led him to deplore the poet's 'many base and vulgar lines', which 'would be a deformity in any prose composition, and even dishonour and debase the tone of familiar conversation' (303). Despite his harsh tone, Godwin is not here referring to obscenity in *Troilus*, but to such vivacious examples of the low style as 'The wrecche is ded, the devel have his bones' (I.805) and 'Ne knewe hem more than myn olde hat' (III.320).

4   Muscatine himself notes the flexibility of his conception of the two styles when discussing Criseyde, whom he argues 'speaks in both

idioms' (*French*, 153). I would suggest that Troilus and Pandarus also each sometimes adopt the other's idiom.

5 Two major anthologies of articles on reader-response theory have appeared (Tompkins; Suleiman and Crosman). Affective stylistics or reader-response criticism tends to be more varied and less rigid than some other contemporary theoretical schools, with practitioners who vigourously attack one another and draw on the insights of such diverse fields as literary history, psychology, aesthetics, politics and phenomenology. Stanley Fish, for instance, has remained a central, even notorious, figure even as he has moved from the examination of specific reading experience in his early writing (*Surprised*) to his more recent work on the determining role of specific 'interpretative communities' in producing literary meaning (*Text*). Although work on the role of the reader was probably at its most innovative in the 1970s, interest in the reader has not died out but has been absorbed into more general critical practices. For the particular importance of affective stylistics in Chaucer studies, see Wood, 'Affective', and Travis.

6 Although Fish ('Why') has attacked the liberality and generosity of Iser's work, its humane lack of theoretical rigidity may explain its appeal for actual readers. Scholes has recently noted the imprecision of Fish's concept of 'interpretive communities' and, like Iser, makes an argument for preserving the integrity of the text itself.

7 This paragraph generally follows Peter Travis's discussion of the proem to book II (204), but Travis's subsequent suggestion that Chaucer wishes to 'guide the reader in the direction of right reading' and that his poetry has an 'intended effect' (205) grants the poet more authority (and readers less) over the way that *Troilus* is to be interpreted than I believe is warranted. Later in this chapter I shall argue for a clear distinction between Chaucer as producer of poetry and the reader as producer of meaning.

8 The concept of reading as a woman has been discussed by Culler, 43–64, and by Schweickart.

4

Troy

Troy and its history are largely incidental to Boccaccio's poem, and the Italian poet makes little effort to present the city as anything more than a vague backdrop for his love-story. Not so Chaucer. *Troilus and Criseyde* contains tangible buildings, streets and gardens, and it is peopled with men and women who form intricate social and personal relationships. Chaucer's city has what Spearing calls a 'material realism' (*Troilus*, 55) and is located in a specific historical period. Its residents follow pagan customs and are always conscious of the besieging Greek army. Yet, if Chaucer gives a sense of reality and history to the nominal setting of *Filostrato*, the result is no simple exercise in antiquarianism. The Troy of *Troilus and Criseyde* is also familiar and medieval. Its architecture and furnishings are those of fourteenth-century London, and the royal family is seen in the intimate domesticity of courtly private life. Although Boccaccio provides some suggestion for many of the Trojan elements in *Troilus*, Chaucer repeatedly makes actual what is only potential in *Filostrato* as he deepens and complicates his portrait of the city. Chaucer's Troy is simultaneously more believably ancient and more contemporary than its source, more political and more personal, more historical and more exemplary, more Christian and more pagan. The world of Troy is an excellent introduction to Chaucer's varied transformations of *Filostrato*. My purpose in the following pages is to identify a few of the many contrasting elements that Chaucer has added to his source in order to create a powerful experience of Troy for his readers.

Chaucer's Troy in History and Myth

One element that Chaucer added to his account of Troy is a much greater sense of the historical reality of the Trojan War.

Whereas *Filostrato* purports to be a version of Boccaccio's own adventures in love, a central role adopted by the narrator of *Troilus and Criseyde* is that of ancient historian (Lewis, 'What Chaucer', 59–60; Bloomfield, 'Distance', 14). Instead of using the story of Troilus and Criseyde as covert autobiography, Chaucer announces that he draws on ancient written sources, especially the Latin work of a certain Lollius (I.394 and V.1653). Such claims to history would not have seemed preposterous to medieval readers, who believed they possessed eyewitness testimony about the Trojan War ultimately derived from Dares and Dictys and preserved in works such as Benoît's *Roman de Troie* and Guido's *Historia Destructionis Troiae*.[1] Unlike Benoît and Guido, Chaucer declines to retell the complete history of the Trojan War (I.141–7), but, to a far greater extent than Boccaccio, he borrows their facts and mimics their perspective.

The Trojan War is especially prominent in the early part of *Troilus and Criseyde*. Whereas *Filostrato* opens with only the most general account of the Greek siege to avenge the rape of Helen (1.7), Chaucer fills out this setting with traditional details about the number of ships that came from Greece (one thousand) and the ten-year length of the siege (I.57–63). Some of Chaucer's information derives specifically from the medieval historical tradition. To Boccaccio's general statement that Calchas understood every secret of Apollo (1.8), Chaucer adds the scholarly detail that Apollo was called Phoebus or 'Appollo Delphicus' (I.70), just as he later has Criseyde mention that her father discovered the city's doom from his god at Delphos (IV.1411), an incident not in *Filostrato* but related by both Benoît and Guido. From them Chaucer probably also learned that one of the Trojan gates was called 'Dardanus' (II.618), a name that appears nowhere in *Filostrato*.

Chaucer continually reminds us that his story takes place in the midst of a genuine military conflict. In addition to being a lover, Troilus is also portrayed as a warrior with an important role in the defence of the city. Several passages added to *Filostrato*, which are reminiscent of episodes in the medieval Trojan historical narratives, show the prince either conquering on the battlefield or returning triumphant to Troy.[2] As Geoffrey Shepherd has noted: 'The background of war is much more prominent in Chaucer's telling of the story than in Boccaccio's. The confrontation of the nations, the everlasting state of siege, the daily skirmishes and the truces, the counsels of state and the debates on policy, these constitute a great stable pattern to the life imagined in the story' (*'Troilus'*, 68). Casual references to the war, without parallel in Boccaccio, occur often. For instance, Pandarus tells his niece that he first learned Troilus was in love while they were in a garden planning how 'we the Grekes myghten disavaunce' (II.511), and he later mentions a mysterious 'Greek espie', reminiscent of Sinon, in order to be able to talk privately with Criseyde (II.1112).

The effect of this added historical material is far from simple. Even though the city is encircled by a hostile army, the general attitude towards the war is optimistic in the first half of the poem because the Trojans are never shown in defeat. Hector is described as 'the townes wal and Grekes yerde' (II.154), and Troilus is apparently irresistible: 'in the feld he pleyde tho leoun' (I.1074). To impress his niece, Pandarus recounts his friend's success the day before in making the Greeks flee like a swarm of bees (II.190–203), and Criseyde herself later witnesses a public celebration following another victory as the townspeople declare: 'Se, Troilus/Hath right now put to flighte the Grekes route!' (II.612–13).

Yet more ominous suggestions may be found within the dominant optimism. The opening lines of the poem remind the reader of the eventual destruction of the city (I.68, I.74, I.76–7), and we are shown the social strains caused by the war. After Calchas's desertion to the Greeks, the Trojans are so indignant that they want to burn 'al his kyn at-ones' (I.90), and the helpless isolation of the abandoned Criseyde is insisted upon: 'For bothe a widewe was she and allone/Of any frend to whom she dorste hir mone' (I.97–8). The sense of betrayal and anxiety created in this opening scene is never completely relieved. Although the narrator shortly thereafter declares that his 'matere' is not 'how this town com to destruccion' (I.141–4) and does not directly mention the fall of Troy again until book IV, the doom predicted by Calchas always remains just below the surface as part of the reader's response to the subsequent narrative. Whatever the power and nobility of Troy, it is a civilization whose end is near and certain.

Criseyde herself is also in a precarious position. The immediate danger to her because of her father's desertion is removed by Hector's intervention, which allows her to dwell honourably in Troy beloved by all (I.127–31), but her unease about the

war remains. When Pandarus first comes to her and announces
that he brings good news, she responds, in lines original with
Chaucer: 'For Goddes love; is than th'assege aweye?/I am of
Grekes so fered that I deye' (II.123–4). The fear that Criseyde
so powerfully expresses is quickly, if perhaps too easily, dismissed by Pandarus' extravagant claim that what he has to
say is fully five times better than peace (II.126). Pandarus has
come with a message about love, which will be the principal
subject of the poem, but at the same time *Troilus* never lets
us completely forget that love in Troy exists within the context
of war.

The addition of classical myth and legend even more powerfully
situates Chaucer's Troy in the ancient past. *Filostrato* contains
several casual citations of the most prominent pagan deities,
especially Jove and Apollo, and on rare occasions mentions heroes
such as Hercules, but the range and number of its allusions
are severely limited. In contrast to the sprinkling of classical
references in *Filostrato*, *Troilus and Criseyde* is saturated with
mythological allusions, most of which are relatively brief. As
John McCall argues, these additions are made to seem 'real'
rather than merely rhetorical from the start: 'They are justified
by history, and they help make history live so that – aside from
the narrator's own uses – many of the mythological references
appear to be elements of everyday discourse rather than "classical
allusions" ' (*Gods*, 22).

The characters of *Troilus and Criseyde* refer easily and often to
the pagan deities. When Pandarus tells Criseyde that she is the
woman, except for romantic attachments, whom he loves best,
he swears the truth of his assertion with an impressive list of
divine names:

> by the goddesse Mynerve,
> And Jupiter, that maketh the thondre rynge,
> And by the blisful Venus that I serve.
> (II.232–4)

When the occasion demands, any of Chaucer's Trojans is capable
of producing a roll-call of immortals. Bereft of Criseyde, Troilus
curses everything and everyone, including 'Jove, Appollo, and
ek Cupide . . . Ceres, Bacus, and Cipride' (V.207–8). More
poignantly, Criseyde calls on Juno to make her dwell in hellish

Styx like mad Athamas and asks Atropos to end her life if she is
ever false to Troilus, swearing to be true by the River Symois and
by 'every god celestial . . . and ek on eche goddesse', as well as
by every nymph, infernal deity, satyr and faun (IV.1534–54).

The pagan gods and the related world of classical legend are
more familiar to Chaucer's characters than to Boccaccio's. In
an original example early in the poem, Pandarus refers to the
metamorphosed figure of 'Nyobe the queene' as if one could
still visit it: 'Whos teres yet in marble ben yseene' (I.699–700).
Although Troilus irritably replies that he cares nothing about
Niobe and tells his friend to 'lat be thyne olde ensaumples'
(I.759–60), an undeterred Pandarus goes on to cite, with no source
in *Filostrato*, Tityus, perpetually tormented by vultures (I.786–8),
and Cerberus, the hellish hound (I.859). Even Troilus uses such
'olde ensaumples' easily: he refers to several mythological love-
stories not mentioned by Boccaccio just before he approaches
Criseyde's bed (III.720–30) and associates himself with the fate
of blind Oedipus (IV.300–1), as well as imagining that he will
dwell 'in pyne' with Proserpina (IV.473–4), an expansion from the
Italian hero's vague forecast of suffering torments 'nello 'nferno'
('in hell', 4.54). Criseyde is also familiar with ancient stories of
love unknown to her Italian original: she wishes her first night
of passion with Troilus could last 'as longe as whan Almena lay
by Jove' (III.1428) and later compares the threatened separation
from her lover to that of Orpheus from Eurydice (IV.790–1).[3]

The many mythological and legendary allusions added to *Troilus
and Criseyde* help to locate Troy in history and convince us that
we are reading about an ancient pre-Christian civilization. But, as
with Chaucer's use of material about the Trojan War, these original
passages are capable of producing a variety of different effects. One
such is a strong statement of Chaucer's literary ambition. Myth is
an important device by which *Troilus and Criseyde*, in contrast to
most other English writing of the time, declares its intent to imitate
the achievement of the great Latin poets.[4] The elaborate proems,
especially, stake out such a claim, as in the opening invocation to
Thesiphone (Tisiphone), 'sorwynge evere in peyne' (I.9), probably
influenced by Statius' *Thebaïd*, an invocation which announces
both a desire to follow in the classical tradition and the poem's
concern with pain and suffering.

Myth also has thematic functions in *Troilus*, though we should
never assume the meanings it suggests are obvious or unitary.

Given the widespread medieval practice of allegorizing myth for
Christian ends, a reader might conclude that the many allusions
to infernal figures in the early books of the poem indicate that
the love of Troilus and Criseyde is damned and sinful. Such an
interpretation has some justification but ignores the multiplicity
in both the mythographic tradition and in Chaucer's poetic practice. Medieval mythographers drew secular as well as religious
lessons from the stories they analysed and often provided a
series of different explanations for a single episode. Moreover,
the reader must constantly decide whether particular allusions
in *Troilus* should be interpreted as a moral judgement or only
as establishing a certain tone. A brief infernal image might
suggest unease about the outcome of the love between Troilus and
Criseyde without necessarily condemning the affair as absolutely
evil. Finally, we must consider the context of the images. John
McCall cautions against assuming that the hellish allusions in the
poem necessarily produce an unambiguous moral lesson, 'for they
stand against another cluster of joyous mythical allusions which
suggest that earthly love is like a paradise' (*Gods*, 30). In its use
of myth, as in the other elements added to its account of Troy,
Troilus offers a rich literary experience, including the potential of
allegory, whose meanings must be realized by individual readers.
The text is constructed so as to offer a range of possibilities.

The significance as well as the openness of myth in *Troilus
and Criseyde* can be seen near the very beginning of book II,
as Pandarus arises from a night's sleep and prepares to set out
on the 'grete emprise' (II.73) of wooing Criseyde for Troilus as
he had promised the day before. The entire passage is original
with Chaucer (Boccaccio has Pandaro pass directly from Troiolo's
dwelling to Criseida's), and the mythological allusion is insistent:

> The swalowe Proigne, with a sorowful lay,
> Whan morwen com, gan make hire waymentynge
> Whi she forshapen was; and ever lay
> Pandare abedde, half in a slomberynge,
> Til she so neigh hym made hire cheterynge
> How Tereus gan forth hire suster take,
> That with the noyse of hire he gan awake.
>   (II.64–70)

The story referred to here, which Chaucer could have found
in Dante, Ovid and elsewhere, is one of the most horrible in

classical literature: Tereus has been sent by his wife, Procne, to bring back her sister Philomela for a visit; but Tereus, overcome by lust, instead rapes and mutilates his sister-in-law. In response, Procne and Philomela exact a grisly revenge by making Tereus unknowingly eat his own son in a meal they have prepared, following which they themselves are metamorphosed into a nightingale and swallow respectively.

Chaucer's reference to Procne at the beginning of book II is prominent even if its precise significance is uncertain. We can safely say that the association of the swallow with the ancient story of Procne contributes to the historical setting of *Troilus* and displays the poem's learning and literary ambition: two of the functions of myth already discussed. The problem comes when we try to determine how the allusion affects our understanding of the events and characters in the poem. Comparing Chaucer's passage with a similar one at the beginning of Dante's *Purgatorio* (9), Wetherbee concludes that the effect is to contrast Virgil's spiritual mission with Pandarus' very different enterprise (155–6). The lines could be read even more negatively, as indicating that Pandarus' involvement in the affair is wicked even to the point of incest. The text certainly permits such interpretations (especially for the modern reader trained in close reading and alert for the subversive), but it does not demand it.

Although this terrifying example of the consequences of lust 'introduces an ominous note' to Pandarus' amorous errand (Windeatt, *Troilus* edition, 155nII.64–70), the poem frustrates any attempt to forge a direct and irrefutable connection between the two episodes. The gap is simply too large. Whatever his other faults, and however unsavoury his interest in the lovers, Chaucer's Pandarus is not guilty of physical rape and mutilation, nor do his actions provoke a retaliatory murder. Although it may be too much to say that the reference to Procne turns out to be a 'false clue' (Miller, 65), because in literature all clues have potential meaning, *Troilus* does not itself develop the negative associations suggested by the mythological story. Indeed, when a nightingale is mentioned as Criseyde falls asleep at the end of the same day, no reference at all is made to Philomela, though we might well expect it: instead we are shown an apparently literal bird in nature ('upon a cedre grene') without mythological association, whose singing 'ful loude . . . ayein the moone shene' makes Criseyde's 'herte fressh and gay' (II.918–22). The ominous note at the beginning of book II appears to have metamorphosed into a delightful song of spring. Sexual tragedy has given way to courtly lyric. Of course, if a reader chooses to take these passages more darkly, bringing to bear the full horror of the mythological story, the text allows it, but the result is only indirectly due to Chaucer. The poet has deepened and complicated the narrative texture of the episode, but the exact relationship between Procne and Pandarus is left to individual readers. The only danger here and elsewhere is that the reader may too quickly rush to judgement without considering the full range of interpretations made possible by the poem. Although the mythological world of Troy contributes to the experience of *Troilus and Criseyde*, it does not provide a certain guide to meaning.

Ancient and Medieval Troy

The military and mythological additions to *Troilus and Criseyde* we have just discussed locate Chaucer's city in the distant past, but other original materials in the poem make Troy seem remarkably contemporary. Morton Bloomfield is especially sensitive in his analysis of the 'shifting sense of nearness and farness' in the poem ('Distance', 17), but most Chaucerians have usually been content to look at only one temporal element while ignoring the other (McCall, '*Troilus*', 449). One school follows Kittredge in arguing that Chaucer 'Trojanized' *Filostrato* by adding elements 'meant to produce or intensify an atmosphere of high antiquity' ('Lollius', 51–4); whereas others, from a variety of perspectives, claim that what Chaucer accomplished, in the words of C. S. Lewis, is 'first and foremost a process of medievalization' ('What Chaucer', 56). However contradictory these readings may seem, I suggest that both are true. *Filostrato* takes place in a vague atemporal setting that is neither ancient nor modern, but Chaucer's Troy exists in the two worlds simultaneously: more convincingly ancient than Boccaccio's city, it is also more infused with medieval values and practices.

Several famous older scholars, like Kittredge and Tatlock ('Epilog'), recognized a strong antiquarian strain added to *Troilus and Criseyde*: the many original touches designed to convince the reader that the events of the poem had taken place long ago and far away. More recently, John Frankis has noted the amount of pagan 'local colour' in *Troilus* (59), and A. C. Spearing has commented on the poet's 'scholarly interest in the pagan and "classical" details of his story' (*Troilus*, 55). The most casual actions of the characters reveal Chaucer's efforts to establish the pastness of Troy, as when Troilus creates an alibi by saying that he will be doing 'sacrifise' to Apollo (III.537–43) or when Pandarus swears 'by stokkes and by stones' (III.589). In describing the Trojan festival in honour of Pallas, the narrator refers to 'hire olde usage' (I.150) instead of Boccaccio's 'modi usati' ('usual customs', 1.17) and 'hire observaunces olde' (I.160) instead of 'li consueti onori' ('customary devotions', 1.18). The historical remoteness of Troy is further emphasized by repeated references to the even earlier story of Thebes, including mention of 'the geste/Of the siege of Thebes' (II.83–4) to which Criseyde is listening when we first see her at home and the more pointed account that Cassandra later gives Troilus of Theban history (V.1457–1519).[5]

Not all Chaucerians have been convinced by the antiquity of Chaucer's Troy, however. Citing anachronisms like 'hell' and 'bishop', some deny that Chaucer had any genuine sense of the past.[6] In a direct attack on Kittredge and Tatlock, Robert Mayo argues that 'measured by present-day standards' the Trojan setting of *Troilus* is not very prominent or persuasive, nor has it been 'fully *realized* in the nineteenth-century sense' (255–6). Michael West, while noting the addition of 'archaizing detail' in the poem, also asserts that 'Chaucer lacks a modern sense of time as history' (186). By their own words, Mayo and West reveal why such arguments, even if narrowly correct, are irrelevant. Of course Chaucer does not have a modern sense of history that meets the standards of the nineteenth and twentieth centuries. How could he possibly have had such? The most we can ask of an early writer is that his conception of the past be convincing according to contemporary knowledge. By that test, Chaucer is extraordinarily successful. Although Chaucer's Troy seems quite medieval from a modern perspective, Alastair Minnis (*Pagan*), following the pioneering work of Beryl Smalley, has shown that the poet reflects the best English scholarship of his day in portraying the pagan world with sympathy and accuracy.

Perhaps more impressive than Chaucer's many historical and mythological additions is his restraint. He carefully avoids anything that would destroy the antiquity of Troy for his original readers. What may appear to us as anachronisms would not have been seen as such by a medieval audience. 'Hell' is the standard Middle English translation of 'inferno', for instance, just as calling the Theban Amphiorax a bishop points to high ecclesiastic office without implying that the papacy had been established at the time of the siege of Thebes. We may be startled that Pandarus cites the authority of 'clerkes wyse' (I.961) and that Troy is populated by 'many a lusty knyght' (I.165), but the presence of either group in Troy would not have surprised the Middle Ages, which believed in the continuity between ancient and contemporary learning and warfare.

Chaucer always seems to know where to draw the line. His narrator is medieval, of course, and so is historically justified in making Christian comments like 'God foryaf his deth, and she al so' (III.1577), however remarkable the phrase may be in other ways, but the poet is 'careful not to put specifically Christian sentiments into the mouths of his characters' (Dunning, 171). Although 'God' is frequently invoked, even 'almyghty God' (IV.693 and V.1742), and Criseyde mentions 'holy seyntes lyves' (II.118), the divinities actually named are all pagan and the saints never Christian. Antigone says that 'seyntes' know about 'hevene' and 'fendes' about 'helle' (II.894–6), but the only residents of the lower realm we see in the poem are classical, just as when Troilus ascends to the heavens after death he is escorted by Mercury. The apparent exception to the consistent paganism of the characters in *Troilus and Criseyde*, as Bloomfield notes ('Sense', 308n17), is Criseyde's casual reference in some manuscripts to the 'God that bought us bothe two' (III.1165). Knowledge of the Redemption would be undeniably Christian, but we may doubt (with Bloomfield, editors such as Root, and several early manuscripts) that the offending word is truly Chaucerian (they read 'wrought' instead of 'bought'); and, even if it is genuine, the rarity of such a blunder testifies to the care with which Troy is presented as ancient and pagan throughout *Troilus and Criseyde*.

Yet there is also real truth in the view of those who insist that Chaucer's Troy is recognizably medieval: 'only the names are ancient; the characters, the manners, are modern and contemporary' (Root, *Poetry*, 87). Despite the antiquarian information added to *Troilus and Criseyde* and its avoidance of Boccaccio's occasional absurdities (such as having Pandaro refer to Mount Etna), there can be no doubt that 'Chaucer pictured Troy as much like his own London' (Magoun, 160). Both cities have surrounding walls and a river running through them, and, more significantly, the houses of Troilus, Pandarus and Criseyde – with their sparsely furnished bedchambers, paved parlours, gutters and attached gardens – closely resemble the great palaces of fourteenth-century London. As Smyser and Magoun have shown, there is nothing exotic about the domestic architecture of *Troilus and Criseyde*. In keeping with a general amplification of setting, the buildings and rooms of Troy are described in more detail by Chaucer than by Boccaccio, but almost everything would have seemed familiar to the original readers of *Troilus*.

Chaucer's Troy is also more obviously Christian than Boccaccio's city. Although the English poet is careful not to violate the paganism of his characters, he adds many passages that would suggest contemporary practice and beliefs to the medieval (and modern) reader, an aspect of the poem that will be discussed more fully in the final chapter. For example, the characters frequently echo common Christian expressions (though of course they are unaware of the parallel), as when Pandarus refers to Cupid as 'Immortal god . . . that mayst nought deyen' (III.185) or Criseyde swears that she cares more for Troilus than for the whole world 'Or ellis se ich nevere Joves face' (IV.1337). Moreover, as in other medieval courtly works, the love-affair is repeatedly described with a religious vocabulary derived from Christianity. To choose a few brief examples among many, Pandarus urges Troilus to 'repente' and insists that he ask the God of Love for 'grace' (I.932–3), and Troilus himself begs Criseyde for 'mercy' and 'grace' (III.1172–6).

That Chaucer is consciously emphasizing the similarities be-tween Troy's pagan belief and Christianity seems clear when we compare *Troilus and Criseyde* with 'The Knight's Tale', his other adaptation of a Boccaccian poem of antiquity. Pagan worship in 'The Knight's Tale' is always portrayed as exotic, even bizarre, as we see especially in the long accounts of the temples of Mars, Venus and Diana, the sacrifices made there by Arcite, Palamon and Emelye to their respective gods (who actually appear in the poem), and Arcite's funeral. As I have argued elsewhere, Chaucer goes out of his way in 'The Knight's Tale' to insist on the strangeness of these rites by adding obviously non-Christian details such as the 'hornes fulle of meeth' (I.2279) that Emelye brings to her sacrifice (*'Knight's Tale'*). In contrast, there is nothing as unusual as this in the religious world of *Troilus and Criseyde* and much that would have been familiar to a medieval audience. Although Troilus mentions sacrifices, we never actually see any, and the Palladian festival (the only religious rite we see in detail) is described quite blandly and might have reminded the original audience of Easter. Minnis rightly insists on Chaucer's genuine sense of the past, but he over-states the case by claiming that the settings of both *Troilus and Criseyde* and the 'The Knight's Tale' are 'as consciously pagan as he could make them' (*Pagan*, 22). The statement may be true for the latter work, but ignores the prominent strands of 'medievalization' in the former. Whereas Chaucer repeatedly insists on the difference between paganism and Christianity in 'The Knight's Tale', in *Troilus and Criseyde* he suggests continuities as well.[7]

My purpose in discussing some of the competing historical elements added to *Troilus and Criseyde* has been to call attention to their presence and variety rather than to offer any definitive explication. More detailed and specifically realized than Boccaccio's city, Chaucer's Troy allows (indeed, virtually demands) multiple interpretation. In accord with sophisticated contemporary learning, Chaucer created a convincing classical setting, yet the result goes beyond an exercise in antiquarianism, however scholarly. The Troy of *Troilus and Criseyde* would also have been more recognizable and immediate to its original audience than Boccaccio's city would have been to its audience. One result of this familiarity would have been to suggest the exemplary potential of Troy. Its story may be seen to contain pertinent lessons for the contemporary residents of the city often called 'New Troy" – Chaucer's London.[8]

Trojan Courtly Society

The society found within the walls of Troy is more intricate in *Troilus* than in *Filostrato*. Whereas Boccaccio concentrates almost exclusively on the emotions of his two lovers, Chaucer introduces us to other kinds of personal relationship among the aristocracy. His Troy contains several characters who do not appear in its source (Antigone and Helen, for example), and he gives more prominent roles to others (such as Pandarus and Deiphebus). These sympathetic nobles, who live in a luxurious world without the moral restraints of Christianity, represent an ideal of pagan courtliness. The disparity in class between the lovers that made marriage impossible in *Filostrato* is eliminated by Chaucer, who raises in status both Criseyde, who like Troilus lives in a palace, and her uncle, now made an adviser to King Priam. Yet, for all its attractiveness, Trojan society is far from innocent. Its members understand power, practise deceit, and are constrained by political realities.

The charm of Trojan society is apparent early in the poem during the Palladian festival, which the war does not cancel and which allows us to ignore Calchas's prediction of ruin. The season is delightful ('of lusty Veer the pryme'), and the happy citizens include not only romance exemplars ('many a lusty knyght' and 'many a lady fressh and mayden bright'), but also those from other ranks: 'Ful wel arayed, both meeste, mene, and leste,/Ye, bothe for the seson and the feste' (I.155–68). In the rest of *Troilus and Criseyde*, however, it is almost exclusively courtly society that we see. The English poem insists on the ease and comfort of private life for the Trojan élite. When we first see Criseyde at home, in a scene original to *Troilus*, she is sitting with two other ladies 'withinne a paved parlour' listening to a fourth read a romance (II.78–84). Even more than the luxury of her palace, which includes a beautiful formal garden (II.820–3) and such furnishings as an exotic jasper stone chair with a gold cushion (II.1228–9), Chaucer emphasizes her pleasant social intercourse with other women, none of whom appears in *Filostrato*. In addition to frequent mention of a number of unnamed female attendants, Criseyde is shown taking a walk in her garden with three nieces (Flexippe, Tarbe and Antigone) and 'other of hire wommen, a gret route' and playing so 'that it joye was to see' (II.813–19). Antigone then initiates a long discussion about love and later accompanies Criseyde to the dinner-party given by Deiphebus. Similar courtly enjoyments are still to be found near the end of the poem at King Sarpedon's house, which offers the best in wine (as well as in food), women and song (V.435–48).

The virtues of Trojan high society are best represented by Troilus' two brothers, Hector and Deiphebus, especially in their dealings with Criseyde. Left alone and vulnerable after her father's desertion, Criseyde appeals to Hector's mercy and receives a promise of full protection from this paradigm of chivalry (I.106–26). Moved by her beauty, Hector acts primarily out of 'goodnesse' (I.116) when he promises that she may, if she wishes, continue to dwell 'in joie/. . . in Troie' (I.118–19). Hector wants nothing in return for his magnanimity, and Criseyde and Pandarus later praise him for his exceptional combination of military might and moral virtue (II.167 and II.179).

If the behaviour of Chaucer's Hector justifies his traditional inclusion as one of the three pagan Worthies, his brother Deiphebus, who 'comen was of kynde/To alle honour and bounte to consente' (II.1443–4), represents the more domestic virtues of Trojan society. Upon being told of a supposed threat to Criseyde from a certain Poliphete (really an invention by Pandarus to bring the lovers together), the unsuspecting Deiphebus immediately agrees to hold a dinner-party to rally support for what he believes to be a fatherless widow in distress. The long scene at his house extending from the end of book II into book III, which has no source in *Filostrato* and whose 'effect is to enhance the joy, beauty, and easy pleasures that we have already seen in the city' (McCall, *Gods*, 96), offers an intimate glimpse into the private lives of the Trojan royal family and supports Pandarus' judgement that 'Swych love of frendes regneth al this town' (II.379). We learn that Deiphebus is the brother whom Troilus 'lovest best' (II.1396) as well as being Pandarus' 'grete frend' (II.1403). For his part, Deiphebus expresses love for both Troilus and Pandarus, identifies Criseyde as 'my frend' (II.1424), and says that Hector need not be invited because he is already friendly towards the lady (II.1450–6). At the dinner-party itself the royal family acts with generous concern towards both lovers: sympathetic to the bedridden Troilus, who has feigned illness to further Pandarus' scheme, they cannot do too much for Criseyde despite her father's treason. After Pandarus tells the guests about the imaginary outrages of Poliphete, they all rush to Criseyde's defence, promising 'To ben hire help in al that evere they myghten' (II.1624). Deiphebus' dinner-party reveals a web of affectionate Trojan relationships that extends far beyond the passionate love of Troilus and Criseyde.

The response of readers to Chaucer's depiction of Trojan society has not been uniform. Two major critics, for instance, have recently offered radically different views of Deiphebus' dinner-party, though both regard it as an accurate representation of life in the city and note its parallel to the central consumma-tion scene. Mark Lambert stresses the general contentment and kindliness of Chaucer's Troy, which he calls 'one of the wonderful places of our imaginations' (109). In Lambert's view, Chaucer has created 'a town of childhood' in which the usual restrictions of adult society do not apply: absent parental authority is replaced by the indulgent Pandarus and 'no wives, husbands or lovers appear with their partners except for the hero and heroine themselves'. This Troy is populated 'by people for whom friendliness is the principal emotion, people who seem to like simply being in one another's company' (109). In his discussion of the scene at Deiphebus' house, Lambert shows that the lovers are brought together in a context where 'all one's friends turn out to be each other's friends as well' (115). The 'piling up of solicitude' for Troilus and Criseyde (115) is symbolized by the maternal Helen, who appears as friend and sister rather than as *femme fatale*, and causes romantic passion to seem 'cosy' and so 'love blurs into the ordinary and the comforting' (117).

In contrast, John Fleming takes a more censorious view of Troy and of what happens during the dinner for Criseyde. He argues that, despite Deiphebus' goodness, the dinner-party, like the consummation scene that follows directly from it, is dominated by a deceit that produces death and destruction: 'the dynamic power that commands the action is the power of the lie, untruth' (183). If Helen is the paradigmatic character for Lambert, for Fleming that figure is Pandarus. In contrast to Hector, the 'internal moral referent' of *Troilus* (190), Pandarus lies about both Poliphete's threat and Troilus' illness. His actions in arranging for the lovers to meet at Deiphebus' are compared by Fleming to those of Jonadab, 'the perfect paradigm of a false friend', who helped King David's son Amnon incestuously woo his sister Tamar (186–8).[9] Far from seeing the dinner-party as an expression of genuine friendship and human contentment, Fleming argues for an absolute opposition there between *caritas* and *cupiditas* (191). If Deiphebus' presence suggests his later betrayal in Virgil's *Aeneid* by Helen, the 'vilest whore in Latin literature' (193), Fleming also notes that Deiphebus is here betrayed by a man, Pandarus, whose greater goal is the deception of Criseyde: 'And the means of the deception is the obvious and manipulated abuse of brotherly love, Christian charity, the ideal at the heart of Chaucer's society' (197–8).

Although each author asks us to assent to his reading of Deiphebus' dinner-party (and therefore ignore the other), to follow either exclusively would impoverish our experience of the poem. Both readings have something important to tell us about *Troilus and Criseyde*, for each has understood a genuine element (though only one element) in the creation of Chaucer's Troy. The delights of Trojan society are in the text, but so are the dangers. Chaucer goes far beyond anything found in *Filostrato* to portray the joys of private life in Troy: as Lambert shows, the poet describes the pleasures of family and friends, of dinner-parties and intimate conversation. The Trojan nobles who gather at Deiphebus' house are friends with one another and rally round when any is thought to be threatened or merely ill. Theirs is a world of easy luxury, kindliness and generosity, to which many readers warmly respond. At the same time, Fleming is justified in his claim that the dinner-party is built on the lies and duplicity of Pandarus. The reason Pandarus gives to his 'grete frend' Deiphebus for wanting him to invite Criseyde in the first place is simply not true. He then repeatedly and enthusiastically deceives all of the guests of the party, especially Deiphebus, Helen, Criseyde and her nieces, thus making a mockery of all the concern and kind solicitude he has engendered. Even the idealistic Troilus is manoeuvred into lying to family and friends. Fraud and friendliness coexist at Deiphebus' dinner-party. My purpose here is not to adjudicate between the implications of the readings of Lambert and Fleming, but to insist that each responds to one of the contrasting elements that Chaucer has built into this scene.

Chaucer's Helen, who is central to Lambert's interpretation, is a microcosm of the way the episode provokes multiple interpretation. The famous beauty appears here as an affectionate friend and relative, quick in her support for Criseyde (II.1604–10) and anxious to console the sick Troilus 'in al hire goodly softe wyse' (II.1667). She is a wonderfully sympathetic aunt, and yet no reader (then or now) can entirely ignore her traditional role in history. Deiphebus' comment that Helen ought to be invited 'for she may leden Paris as hire leste' (II.1449) is the kind of intimate personal detail that makes us feel close to Trojan high society. Yet the line also carries wider, more fateful implications. How can we ignore the knowledge that Paris's passion for this sweet woman is the cause of the entire war (I.62) and will bring untold ruin to Greek and Trojan alike? Chaucer has added both comic and tragic themes to Boccaccio's narrative, and we do ourselves a disservice if we do not respond to both.

Lambert's humanistic reading and Fleming's moralistic reading do not exhaust the many elements in Chaucer's account
of Deiphebus' dinner-party. Neither critic, for instance, gives
much attention to the intricate machinations by which Pandarus
arranges that Troilus and Criseyde will be brought together
during the party. We may judge these schemes, as does Fleming,
to be those of a false friend and betrayer of brotherly (and
avuncular) love, but they are also very ingenious – many readers
are as delighted as Pandarus himself with their clever execution.
Pandarus' tricking of the royal family can produce appreciation
for its witty skill as well as moral condemnation. Pandarus
describes the plot against Criseyde by Poliphete, which is entirely
his own invention, so well that he utterly convinces his audience
of its reality:

> He rong hem out a proces lik a belle
> Upon hire foo that highte Poliphete,
> So heynous that men myghten on it spete.
> (II.1615–17)

Equally accomplished is the way that Pandarus makes sure that
Troilus and Criseyde will be alone together (with only himself to
move things along). He tells Troilus to arrive at Deiphebus' house
and claim to be ill. Then, having induced Helen and Deiphebus to
visit the sickroom, he has Troilus manoeuvre them into the back
garden by asking for their advice about a matter in a letter from
Hector. When Pandarus returns to the party to escort Criseyde
into Troilus' room, he pretends that Helen and Deiphebus are still
there ('Com, nece myn; my lady queene Eleyne/Abideth yow, and
ek my lordes tweyne', II.1714–15). He then improves on the trick
by first telling Criseyde to bring a companion with her ('youre
nece Antigone,/Or whom yow list', II.1716–17) before smoothly
concluding that the 'lesse prees, the bet' and, taking his niece
into Troilus alone, reminding her to be sure humbly to thank
'alle thre' (II.1720). As a piece of comic stage business, this could
hardly be improved, and to ignore its delight is to diminish the
episode as a whole.

Trojan society in *Troilus* offers more than the setting for
friendliness or clever tricks, however; it also is the site of powerful
political forces. As we might expect, Marxist critics, notably
David Aers and Sheila Delany, have been especially alert to this

dimension, though we find diversity in interpretation even here: Aers says that Criseyde is a victim of society, whereas Delany sees both lovers as escapists from social realities.[10] One need not be a Marxist, however, to recognize that *Troilus*, to a much greater extent than *Filostrato*, shows Trojan society as the product of specific political forces and values. For instance, despite its nobility and kindliness, Troy does not transcend the limits of traditional assumptions about gender. A beautiful high-born woman like Criseyde may have a measure of sovereignty over her lover but, at the same time, as a niece she is expected to be subservient to her uncle Pandarus ('as his nece, obeyed as hire oughte', III.581), and as a daughter she is expected to welcome the reunion with her father despite his previous desertion. Even Hector, whom Fleming identifies as the poem's moral referent, operates within the patriarchal assumptions of his culture. He may be the best that pagan chivalry can produce, but he cannot escape the limitations of chivalry itself. Although he generously protects Criseyde against the mob that would punish her for her father's treason, the way he phrases that protection suggests the essential male bias of chivalry. He says that she may dwell in Troy as long as she likes:

> 'And al th'onour that men may don yow have,
> *As ferforth as youre fader dwelled here,*
> Ye shul have, and youre body shal men save . . .'
> (I.120–2, my emphasis).

Criseyde apparently cannot hope to receive honour and safety in her own right; it must be given in her father's name, *as if* he were still present in Troy and had never betrayed the city. This seems something like the reported practice in some Arab countries of making the Queen of England an 'honorary man' when she visits so that she can participate in public events.

Not only is Hector's mercy towards Criseyde (genuine as it appears) expressed in patriarchal terms, but it also ultimately proves ineffective against the stresses brought about by war – the most violent and most thoroughly masculine manifestation of both politics and chivalry. Hector's principled objection to trading Criseyde for Antenor ('We usen here no wommen for to selle') is ruthlessly swept aside by the Trojan parliament when the opportunity arises to trade a mere female ('this woman') for a 'so bold baroun' (IV.179–95). Hector's courtly ideals, although a permissible luxury in more peaceful times, are regarded in the current military emergency as frivolous – 'O Ector, lat tho fantasies be!' (IV.193).

Thus Deiphebus' dinner-party, in addition to the friendship, moral deceit and clever comedy already discussed, contains a clear political dimension as well. The stated reason for the social gathering is to mount a response to the supposed attack against Criseyde's possessions by Poliphete (II.1419), whom Criseyde fears because of his powerful connections with two Trojan military leaders, Antenor and Aeneas (II.1474). Deiphebus is asked to help not only because of his honour and benevolence, but also because of his exalted rank in the Trojan political hierarchy, as Pandarus underlines by addressing him as 'my lord so dere' (II.1431) and as he himself confirms by promising to be Criseyde's 'champioun with spore and yerde' (II.1427). For all its easy geniality, the party is essentially a power dinner, designed to secure the support of the royal princes, whose control of life and death are casually revealed by the letter from Hector used to distract Helen and Deiphebus that asks if a certain man 'was worthi to ben ded' (II.1699).

As we have seen, the political is only one of several layers that Chaucer has added to his portrait of Troy. The complex society of *Troilus*, which no single interpretive approach can fully analyse, is almost entirely the creation of the English poet. He develops the vague setting he found in *Filostrato* in a variety of specific but contradictory ways, emphasizing the city's private pleasures and wit as well as its political constraints, its betrayals as well as its personal generosity. Chaucer invents an ancient courtly way of life whose richness and depth challenge each reader and every reading.

A significant addition to the portrait of Trojan society in *Troilus and Criseyde* is the account of two intense friendships outside the central love-affair: the friendship between Pandarus and Troilus and the friendship between Pandarus and Criseyde. Both relationships differ from what is found in Boccaccio as well as from each other. For instance, whereas Troilus and Pandarus are virtually identical in *Filostrato*, each is a strikingly distinct character in *Troilus* and their relationship much more dynamic. The English Troilus takes much longer than his

Italian model to tell Pandarus whom he loves, and it is never clear how many values the two actually share. The prince is the most serious and least playful major figure in the poem, whereas Pandarus, who offers a constant stream of jokes, proverbs and schemes, is perhaps best defined by his eager cry, 'Here bygynneth game' (I.868). Yet their devotion to one another is deep, as affirmed by the many emotional expressions of concern and thanks they exchange and the mutual offer of female relatives for one another's romantic enjoyment (offers whose significance is highly problematic). Critical discussion of their friendship has usually dealt with whether it is morally good or bad, with little attention to the various ways that Chaucer makes it more intense and complex than the relationship found in Boccaccio.[11]

A more sophisticated and original example of friendship in *Troilus and Criseyde*, however, is that between Pandarus and Criseyde, which barely exists in Boccaccio. Although it is the most highly developed personal relationship in the first half of Chaucer's poem, its mixture of diverse elements, including affection, manipulation, caution and good fun, is too often ignored or simplified in critical discussions. Niece and uncle deceive each other for their own purposes, but they also share a mutual affection and delight, as seen in their first scene together when Pandarus comes upon Criseyde listening to a romance with her women. Boccaccio's Pandaro at this point is all purposeful efficiency: on learning of Troiolo's passion, he goes straight to Criseida's house; she sees him, they greet one another, and he immediately takes her by the hand and leads her into a private room where he begins to tell her his errand (2.34). The comparable incident in *Troilus and Criseyde*, in addition to being less direct, is warmer and more pleasant, demonstrating the way in which the English poem locates the central love-story within the wider social life of Troy (II.74–91). Pandarus' first words ('Wher is my lady?') reveal that he is well known at his niece's house and very welcome. Criseyde is so happy to see her uncle ('Ey, uncle, myn welcome iwys') that she immediately leaves her reading party. Their close familiarity is further suggested by her statement that she had dreamed of him just the other night: 'to goode mot it turne'. In the English poem it is Criseyde who takes Pandarus by the hand and 'with that word she doun on bench hym sette'.

The dialogue that follows between uncle and niece, which one critic says 'portrays domestic happiness as vividly as it is portrayed anywhere in English literature' (Smyser, 314), continues to define the intimacy of their friendship. In *Filostrato*, Boccaccio briefly reports that Pandaro jokes with Criseida, apparently to warm her up for his message from Troiolo (2.35), but Chaucer provides the reader with the actual banter, which is mutual and far from merely tactical. Pandarus laughs at himself, and Criseyde is capable of answering him in kind (II.96–8). Their ease with one another, which we never see between Pandarus and Troilus, is indicated by the range of their conversation: in addition to exchanging 'wordes glade' and 'merie chiere', they get into 'many an unkouth, glad, and dep matere,/As frendes doon whan thei ben mette yfere' (II.148–52).

When Pandarus visits Criseyde's house a second time, the brief and rather stiff greetings reported in *Filostrato* (2.108) are transformed by Chaucer into another intimate scene. Pandarus immediately begins to 'jape' about his own love-pangs (II.1096–9). Although anxious about the purpose of his visit, Criseyde is able to joke back, wondering, in an echo of their first meeting, how her uncle does in 'loves daunce' (II.1106). His response ('I hoppe alwey byhynde') makes her laugh so much 'it thoughte hire herte brest' (II.1107–8; see also II.1163–9). At Pandarus' house just before the consummation, in a scene with no source in *Filostrato*, we see the free and easy relations of uncle and niece once more, as they rise from dinner 'with herte fresshe and glade' and entertain one another: 'He song; she pleyde; he tolde tale of Wade' (III.610–14).

Pandarus and Criseyde are shown to delight in one another's company (though this is often overlooked), but Chaucer also never lets us forget that their friendship takes place within the structures of Trojan society. Having made them uncle and niece, a much more charged relationship than Boccaccio's cousinage, he repeatedly evokes the obligations and restraints of their kinship. Nor are Pandarus and Criseyde innocent in personal politics, as we see when he carefully considers the best way to approach her (II.267–73) and when she says nothing in response to his first mention of Troilus' love so that she can 'felen what he meneth' (II.387). If Pandarus repeatedly lies to Criseyde (about the purpose of Deiphebus' party and about Troilus' presence when she comes for dinner, for instance), şhe is rarely completely frank with him. As sophisticated members of an aristocratic world, the sincerity of their actions is often in doubt, as when Pandarus threatens to cut his throat if Criseyde does not save Troilus from death (II.325) or when she again and again insists that she will grant nothing further. In such a complex relationship, it is not always clear who is manipulating whom. Does Pandarus trick Criseyde into acting against her will by loving Troilus or is that the impression she carefully creates in order to avoid responsibility for what she wants to do anyway?

The friendship that Chaucer has created between Pandarus and Criseyde is as open to multiple interpretation as are other aspects of the poem. Some readers may choose to emphasize the warmth that has been added to Boccaccio's account of the relationship, others the added subtlety, still others the added manipulation; perhaps the best approach of all is one that keeps these various possibilities in suspension. Chaucer's largely original description of this friendship contributes one more element to his subtle portrait of Trojan society. The city that appears in *Troilus and Criseyde* is not only ancient and strange, not only a place of war and exalted passion, but also a courtly society with complex personal relationships, which the reader is allowed to experience in intimate detail. The central tragedy of *Troilus* is the destruction of the love-story, but Chaucer also shows us the ruin of an aristocratic society and its way of life.

What we learn about Trojan society occurs primarily in the first half of the poem because the lovers' private passion eventually estranges them from their community. Although Troilus is shown early with 'his yonge knyghtes' (I.184) and Criseyde with her reading-party of ladies, each soon withdraws from the group into private rooms and begins to deceive family and friends. As the poem concludes, Criseyde is a stranger among the Greeks, with only her negligent father and the rapacious Diomede to make up for the world she fondly remembers as she looks back at Troy: ' "Allas," quod she, "the plesance and the joie/. . . Have ich had ofte withinne yonder walles!" ' (V.731–3). Troilus becomes alienated from courtly society, as we see in his indifference to the party at Sarpedon's in book V, and then from earthly life itself, which he scorns from his final heavenly perspective. Both lovers give up the pleasures of Trojan society for more intense and tragic experiences.

Notes

1 For an account of this historical tradition in English literature, see my *Medieval History of Troy*.

2 For example, I.1072–5, II.190–203, II.611–44, II.932–44, II.1248–63. The longest passage (II.611–44) may well be an imitation of Benoît's account of Hector's entry into the city after the second battle (Young, *Origin*, 137–8).

3 As well as being much more frequent than in *Filostrato*, the added mythological additions in *Troilus and Criseyde* are often quite sophisticated. Troilus refers to 'Flegitoun [Phlegethon], the fery flood of helle' (III.1600) and soon after to 'Piros [Pyrois] and tho swifte steedes thre' (III.1703), allusions to the chariot of the Sun that confused many of Chaucer's early scribes (Windeatt, *Troilus* edition, 335). As the story draws to an end, Troilus knows he will soon die because of the shrieking of the owl, 'which that hette Escaphilo', and he begs 'god Mercurye' to guide his soul (V.319–22), which the god will, in fact, do. Similarly, Diomede claims that the Greek revenge on Troy will aghast even the 'Manes, which that goddes ben of peyne' (V.892). None of these learned references appears in *Filostrato*.

4 On the whole question of Chaucer's attempts to imitate the classical poets and Dante, see Wetherbee.

5 For a discussion of the role of Thebes in *Troilus*, which may sometimes make too much of individual correspondences, see Anderson.

6 See, for example, Lounsbury, 3.377–80; and Root, *Poetry*, 87; and, more recently, Payne, *Key*, 193 n.

7 A more intimate example of the mixture of past and present in *Troilus* can be found in Chaucer's original reference to the letter that the shepherdess Oënone is supposed to have written to her faithless lover Paris. Oënone's letter, which is based on Ovid's *Heroides*, is the kind of classicizing material that Chaucer frequently adds to Boccaccio to give depth and believability to his ancient setting, but its paradoxical effect here is also to make events at Troy seem remarkably contemporary. Trying to persuade Troilus to accept him as an amatory adviser despite his own failures in love, Pandarus casually refers to the letter:

> 'I woot wel that it fareth thus by me
> As to thi brother, Paris, an herdesse
> Which that icleped was Oënone,
> Wrot in a compleynte of hir hevynesse.
> Yee say the lettre that she wrot, I gesse?'
> 'Nay, nevere yet, ywys,' quod Troilus.

'Now,' quod Pandare, 'herkene, it was thus:'
(I.652–8)

One of the most famous texts in classical literature is thus
presented as a piece of topical family gossip. The distance between
literature and life and between the reader and the distant past is
almost totally erased by a single line: 'Yee say the lettre that she
wrot, I gesse?' Pandarus' reference could not be more offhand,
and his 'I gesse' is balanced by Troilus' equally idiomatic response:
'Nay, nevere yet, ywys.' If the darker themes of misery and betrayal
in Oënone's letter are concealed by Pandarus, as has been suggested
by Arn, this would accord with the generally optimistic tone of the
first part of *Troilus and Criseyde*, which, as we have seen, only hints
at the catastrophes to come.

8   For the connections between Troy and London, which were believed
    to be historical as well as moral and are elaborated by John Gower
    in *Vox Clamantis*, see Robertson, *London*, 2–3.

9   2 Samuel, 13. Fleming, who includes no notes in an article
    that was originally written as a talk, does not mention that
    the Pandarus–Jonadab parallel had been previously discussed by
    Muscatine, 'Feigned Illness'.

10 Aers tends to be somewhat sentimental in his reading of *Troilus*
    and imagines that Chaucer himself has quite modern views about
    women and society. In contrast, Delany reads the poem with the
    aid of Marxist analysis without imagining that Chaucer shares that
    approach.

11 Robert Cook sees the friendship as admirable, whereas Gaylord
    ('Friendship') finds it deceitful; the most sophisticated treatment
    of friendship in the poem, which is not especially judgemental, is
    by Freiwald. The best recent account of the relationship between
    Troilus and Pandarus is by Wetherbee.

5

Character

Troilus and Criseyde is a story about human beings. In contrast to most of Chaucer's earlier poems, which are dream visions populated by animals and allegorical figures, *Troilus* follows *Filostrato* in emphasizing character over plot and in describing these characters as fully developed, naturalistic men and women. For all the skill of the historical background created by Chaucer, the epic events of the Trojan War occur largely off-stage; instead of battle we are shown in detail the private lives and feelings of a small number of individuals: the two lovers especially and, to a lesser extent, Pandarus. *Troilus* also contains more minor characters than its source and expands the roles of others, though their primary function is to support the principal actors. Character has always been at the centre of criticism of *Troilus*. Chaucerians as diverse as Aers, Bishop, McAlpine and Wetherbee – like Donaldson, Muscatine and Robertson before them, and Kittredge and Lewis before *them* – pay special attention to the people in Chaucer's poem.

Although ordinary readers tend to respond more immediately and more strongly to character than to any other aspect of fiction, theoretical work on the topic has languished for decades. In the 1960s W. J. Harvey complained that 'modern criticism, by and large, has relegated the treatment of character to the periphery of its attention' (192). Things have not improved much since, despite periodic calls to action: in the 1970s Rawdon Wilson identified characterization as 'the least successfully treated of all literary concepts' (191), and Thomas Leitch has recently noted that 'character has become unfashionable in postwar criticism' (148).[1] Indifference to literary characterization is something shared by the old 'New Critics', with their interest in formal textual analysis and *persona*, and by modern Structuralists and Post-Structuralists (Hochman, 20 ff.; Rimmon-Kenan, 29–36). Many important contemporary theorists, such as Hélène Cixous, even question whether the idea of a coherent human subject, in life or in literature, is anything more than a passing bourgeois illusion (Leitch, 148; Hochman, 26).

The traditional critical debate about literary character, which goes back at least to Aristotle, is whether such figures are merely plot functions, whose being is expressed entirely in what they do, or whether they can achieve an independent existence beyond the text and can be said somehow to resemble living human beings (Leitch, 148–65; Rimmon-Kenan, 31–6). The distinction here is something like E. M. Forster's famous division of characters into 'round' and 'flat', which, despite its impressionism and inadequacy, continues to be a starting-place for contemporary discussion.[2] According to Forster, flat characters, who are sometimes called types, 'are constructed round a single idea or quality' (67), whereas the truly round character is 'capable of surprising' because it has the 'incalculability of life about it – life within the pages of a novel' (78).

The characters in *Troilus* have been treated by Chaucerians as both round and flat. Their realism and individuality were insisted upon by early critics such as Kittredge, who called the poem 'a masterpiece of psychological fiction' and the 'first novel' (*Poetry*, 109), and Patch, who asserted that the characters 'truly live' and can be analysed with 'direct reference to life' (*Rereading*, 65). Naïve as these statements may seem today, they announce a belief in the humanity of Chaucer's people that has led some critics to claim to have 'fallen in love' with Criseyde or to feel justified in analysing such things as the psycho-sexual maladjustments of Pandarus.

Other Chaucerians, however, from a variety of critical schools, deny that the characters should be treated as real people. The most influential statement of this position is by Mizener, who adopts the Aristotelian view that 'Chaucer's chief interest was in the action rather than in the characters' and that the latter are therefore static figures incapable of change or development (67). Shepherd also doubts the psychological coherence of even Troilus and Criseyde, seeing each instead as a 'function of the plot' ('*Troilus*', 78–80), and exegetical interpreters inspired by D. W. Robertson argue that Chaucer's people are typological moral constructs (Troilus is said to re-enact the story of Adam) with none of the depth, autonomy or individuality of post-Romantic creations. Like Robertson, Payne notes the strength of such fixed characterization, which allows Chaucer to make statements of general significance 'without the chance inconsistencies and non sequiturs of actual existence' (*Key*, 223).

Both approaches to characterization in *Troilus and Criseyde* are justified. Certainly the poem contains many flat or type characters. Hector, for instance, possesses almost no individuality, but always appears as the perfect model of a *gentil* and generous knight. Diomede is equally and oppositely representational. We never see him as anything but a self-interested pragmatist. Neither surprises us for an instant. Even the three main characters can be viewed as types, or at least as characters playing clearly defined, traditional roles, which Miskimin identifies as lover (Troilus), lady (Criseyde) and go-between (Pandarus) (198). Most English poets in the late Middle Ages and Renaissance treat the characters thus and are content to turn Pandarus into a common noun and see the lovers as 'true' Troilus' and 'false' Criseyde.

But neither 'type' nor 'plot function' explains the range of Chaucer's characterization in *Troilus and Criseyde*. Even figures we would expect to appear as conventional caricatures, like Helen of Troy, prove elusive and surprising, as we saw in the previous chapter. Certainly none of the major actors can be satisfactorily reduced to a single idea or quality, despite a recent attempt to provide a 'keyword' to 'help readers get started in forming judgments about each character' (Shoaf, xxi). The words proposed include *changeable* for Criseyde, *idealist* for Troilus and *expedient* for Pandarus; but, while each is relevant, none captures, even preliminarily, the distinctiveness of Chaucer's creations. *Expedient* is the least inadequate, but does not suggest Pandarus' humour or differentiate him from Diomede; *idealist* is much too general for Troilus (it would work better for either Hector or Antigone) and ignores his sensuality and complicity in deceit; *changeable* is appropriate for almost every *other* representation of Criseyde in literature, but Chaucer repeatedly shows the limitation of this traditional anti-feminist label.

The achievement of Chaucer's major figures, as some critics have noted, is that they successfully combine qualities of both flat and round characterization. Being 'conventional and original at once' (Ginsberg, 135), they are recognizably familiar as well as capable of surprise. They unite the clarity and general application of medieval allegorical portraits with a new immediacy and realism that was beginning to dominate Western art (Rowe,

57–8).[3] By drawing on the strengths of both abstract and mimetic characterization, Chaucer is able to create figures richer and more powerful than those found in either tradition alone (Scholes and Kellogg, 89–98). Troilus, for instance, is somewhat more conventional in Chaucer than in Boccaccio – he becomes the very archetype of the courtly lover – while, at the same time, he is given more individual qualities, like his shyness. Despite the apparent clarity of their roles, Chaucer's major characters are indeed capable of surprising the reader, for they are what one theorist calls 'open constructs', who are capable of existing outside the text: 'The character may haunt us for days or years as we try to account for discrepancies or lacunae in terms of our changing and growing insight into ourselves and our fellow human beings' (Chatman, 132–3).

That the principal actors in *Troilus and Criseyde* can be treated as both believable human beings and artificial literary types suggests that, while Chaucer learned from Boccaccio's emphasis on character over plot, he nevertheless radically transformed the Italian text. In *Filostrato* Troiolo, Criseida, Pandaro and even Diomede are about the same age and share essentially the same worldly, if elegant, values and desires. Any apparent dissimilarities, such as Criseida's discretion or Pandaro's deference, are the result of social position or narrative role and are not innate. If he were to fall in love, Boccaccio's Pandaro would probably act much like Troiolo, as Boccaccio's Diomede in fact does. The characters in *Troilus and Criseyde*, however, are described with an increased thickness and variety of detail that distinguishes one from the other. Chaucer's Pandarus is made older than his Italian model and given unparalleled verbal skills; Troilus is less experienced in love and more of a chivalric knight; Criseyde is wittier, more courtly, and less directly passionate than Boccaccio's heroine. Many of these added qualities appear to be in conflict with one another; thus Troilus' greater activity as a warrior contrasts with his passivity as a lover, just as Pandarus seems to care more deeply about the lovers even as he shamelessly manipulates them.

Even more significant than the individual qualities given to each character in *Troilus* are the radically different ways in which each is constructed. Troilus, Criseyde and Pandarus each has his or her own particular mixture of type and individuality, and each is so drawn that the reader is permitted to observe the figure only from a certain clearly defined perspective, as we shall see below. By presenting his characters so artificially, Chaucer reminds us that, however real they may become to us, each exists first as a text. Pandarus, for instance, is the most like a type: a vivid but shallow figure almost always viewed in action from the outside. In contrast, we are allowed to see deeply into the heart and mind of Troilus, whose emotions we can directly apprehend. The presentation of Criseyde is different again and more demanding still because at crucial moments we are denied access to her complex inner life and have to imagine what she is really thinking and feeling. Chaucer's Criseyde is not the conventional emblem of female instability that she is elsewhere; instead she is an opaque but generative figure who must be created by each reader.

Pandarus

Pandarus is the most superficial of the three main characters in *Troilus and Criseyde*, as well as being the liveliest and most entertaining. Although he is the easiest to sum up in a single sentence or even a word (his own name), he also shows how vivid a type figure can be. Boccaccio, who invented the character of Pandarus as we know him (though a warrior of that name appears in Homer), uses him primarily as a bland plot device. A pale copy of Troiolo with little that makes him individual, Pandaro is what Henry James called a 'ficelle' (Harvey, 58), a minor character whose only real function is to advance the story. Although Pandarus continues to function as a go-between in *Troilus*, his role and characterization are greatly expanded and complicated by Chaucer. He is so central to the action that the English poem might plausibly include his name in the title with Troilus and Criseyde. In contrast to *Filostrato*, whose lovers arrange the consummation by themselves with Pandaro as little more than a messenger, it is hard to believe that Troilus and Criseyde would have managed to come together in *Troilus* without the relentless pressure of Pandarus, who at last succeeds in getting his passive friend and reluctant niece into bed. He is the driving force behind their affair, and his efforts allow them both to act with more delicacy than their Italian models.

Pandarus is one of those striking figures, intermediate between a protagonist and a background character, whom Harvey has

labelled 'the Card, the character who is a "character" ' (58).
These exuberant, 'larger than life' type figures, common in
the novels of Dickens, tend to be comic rather than heroic,
though their comedy is frequently mixed with the pathetic or the
sinister. 'Part of the joy of these characters lies in their immunity
to the knocks and buffets doled out to them, in their ultimate
reassertion of their own nature' (61). The advantage of a Card is
that the writer can release through him 'a vividness, an energy, an
abundance that would submerge and obscure the more intricate
contours of the protagonist' (62). Chaucer's Pandarus exemplifies
this single-minded intensity to such a degree that he sometimes
threatens to overshadow the lovers themselves.

Pandarus has been the object of extreme judgements by readers
of *Troilus*. Early in the century one major Chaucerian called him
'the most charming of companions' (Root, *Troilus* edition, xxxiii),
whereas another found him a 'corrupter of virtue' whose nastiness
is only tolerable because of Chaucer's ridicule (Legouis, 128).
Critical opinion has continued to be sharply divided, although
the debate is not so much about what Pandarus actually does
as about the standards that are appropriate to interpret those
actions. For example, both C. S. Lewis and D. W. Robertson
agree that Pandarus is responsible for the sexual union of Troilus
and Criseyde, but whereas Lewis sees this as the action of 'a
friend according to the old, high code of friendship' and 'a
convinced servant of the god of Love' (*Allegory*, 191), behaviour
quite appropriate to one whom a more recent critic calls a
'priest of Cupid and Venus' (Bishop, 37), Robertson denounces
Pandarus' efforts as the sinful work of 'a priest of Satan' (*Preface*, 479). If *Troilus and Criseyde* is read as a Boethian poem,
Pandarus must be condemned, but if it is read as a courtly love
romance, he will be excused, even admired. Pandarus makes a
successful considerate *ami*, but a wholly inadequate Lady Philosophy. Both interpretations are valid as far as they go, but
because of their generic presuppositions each responds to only
a few of the many facets that Chaucer has given this character.

Although the English Pandarus never abandons the role of
pander (indeed, he is more active in that office than his Italian predecessor), Chaucer nevertheless adds a rich variety of competing
traits to the portrait he inherited from Boccaccio. As we have
seen, he makes Pandarus the uncle of Criseyde rather than her
cousin. Thus Pandarus is presumably older than the lovers and

has some justification for his attempts to arrange things for them. He is also given greater social status, as indicated by the mention that he is an adviser to King Priam (V.284). This more dignified Pandarus is also, at the same time, made more subversive of the established order: one who has no hesitation in deceiving the Trojan royal family with the false story about Poliphete, and one who repeatedly urges Troilus to prevent by force Criseyde's departure to the Greeks regardless of the consequences to civic order (see IV.621–30). Further complexity results from Pandarus' increased involvement with the lovers (to the point of voyeurism), even as the English poet shows him to be more manipulative, gives him an arsenal of verbal skills of which there is no hint in Boccaccio, and makes him funnier.

Chaucer's Pandarus is one of the great comic characters in English literature, whom even Shakespeare could not improve upon when he came to portray him in his play. He is the focus and source of much of what is most amusing in *Troilus and Criseyde*, virtually all of which is original. He is never afraid to make a joke at his own expense, and he plays the clown even during the consummation scene. We laugh with him as well as at him, though his humour often has a leering cynical element (III.1557–61). In contrast, Troilus' laments and tears leave little room for humour (though Pandarus is able to raise a smile from him at II.1639), and Criseyde laughs only when she is with her uncle. The cleverness of Pandarus' many schemes and his irrepressible energy in promoting them are also delightful for the reader, as long as we are not offended by their amorality. He tricks Deiphebus into holding and Criseyde into attending a dinner-party at which his intricate manoeuvres and outright lies permit the lovers to be alone together without any of the other guests suspecting, and later he puts Troilus into Criseyde's bed with equally bold and hilarious stratagems, which involve a rainstorm, an invented rival, a trap-door and the hero's swoon.

Pandarus is more comic in *Troilus* than in *Filostrato*, but he is also given other, competing traits, such as his expressions of extreme emotion. We have already noted his affection towards Criseyde, but his concern for Troilus is especially intense. When he first comes upon his miserable friend lying prostrate and alone, Pandarus is described as having 'neigh malt for wo and routhe' (I.582), just as in response to the prince's later sufferings he 'Wex wel neigh ded for routhe, sooth to seyne' (II.1356). When

he learns that the lovers will be parted, Pandarus 'Gan wel neigh
wood out of his wit to breyde,/So that for wo he nyste what
he mente' (IV.348–9). None of these extravagant expressions
appears in *Filostrato*. Yet Pandarus' increased emotionalism is
no simple counter to his wit. Although his sympathy is prompt
and dramatic, we are never able to measure its depth or be sure
that it is totally separate from his gamesmanship. The passages
quoted above, which describe him as being on the point of
death or madness, can be read as either sincere empathy or
melodramatic playacting, and Chaucer gives us little reason to
choose one interpretation over the other.[4] In the face of Troilus'
'manly sorwe' when first in the presence of Criseyde, 'Pandare
wep as he to water wolde,/And poked evere his nece new and
newe' (III.115–16). Pandarus' warm sympathy is inextricably
mixed in with his cool scheming – he weeps even as he pokes.

As suggested by the above, a further complicating trait added
to the English Pandarus is his virtuosity at manipulating others,
which hardly exists in *Filostrato*. Both Muscatine (*French*, 136)
and Spearing (*Troilus*, 43) call him a 'fixer'. Although professing
to serve Troilus and Criseyde, Pandarus is incapable of being
honest with either. Despite the deep sympathy we are told he feels
when he comes upon the love-stricken Troilus, the first words out
of his mouth, which attribute his friend's distress to fear of the
Greeks, are insincere but meant only to rouse the prince: 'Thise
wordes seyde he for the nones alle' (I.551–61). Throughout the
rest of the poem, we continue to observe his trickiness and lack
of frankness in the pursuit of some immediate end. Professing
openness, he carefully finds the most artful way to tell Criseyde
of Troilus' passion (II.255–73); in so doing, he uses a technical
rhetorical vocabulary that, as David Burnley has shown, reveals a
'deliberate display of duplicity' towards one he claims to love and
respect (*Guide*, 173–4). Later he creates the fictions of Poliphete
and Horaste to further the love-affair, and, at the end, when he
knows Criseyde will not return, he still cannot bring himself to
be candid with Troilus (V.505–11). Pandarus' motto, expressed
at Deiphebus' house, always seems to be: 'While folk is blent,
lo, al the tyme is wonne' (II.1743).

Larger questions of social or moral ethics do not seem relevant
to Pandarus. He tells Troilus he will help him pursue his passion
even if it is incestuous ('Be what she be, and love hire as the
liste!', I.679), and Criseyde indignantly charges that he, who as

uncle and friend ought to prevent her from loving, is instead its principal advocate (II.409–27). His help for the lovesick Troilus is inventive but relentlessly practical. He scorns his friend's passive suffering – repeatedly labelling it the behaviour of a fool (I.618, I.705, I.762) – and instead looks to what can be done. Far from leading Troilus to the summit of *amicitia*,[5] as some moralistic critics think he should, Pandarus appears not to take seriously even the higher reaches of romantic love. From the first, his clear goal is the limited one of bringing his friend and niece to bed. When it is known that Criseyde will be sent to the Greeks, Pandarus recommends, whether joking or not, that Troilus find a new woman (IV.400-6) or that he ravish Criseyde (IV.530). Despite occasional talk of service and devotion, Pandarus appears to regard love as no more than 'casuel plesaunce' (IV.419).

Chaucer characterizes Pandarus not only by giving him a number of different traits whose wide range is often ignored, but also by constructing him in a certain way that is unlike the method used for the other two principal characters. Pandarus is more superficially drawn than either Troilus and Criseyde and is given no more depth than his own fictional creations. Despite his feverish activity, his motives and inner being remain absent, and the few times we are allowed into his mind all that we find there are the mechanisms of plots and schemes, as when he leaves Troilus' palace after having promised to speak to Criseyde:

> And went his wey, thenkyng on this matere,
> And how he best myghte hire biseche of grace,
> And fynde a tyme therto, and a place.
>
> For everi wight that hath an hous to founde
> Ne renneth naught the werk for to bygynne
> With rakel hond, but he wol bide a stounde,
> And sende his hertes line out fro withinne
> Aldirfirst his purpos for to wynne.
> Al this Pandare in his herte thoughte,
> And caste his werk ful wisly or he wroughte.
>
> (I.1062–71)

This passage, derived ultimately from Geoffrey of Vinsauf's *Poetria Nova*, suggests that here as elsewhere (II.266–73) what is meant by

Pandarus' inner self or 'herte' is less human feelings and desires than literary and rhetorical theory.

Pandarus is essential in getting Troilus and Criseyde together, but he becomes increasingly irrelevant as the story continues and deepens. He is an impresario rather than an actor – a brilliant initiator of events, but not a full participant. He shares neither the lovers' profound satisfaction nor their tragedy. The larger forces at work in the story are beyond Pandarus. As a practical man of the world, he derides Troilus' fatalism, believing that Fortune helps those who help themselves (IV.600-2), and he scorns belief in dreams and auguries as unworthy of 'so noble a creature/As is a man' (V.384–5). If he is a kind of humanist, as some have suggested (Howard and Dean, *Troilus* edition, xxvii-viii), that worldly philosophy proves inadequate to the desperate course of events. In the last two books, Pandarus is able to accomplish almost nothing, though he is increasingly scornful of Troilus' hopeless faithfulness. He begins his final speech with 'I may do the namore' (V.1731), and he concludes it with 'I kan namore seye' (V.1743). Because Pandarus realizes himself almost entirely through practical action and language meant to influence others, his announcement that both are lost means his extinction as a character.

The attractiveness and limitation of Pandarus is that he seems to turn everything, including the love-affair, into an occasion for play. In response to Troilus' blushes when asked about his lover's name, Pandarus crows: 'Here bygynneth game' (I.868). Because of his inventiveness, Pandarus has often been seen as a figure of the artist and thus compared to Chaucer himself (Fyler; Bloomfield, 'Distance', 26n14; Donaldson, 'Three', 282). As we have seen, there is much truth in this: his stories of Poliphete and Horaste, which are crucial to advancing the love-affair, are sheer fiction, yet Pandarus manages to convince others of their reality. He is similarly skilful in creating a heroic picture of Troilus on the battlefield to impress Criseyde (II.190–203) and may have invented the garden scene during which he says he first learned about Troilus' love (II.505–53; Donaldson, *Chaucer's Poetry*, 972).

For all his imaginative skills, however, Pandarus is limited as an artist. He is a manipulative storyteller, like Nicholas in 'The Miller's Tale' (Bishop, 40), rather than a great poet. Pandarus' fictions, for all their wit, are shrewdly crafted to produce a predetermined result. As he explains to Criseyde, although some men 'delite' in narrating their stories with 'subtyl art', yet 'in hire entencioun/Hire tale is al for som conclusioun' (II.256–9). He cannot imagine a fiction that is not utilitarian. The hostility of moralistic critics like Robertson against Pandarus may reflect their awareness that his view of art is quite similar to their own, though in the service of different values. In Pandarus' creations there is no post-Romantic nonsense about ambiguity or complexity of meaning; instead they are deliberately closed works whose every effect is tightly controlled by the author for a specific practical end – to make Deiphebus give a dinner-party, for instance, or to make Criseyde receive Troilus into her bedchamber. Pandarus' fictions are calculated indoctrination, a kind of art all too common in medieval (and modern) literature, but which some writers, like Chaucer himself, were able to transcend.

Although Pandarus is the most superficially drawn of the major characters in *Troilus and Criseyde*, Chaucer adds a few passages with no precedent in *Filostrato* that hint that even he has an independent private life, which we might have been told more about if the poet had so chosen. Both Troilus and Criseyde make brief reference to Pandarus' amorous misadventures as if they were well known, and book II opens with mention of his having felt 'loves shotes keene' (II.58). The mysterious mistress is never named, however, and her reality remains shadowy. It must be some other aspect in the characterization of Pandarus that has led critics to treat him, not always successfully, as if he had a genuine psyche. We may be helped in understanding this supplementary quality in Chaucer's Pandarus by Baruch Hochman's observation that even a stylized character like the silly Mrs Bennet in *Pride and Prejudice* ought not to be classified as a simple type because her admittedly limited number of traits are so arranged that they implicitly 'form a dynamic system of stresses that suggest greater complexity – that is, a high degree of inner tension and self-contradiction in enacting herself' (124). Pandarus may be another such character. The variety of original, sometimes conflicting traits he is given in *Troilus* suggests a dynamic system of stresses that we sense even if we cannot fully explain. Something must be fuelling the manic energy with which Pandarus promotes, even invents, the love-affair, but we can only guess, to use Harvey's terms from the beginning of this section, whether Pandarus the comic Card may also be pathetic or sinister.

The possible existence of such inner tensions in Pandarus is implied most clearly by an original and now notorious scene in which he visits his niece's bedroom on the morning following her first night with Troilus (III.1555–82). Pandarus coarsely jokes that he hopes the rain has not kept Criseyde awake and asks how she is. When she calls him a fox and hides under the sheet, we are told that Pandarus 'gan under for to prie', urges her to cut off his head with a sword if he is guilty, and 'his arm al sodeynly he thriste/Under hire nekke, and at the laste hire kyste'. After these melodramatic acts, the poet blandly states, 'I passe all that which chargeth nought to seye,' notes that Criseyde 'with here uncle gan to pleye', and concludes by asserting that 'Pandarus hath fully his entente'.

The explanatory note in the *Riverside Chaucer* to this odd scene is uncharacteristically dogmatic: 'The now widespread view that Pandarus here seduces or rapes Criseyde, or that Chaucer hints at such an action, is baseless and absurd' (1043). Those critics who find actual incest here are obviously claiming something that goes far beyond anything in the text; but, in contrast to the apparent innocence of the events themselves (nothing much actually happens with respect to action), the violent, even sexual language and images ('prie', the phallic sword, 'thriste', 'kyste' and 'pleye') provoke us to wonder about the motives that are driving Pandarus, which the narrator so deliberately refuses to discuss. We are left to guess whether some powerful inner needs (pathetic or sinister) are fulfilled by Pandarus' close involvement in the love-affair that he has now brought to success. By calling attention to such questions without resolving them, by such a 'presence of absence', *Troilus* occasionally implies that even Pandarus, the most superficial of the major characters, has a self more profound than that revealed by his delightful japes and amoral schemes.

Troilus

Despite the efforts of some to establish him as the hero of the poem, Troilus is usually slighted by critics (David, 'Hero'). Tatlock scorned him as 'the least lifelike' of the principal figures

('People', 335), and current students of both sexes tend to find him weak and foolish. The recent *Riverside Chaucer* cites intense critical debate over the characters of Criseyde and Pandarus, but does not consider discussions of Troilus worth recording (1022–3). He has not always been overlooked, however. The Trojan prince was regularly celebrated as an exemplary knightly lover by English poets in the fifteenth and sixteenth centuries, and his emotional sensitivity and lack of male assertiveness may make him an ideal once again. Troilus, of course, may also be regarded as little more than a type character. Just as Pandarus never transcends his role of pander, so Troilus, once he sees Criseyde, always plays the lover. He has even been accused of overplaying this role, and Muscatine calls him '*too* perfect a courtly lover' (*French*, 137, original emphasis).

Chaucer's Troilus is not the rounded, psychologically believable character expected of modern realistic fiction, but he is far from simple. Although far closer to Boccaccio's original than any of the other major characters in *Troilus and Criseyde*, he, like Pandarus, has been given a variety of new and contradictory traits. For instance, as I suggested earlier, he is more active as a warrior while being more passive as a lover. Early in the poem Chaucer adds a scene, reminiscent of the medieval histories of Troy, that describes the victorious prince riding wounded from battle (II.610–44), and near the end he supplements *Filostrato* with a formal portrait that reminds us again of Troilus' masculine energy: 'Yong, fressh, strong, and hardy as lyoun' (V.830). If the prince is a lion on the battlefield, he is a lamb in the bedroom. In contrast to the amorous experience and competence of Boccaccio's hero, Chaucer's Troilus is innocent in love and hesitant in the pursuit of Criseyde. Not long before the consummation, both Pandarus and Criseyde are so dismayed by his supine inertness that they separately ask him 'is this a mannes herte?' (III.1098) and 'is this a mannes game?' (III.1126).

Chaucer gives other contrasting qualities to the character he inherited from Boccaccio. Troilus' falling in love is treated with greater respect by means of a lengthy exploration of his physical and psychological responses, as we shall see in the next chapter; but, at the same time, moral criticism is stimulated by associating him with an original series of bestial images (Rowe, 74). Moreover, though Troilus' conception of love is more idealistic and delicate in the English poem (service means at least as much to

him as sex), he nevertheless participates eagerly in Pandarus'
schemes to deceive Criseyde, almost all of which are original in
Troilus.

Given the range of traits that Chaucer has added to his
Troilus, it is no surprise that the prince has been judged by
critics as everything from a lovesick boy to a perfect lover,
from a noble pagan deserving of heaven to an archetypal sinner.
Early in the nineteenth century, in an echo of earlier views,
William Godwin found him 'the model of a true, a constant
and a loyal lover' (1.459); in our time, Donaldson has called
him 'the only unequivocally worthwhile person in the poem'
(*Chaucer's Poetry*, 974), and Robert Burlin believes that he is an
intellectual who merits a celestial seat (120–1). The prosecution,
as we might expect, has been led by Robertson, who insists
that the 'heroic potentialities' of Troilus are 'undercut whenever
they appear' (*Preface*, 285) and who argues that his tragedy
is 'in an extreme form, the tragedy of every mortal sinner'
('Tragedy', 36; see also Wood, *Elements*). Others have attacked
Troilus more personally. Patch thinks that he is not masculine
enough to satisfy Criseyde (*Rereading*, 89), Delany says that his
'self-pity, self-deception and passivity become more and more
prominent' (84), and Stanley calls him 'a poor fish' (102).

Such disparate conclusions result from the preconceptions of
individual critics and from their granting special privilege to
one or two of the several elements that Chaucer has added to
the characterization of Troilus, while ignoring or ironizing the
others. None of these judgements is without some justification
but, as so often with *Troilus and Criseyde*, each is limited. Such
selective interpretation results in part from the pressure most
academic readers feel to arrive at a definitive and total assessment
of Troilus. Is he the model lover or a pattern of sin? Is he noble,
comic or crazy? Is he to be admired or blamed? Even the few
critics who find complexity in Troilus usually settle for some clear
binary opposition, such as the contrast Wenzel develops between
Troilus' moral goodness in reference to chivalry as opposed to
his moral blindness in relation to divine philosophy. Although
Troilus, like the other major characters in Chaucer's poem, has
often been reduced to an ethical *exemplum* – or, rather, to a
number of conflicting *exempla* – his greatest achievement is not
in any lesson he can teach us, but in the depth and power of his
experience.

The reader is allowed full access to Troilus' psyche. In contrast to what is found in *Filostrato*, which tells us what all of its major figures are thinking and feeling, Troilus is the only character in *Troilus and Criseyde* whose consciousness is truly open. The extraordinary entry given to Troilus' inner being is in keeping with the Chaucerian practice noted above of reconstructing each of Boccaccio's similar major characters in a particular way. Unlike the deliberately restricted accounts of the hearts and minds of Pandarus and Criseyde (the former because he is relatively shallow and the latter because she is so deep), Chaucer allows us unrestricted admission to his hero's mental and emotional life so that we always know his response to both suffering and joy. When the lovers first meet at Deiphebus' house, we hear the public words of Pandarus and Criseyde, but the private musings of only Troilus (III.50–8). Later at Pandarus' house the motives and sincerity behind Criseyde's speech on jealousy are hard to determine (see especially III.1051–7), whereas the forces within Troilus that produce his answering swoon are explicated at length (III.1065–92).

Although rightly praised for his constancy, Troilus undergoes a radical change at the beginning of the poem from prince to lover, which the reader is able to follow closely. When we first see Troilus, he is a conventional member of a ruling élite, 'kyng Priamus sone of Troye' (I.2). Born to command, he leads his knights around the temple of Pallas (I.183–5), uttering words that are confident and smug in their criticism of any man who shows the slightest interest in women (I.194–203). As befits one so completely in control, he smiles, indulges in scornful irony, and is very pleased with himself: 'And with that word he gan caste up the browe,/Ascaunces, "Loo! is this naught wisely spoken?"' (I.204–5).

Once Troilus sees Criseyde, however, he is utterly transformed. Instead of an independent leader, the prince becomes 'subgit unto love' (I.231) and a 'thralle' (I.235, I.439), like other strong, worthy and high-born folk who have been 'overcome' by love (I.243–4). Attacked by Cupid, Troilus retreats from the temple 'thorugh-shoten and thorugh-darted', as though he had been defeated on the battlefield (I.325). The change in his speech is especially revealing. He attempts to conceal his passion under cover of more blame of lovers (I.330–50), but he cannot sustain his old confident superiority and when he reaches the privacy of his bedroom we hear a new note: the 'Canticus Troili', which Chaucer adapted from a sonnet of Petrarch (I.400–20). Troilus moves from scorn to song (I.386–9), from a language of command and control to a questioning language of confusion and paradox: 'If no love is, O God, what fele I so?/And if love is, what thing and which is he?' (I.400-1). The oxymorons we now hear ('O quike deth, O swete harm so queynte', I.411) are repeated when Troilus first describes Criseyde to Pandarus: 'my swete fo' (I.874). He has experienced something overwhelming and indecipherable.

Troilus exchanges his public role as prince of Troy for the uncertainties of a lover. He enters a new and secret world when he decides 'loves craft to suwe' (I.379). Troilus remains a knight, but his real combat is now inward – not with the Greeks but with love. The proem to book I speaks of his 'aventures' in loving (I.3) and of his 'unsely aventure' (I.35), just as after first seeing Criseyde he privately concludes it was 'to hym a right good aventure/To love swich oon' (I.368–9). 'Aventure' is often glossed as simply good or bad 'fortune' or 'chance', which is its obvious meaning at I.568 and elsewhere, but I would suggest the word also carries its full romance significance: 'adventures' are those extraordinary events by which a chivalric hero defines and realizes his high destiny, which is how Chaucer uses the word in *The House of Fame* (463) and 'The Squire's Tale' (659). When Troilus commits himself to loving Criseyde, he embarks on a great adventure, which, as the Petrarchan song informs us, is as arduous as any war and equally associated with death and suffering. The riddling paradoxes of the song suggest that Troilus' adventure in love will be one of exploration, a quest with no certain paths or easy answers. In contrast to the assured military commander we first saw, Troilus is now, after seeing Criseyde, 'al stereles withinne a boot' (I.416). The familiar stilnovistic image might remind us of the lordless solitary of Old English poetry as Stephen Knight argues (43), but it could also suggest the more positive daring of those, like Constance in 'The Man of Law's Tale', who commit themselves entirely to the will of God.[6] Troilus' God is Cupid, of course, and not the Christian Lord, but the knight's worship is absolute when, at the very end of book I, he 'dryeth forth his aventure' (I.1092).[7]

The extent to which Troilus' devotion leads him to reject all other values (I.463–8) is sometimes not sufficiently acknowledged. Patricia Kean declares that Troilus does not try to stop parliament from exchanging Criseyde because 'he [puts] the commonweal before his private passion' (*Making*, 130), and Donaldson similarly argues that Troilus' integrity and 'trouthe' will not allow him 'to substitute anarchy for law' (*Chaucer's Poetry*, 974). Criseyde will make such civicly responsible arguments, but never Troilus. He cares nothing for king, family, fellow-citizens, law or knightly reputation – only for his beloved.[8] Hearing in the Trojan parliament that Criseyde will be exchanged for Antenor, Troilus wants to act, but first he thinks of her honour (IV.159). Then, in a passage added to Boccaccio, he vows that not his but her will be done: 'And whan that she hadde seyd hym hire entente,/Therafter wolde he werken also blyve,/Theigh al the world ayeyn it wolde stryve' (IV.173–5). His principal reason for not accepting Pandarus' advice to steal her away is the injury it might do to her good name: 'As nolde God but if I sholde have/Hire honour levere than my lif to save!' (IV.566–7). Although he is always ready to sacrifice Troy and his own honour, not to mention his life, Troilus will not risk Criseyde's slightest disapproval. When he reluctantly accepts the exchange, it is only because she wishes it so.

Our access to the inner drama of Troilus' love-adventure and awareness of its intensity do not preclude the possibility of different interpretations. For some his unshaken constancy in love makes him a romance ideal, and the English poets of the centuries immediately after Chaucer often referred to him alliteratively as 'true' or 'trusty' Troilus (Benson, 'True Troilus', 159). His sometimes painful sincerity is in sharp contrast to the artful pragmatism of Pandarus and Diomede. For example, although Troilus carefully rehearses what he plans to say to Criseyde at their first private meeting, he instantly forgets his planned speech once she actually arrives (III.78–84). He is incapable of carrying out an Ovidian plan of calculated seduction, for his is a genuine devotion. As a true believer, he dedicates his spirit to the God of Love, whom, along with Criseyde, he wishes to 'serve' (I.426, I.430, I.458). Some readers, however, attack the very nature of Troilus' faith. Moralistic critics, for instance, find his 'religion of love' blasphemous at best and note its resemblance to Adam's Original Sin (Wood, *Elements*, 99–128; Robertson, 'Tragedy').

Whether we think that the suffering and death associated with Troilus' worship are signs of his nobility or his immorality, we must acknowledge that Troilus practises no comforting creed. Even when Pandarus announces that all is arranged for the consummation, Troilus' immediate response, in a scene original with Chaucer, is 'drede' (III.707). His subsequent prayer to an array of pagan deities, during which he solicits their help in the name of their own unhappy love-affairs, prompts Pandarus' disgusted response: 'Thow wrecched mouses herte' (III.736). This wonderful comic insult suggests another possible response to Troilus' fervent religion of love: its extremism permits scepticism and even amusement. The reader may also have smiled earlier in the poem when Pandarus, in a parody of sacramental confession, urges Troilus to repent his past sins to the God of Love ('Now bet thi brest, and sey to God of Love,/Thy grace, lord, for now I me repente'), though Troilus takes the advice very seriously indeed (I.932–8).

Although the intensity of Troilus' love-adventure is undeniable, the prince evades unitary definition because Chaucer's wide range of additions encourages us to interpret his character in different ways. If Pandarus is an author of texts, Troilus himself becomes a kind of text, even a textbook, of the lover, as he himself recognizes. Looking back over his life, Troilus addresses his god and declares:

> 'O blisful lord Cupide,
> Whan I the proces have in my memorie
> How thow me hast wereyed on every syde,
> Men myght a book make of it, lik a storie.'
> (V.582–5)

As these lines suggest, the heart of the Book of Troilus is his transformation from knight to lover. His story is not about military conflict but about being 'wereyed on every syde' by Cupid: it is a narrative less of public chivalric deeds than of private amatory experiences. But if we know the subject of the text of Troilus, its literary genre remains in flux and so we are allowed to read it in many different ways.

Once the exchange for Criseyde is announced, destroying the happy ending that Troilus had seemingly achieved in his love-adventure ('And Troilus in lust and in quiete/Is with Criseyde, his owen herte swete', III.1819–20), the reader is offered a number of possible literary genres by which to understand the Book of Troilus. In keeping with the religion of love, the prince initially suggests that the story of his life be treated as hagiography: he imagines himself as dead and buried in a sepulcre that fellow-lovers come to visit (IV.327–9). The vision of himself as a martyred saint of love almost comes to pass. During the lovers' final night together, the distraught Criseyde faints, and Troilus, assuming she is dead, draws his sword and resolves to join her: 'Shal nevere lovere seyn that Troilus/Dar nat for fere with his lady dye' (IV.1200-1). Had he fulfilled his intent at this point, Troilus would have indeed inscribed himself on the roll of those who died for love along with such as Pyramus, and we would be satisfied about the kind of story we were reading. Such a clear resolution is denied him (and us), however, as the genre of his life suddenly switches to something more like sentimental melodrama or farce. Criseyde regains consciousness, and his sword is put away amidst a flood of tears on both sides, leaving Troilus to act out a more problematic story.

Pandarus, as befits a maker of fictions, offers a number of genres that might be appropriate for the Book of Troilus. One of his suggestions, that Troilus find another woman, is reminiscent of Ovid's love-manuals or of the fabliaux, whereas another, that Criseyde be stolen away, evokes the direct action of epic or romance, such as Paris's rape of Helen. A more ominous genre for Troilus' life is provided by his sister Cassandra: not romance of any kind, but *de casibus* tragedy. When asked to interpret Troilus' dream of the boar, she tells him 'a fewe of olde stories' about how 'Fortune overthrowe/Hath lordes olde' (V.1459–61), the final victim of the wheel of Fortune being himself: 'This Diomede is inne, and thow art oute' (V.1519).[9] The end of *Troilus and Criseyde* suggests at least two other literary forms that the Book of Troilus might take: military history and a sermon in contempt of the world. Having tried to be Pyramus, Troilus finally returns again to being the son of Priamus. Changed back into 'this ilke noble knyght' and no longer a lover, his life is now taken up with 'many cruel bataille' that 'men may in thise olde bokes rede' (V.1751–3). After Troilus' death and ascent to the eighth sphere, Troilus is associated with a final genre. From his celestial perch he looks down with disgust and in the accents of a *de contemptu* preacher damns the 'blynde lust' of this world (V.1821–5). Although many in the last generation have accepted these final words as the correct way to understand the character of Troilus, they need not be given special precedence over any of the other literary genres we have noted. There are many ways to read the Book of Troilus.

Criseyde

Readers of *Troilus and Criseyde* have usually found Criseyde to be its most fascinating character. Henryson chose her as the protagonist for his powerful continuation of Chaucer's story, and David Daiches has called her 'the first truly complex heroine in post-classical European literature' (100). She is complex even on the level of plot. Whereas Pandarus always plays the pander and Troilus, after the first few lines, the lover, she moves from reluctant object of desire to false betrayer after an intermediate period of amorous fulfilment. The English poets of the sixteenth century understood some of her possibilities: although they most commonly portray her as a type of the inconstant whore, she also appears as both an ideal sweetheart and a pitiable victim (Rollins; Benson, 'True Troilus'). Modern Chaucerians also acknowledge the intricacy of Criseyde's characterization, but their frequent practice, as we have just seen with Troilus, is to emphasize one or two dominant traits in order to produce a coherent interpretation. Few agree on which traits are most significant, however, with the result that the critical tradition offers us a number of radically different Criseydes.

The 'false Cresseid' suggested by Henryson's *Testament* continues to be popular. In our time, Robertson has denounced her 'pride and self-love', though he finds her less guilty (because less serious) than Troilus (*Preface*, 487). Burnley notes that her refusal to accept responsibility and 'a pervasive moral weakness in her character' echo standard medieval attitudes towards women ('Heart', 32; cf. 38). Other critics stress her positive qualities. Tatlock called her 'sweet, loving, and essentially good' (*Mind*, 46), and more recently Mark Lambert says that she reveals the charms of the unheroic and is the Chaucerian character most like the poet himself (107, 125; see also David, 'Comedy'). Even the most influential studies tend to deal with only a few of Criseyde's qualities. In a brilliant analysis, C. S. Lewis argues (*Allegory*, 185) that her ruling passion is fear ('fear of loneliness, of old age, of death, of love, and of hostility; of everything, indeed, that can be feared'); but, even if we admit some pervasive fearfulness in her character, it is not hard to find Chaucer's Criseyde in more comfortable moods, including her lively curiosity about Troilus as a lover (II.498–504), appreciation of her own desirability (II.743–9), and self-confidence in her ability to trick her father and return to Troy (book IV).

The most satisfying analyses of Chaucer's Criseyde are those that insist on how much more various her character is than that of Boccaccio's heroine. Muscatine shows that she uses one idiom to speak with Troilus and another to speak with Pandarus (*French*, 153ff.), Lanham refers to her 'multiple self' and stresses the different ways she responds to different situations ('Game', 21–2), and Frank notes that Chaucer in the first three books has made her at once more sensitively emotional and calculatingly controlled (163). Her most sympathetic interpreter in this century, E. T. Donaldson, aptly calls her 'a mystery', which each reader will solve differently, but I would maintain that she is even more elusive than the 'paradox' he defines.[10]

Criseyde is not so much a collection of discrete traits, however diverse, as an endlessly protean figure who must be created anew with each reading. Troilus and Pandarus are complex characters because their thoughts and actions can be interpreted in different ways, but with Criseyde we must first decide what it is that she in fact thinks and does. Although we are constantly made aware, as is only rarely true with Pandarus, that Criseyde has psychological depth, the exact nature of this inner self, in contrast to the portrayal of Troilus, is often tantalizingly hidden from the reader. Many male critics claim that they have fallen 'in love' with Criseyde, but her real fascination is less erotic than literary. Her textuality dominates her sexuality. Criseyde may have no children, but with the reader's help she is endlessly generative of fictions about herself.

Book I of *Troilus* suggests how we must read its heroine by repeatedly portraying her through the eyes of others who create their own individual Criseydes. Her public appearance and actions are fully available to these observers, but her inner being, whose depth is repeatedly insisted upon, remains largely hidden from view. The very first mention of Criseyde in *Troilus* adds a few lines to the account in *Filostrato* of her 'drede' and indecision after Calchas's desertion (I.94–8, I.108), as if to assure us of the existence of her psychological life, but the stanza-length portrait that follows is drawn entirely from the outside, as revealed in the phrases 'as to my doom' and 'seemed' (I.99–105). The Criseyde thus seen or, rather, created by the narrator is a divine being ('like a thing immortal') of 'aungelik' beauty whose transcendent artificiality is stressed by the claim that she was 'sent in scornynge of nature'.

In the following stanza we are shown another, more earthly Criseyde – this time from the perspective of Hector:

> In widewes habit large of samyt broun,
> On knees she fil biforn Ector adown
> With pitous vois, and tendrely wepynge,
> His mercy bad, hirselven excusynge.
>
> (I.109–12)

Her dress and actions (kneeling, weeping) are emblematic rather than individual or personal and again observed only from afar. She resembles the very model of an innocent young widow, and this is how Hector envisions her: '[He] saugh that she was sorwfully bigon,/And that she was so fair a creature' (I.114–15).

Our next view of the heroine is through the eyes of Troilus ('His eye percede, and so depe it wente,/Til on Criseyde it smot', I.272–3); this third male observer perceives a third Criseyde: not an angel or widow but a physical if courtly being.

> She nas nat with the leste of hire stature,
> But alle hire lymes so wel answerynge
> Weren to wommanhod, that creature
> Was nevere lasse mannyssh in semynge;
> And ek the pure wise of hire mevynge
> Shewed wel that men myght in hire gesse
> Honour, estat, and wommanly noblesse.
>
> (I.281–7)

The distant point of view, which is generalized to include that of any man (I.286), is insisted upon with words like 'semynge', 'shewed' and 'gesse'. The passage is silent about Criseyde's own feelings, and her single public action in this scene, a sideways glance, is tentatively interpreted by the narrator ('ascaunces') in a following stanza that begins and ends with accounts of Troilus's emotions (I.288–94). In contrast to our full knowledge of the prince's feelings, Criseyde's inner being, here and elsewhere in book I, is largely inaccessible. Lacking a fixed human identity, she appears as a beautiful distant object, whose true character must be created by her readers. Like the three male observers within the text, each of us must construct our own Criseyde from the deliberately limited exterior information provided in the poem.

Criseyde's lack of identity and her dependence on others for definition may be a result of her gender. In a pioneering article, David Aers sees her as a victim of male oppression and argues that the inferior condition of women in Trojan society denies her any chance to become a genuine individual. Such a feminist analysis, which continues to be developed in current criticism (Diamond; Dinshaw), is persuasive. Criseyde can be seen as a victim in both Troy and the Greek camp. Her father selfishly leaves her behind when he goes over to the Greeks, Pandarus dishonestly manipulates her into a relationship with his friend, the Trojan parliament treats her like a prisoner, and Diomede callously takes advantage of her vulnerability for his own selfish pleasure. Criseyde seems to achieve some measure of security only during the love-affair with Troilus, which occurs during the absence of her father. Once Calchas demands her back, however (his paternal rights in no way abrogated by his long neglect), Criseyde is once again described as her father's daughter (IV.92, IV.663), as she has not been since early in book I (I.94), signalling both a renewed dependence, seen when she returns to in the presence of Calchas ('And stood forth muwet, milde, and mansuete', V.194), and her coming victimization by the predatory Diomede.

Feminist readings of *Troilus* emphasize the difficulty of Criseyde's life in a patriarchal society, though their understandable political indignation need not obcure her triumph as a literary character. Chaucer seems sensitive to the social marginality of women, but he uses that historical condition to create a fictional heroine of extraordinary power and creativity. In contrast to Boccaccio's Criseida, whose consciousness is fully as transparent as that of his other principal characters, Chaucer's heroine is largely hidden from the reader. Her silence and lack of self-assertion, which accurately represent the traditional political state of women, have a positive artistic result because they create a space for readers to produce their own Criseydes. With respect to Chaucer's characterization of Criseyde, less is certainly more.

As Leo Braudy notes, this is also true for the characters in film, who, though apparently more limited and distant than characters in the standard realistic novel, are not necessarily inferior. More easily than novelistic characters, 'film characters can leave their plots and inhabit our dreams, so free because they are so elusive' (Braudy, 184). The elusiveness of Criseyde's inner self makes her equally free and haunting.

My claim that the reader is frequently excluded from Criseyde's psyche is not the dominant critical view. Many of the best Chaucerians have argued that we are able to see clearly into the heroine's mind and heart, especially during her long inner soliloquy in book II. For instance, Jill Mann writes that Criseyde is unique in *Troilus and Criseyde* because 'we are introduced to the minute-by-minute workings of her mind, to a complex notion of her psychological processes' (Mann, *Estates*, 199).[11] I would argue instead that we are only sporadically allowed into Criseyde's mind and that even her private soliloquy, to be discussed further in the next chapter, provides little more than the *illusion* of interiority: we hear some conventional calculations rather than see her genuine feelings. A few critics have noted the lack of access to Criseyde's inner being without discussing it fully, as in Robert Payne's shrewd observation that 'we are always moved outside her at critical moments' (*Key*, 201; cf. Donaldson, *Chaucer's Poetry*, 969). Again we may note the unique construction of Chaucer's principal characters. His Criseyde differs from both Troilus, whose consciousness is continually on display, and from Pandarus, whose intentions are usually clear if rarely more than superficial. In keeping with our experience of most people in real life, Criseyde's deepest self is deliberately withheld from us.

Troilus and Criseyde repeatedly incites us to wonder what its heroine is thinking and feeling while preventing us from certain knowledge. Such passages, almost invariably added to *Filostrato*, oblige readers to fill in the gaps for themselves and by so doing create their own heroine. For instance, soon after Criseyde is first told that she is loved by Troilus, Pandarus looks to a future time: 'Whan ye ben his al hool as he is youre;/Ther myghty God graunte us see that houre!' (II.587–8). The poem then gives Criseyde's provocative spoken words in response (' "Nay, therof spak I nought, ha, ha!" quod she;/"As helpe me God, ye shenden every deel!" ', II.589–90), but we are told nothing about her private thoughts. At least one critic, however, is confident that he knows what Criseyde is thinking: she now fully understands that Pandarus' intent is to bring the proposed affair to a physical union and is both pleased and offended by that knowledge (Markland, 'Pilgrims', 74). This is a plausible interpretation, to be sure, but by no means the only one. The text incites interpretation but prevents certainty.

Other important scenes also keep readers at a distance from Criseyde's private thoughts. When Pandarus brings his niece to speak with Troilus for the first time, he begs her to act boldly and secretly to cure her lover's pain (II.1730–50). Immediately before her uncle's words, we are told that Criseyde is 'al innocent of Pandarus entente' (II.1723), but we are not permitted to observe her response once that intent has been made clear. When Pandarus a few lines later puts the lovers on notice that he will soon summon them for a longer private meeting at his house, Troilus eagerly responds, 'How longe shal I dwelle,/Er this be don?' (III.201–2), but the text again provides not the slightest indication of Criseyde's reaction to her uncle's promise.

The most famous instance in which we are kept out of Criseyde's mind at a crucial moment in the story occurs just after Pandarus finally does invite Criseyde to his house, though ostensibly only for dinner. When Criseyde asks whether Troilus will be there, Pandarus says that he will not be, but adds that she would have nothing to fear even if he were (III.568–74). The narrator then addresses us directly:

> Nought list myn auctour fully to declare
> What that she thoughte whan he seyde so,
> That Troilus was out of towne yfare,
> As if he seyde therof soth or no;
> But that, withowten await, with hym to go,
> She graunted hym, sith he hire that bisoughte,
> And, as his nece, obeyed as hire oughte.
> (III.575–81)

Many have assumed that they knew precisely what 'she thoughte'. In 1913, William Dodd suggested that 'on the whole, the poet subtly makes us feel that Pandarus's reassurances are sufficient to allay the heroine's suspicions, and that she went to his house in innocence' (170), but during the same decade Kittredge expressed what has become the majority view: 'Pandarus lies, of course, but it is perfectly clear that she does not believe his protestations'

(*Poetry*, 132). The lines themselves support neither opinion; or, rather, they are capable of supporting either and several others as well. The only interpretation offered in the text itself is purely conventional (if slyly humorous) and exterior: Criseyde obeyed her uncle as a niece should. Yet, even though the passage keeps us in ignorance, we cannot easily dismiss the problem of what Criseyde really thought because, here and elsewhere, the lines provoke us to seek an answer. The 'author' invoked at the beginning of the stanza is no help, for the entire scene is original with Chaucer. Once again it is the reader, each individual reader, who is left 'fully to declare' what lies behind Criseyde's public words and behaviour.[12]

Our distance from Criseyde is especially pronounced during her betrayal of Troilus in book V, which is narrated largely from outside. Although Chaucer provides some of her public words and actions, he continually makes us guess what is occurring in her mind and heart at this crucial point in the narrative. For example, soon after her arrival in the Greek camp, Criseyde states her resolve to return: 'To Troie I wole, as for conclusioun' (V.765). The narrator then informs us that before two months were over she was very far from such an intention and had let both Troy and Troilus 'knotteles thorughout hire herte slide' (V.766–70), but he never shows how and why that change occurred.[13] The closest he comes to an explanation is a single stanza describing her response after Diomede has both predicted the utter destruction of Troy and offered to serve her in love:

> Retornyng in hire soule ay up and down
> The wordes of this sodeyn Diomede,
> His grete estat, and perel of the town,
> And that she was allone and hadde nede
> Of frendes help; and thus bygan to brede
> The cause whi, the sothe for to telle,
> That she took fully purpos for to dwelle.
>
> (V.1023–9)

The stanza is more of a list than an analysis, in which it is difficult to determine the relative significance of the forces that are noted. For instance, is Criseyde's fear of the fall of Troy more or less important than the attractions of the friendship of the forceful high-born Diomede? Furthermore, even this rare insight into the heroine's consciousness is severely limited. The thoughts are only

an early stage in her change of resolve: they only 'bygan to brede'
the reason that she decided to dwell among the Greeks, and they
say nothing directly about how she comes to love Diomede, if,
in fact, she ever does.

The narrator earnestly tries to makes sense of and mitigate
blame for Criseyde's actions in the Greek camp, but his confusion
and bafflement only underline the elusiveness of her character.
He reminds us that his knowledge of his heroine comes from the
writings (often incomplete) of others, and he is thus reduced to
interpreting a variety of public symbols:

> And after this the storie telleth us
> That she hym yaf the faire baye stede
> The which he ones wan of Troilus;
> And ek a broche – and that was litel nede –
> That Troilus was, she yaf this Diomede.
>
> (V.1037–41)

Like a good semiologist, the narrator examines the signs provided
by other accounts (her giving Diomede a sleeve as a pennon
and weeping over his wounds), but he admits that he has no
authoritative access to her deepest feelings: 'Men seyn – I not
– that she yaf hym hire herte' (V.1050). Whatever others say,
he does not know what she did with her heart. Soon after this,
Criseyde herself disappears from the narrative except for one last
appearance: Chaucer gives verbatim a final letter to Troilus (it is
only summarized in Boccaccio), which is so cold and written in
such apparent bad faith that we realize that we no longer have
any idea what Criseyde is doing in the Greek camp, let alone
what she is really feeling and thinking (V.1590–1631). She has
become almost totally opaque.

On one of the few occasions that we are allowed any access into
Criseyde's mind during book V, we discover that she imagines
herself becoming a literary text. After her betrayal of Troilus,
Chaucer adds lines to Boccaccio based on Benoît's *Roman de
Troie* in which Criseyde predicts her metamorphosis into a lesson
of falseness in any number of forms:

> 'Allas, of me, unto the worldes ende,
> Shal neyther ben ywriten nor ysonge
> No good word, for thise bokes wol me shende.
> O, rolled shal I ben on many a tonge! . . .'
>
> (V.1058–61)

We will remember that Troilus also imagines his life becoming a text in book V (V.583–5). But, whereas Troilus proudly declares that his amorous sufferings are worthy of being enshrined in writing, Criseyde is terrified of what books will do to her. She fears that she will be made into a *exemplum* that will only present her negatively: everything said about her until the end of the world will be only bad ('no good word'). This is an accurate description of how her character appears in most literary works, but not in *Troilus and Criseyde*, where she has proved capable of generating stories 'on many a tonge' that range throughout the spectrum from good to bad.

Chaucer's Criseyde herself is what recent literary theory would call an open text – in absolute contrast to the closed fictions of Pandarus that are designed to produce a single practical end. The same lack of consistent identity ('slydynge of corage', V.825) that Criseyde rightly fears will bring her moral condemnation is used in *Troilus* to produce a brilliant literary success. Using the familiar, if overly rigid (Kermode), terminology of Roland Barthes, we might see Chaucer's Criseyde as a supreme example of a *scriptible* rather than a *lisible* text. She does not represent a unified or even complex authorial statement whose meaning we must passively accept, but is instead a stimulating figure that challenges each reader to make her new.

My claim that Chaucer's Criseyde is an open character who is capable of generating multiple texts may seem inappropriately modern, but there seems some evidence for it in the work that first told of her love for Troilus: Benoît's twelfth-century *Roman de Troie*. In the long final speech of his heroine, Benoît has her utter a series of contradictory statements, which he makes no attempt to resolve: she says nothing good will ever be said about her, that she acted wrongly and stupidly in abandoning Troilus, that she was ruined by listening to Diomede's speeches, that she has brought disgrace upon womankind, that she had the best lover a woman ever had, that there is no reason to repent, that she should be true to the valiant and worthy Diomede, that she never would have deceived Troilus if she had remained in Troy, that she has conquered her lonely state in the enemy camp and achieved contentment, that one should never suffer because of what people might say, that she is now both happy and sad, that she wishes Troilus well, that she must grant Diomede all that he wishes to keep him in love with

her, and finally that she hopes to achieve joy and happiness
(lines 20, 237–340).

The speech in Benoît does not characterize a single person;
rather, it sketches an anthology of diverse attitudes to what
has happened (fearful, hopeful, repentant, triumphant, oppor-
tunistic, satisfied, deceived, conflicted, nostalgic, scheming and
proud), each one of which has the potential to be developed
into the portrait of a different kind of woman. In addition to
supplementing Boccaccio with individual lines from this powerful
speech, which is not reproduced in *Filostrato*, Chaucer seems to
have been inspired by its variety to create an even more open
Criseyde in *Troilus and Criseyde*. Although Benoît eventually
draws the standard moral about female unfaithfulness from the
action of the episode, the words he gives to his heroine suggest
an infinite number of narratives. Chaucer does not himself write
these stories (what single author could?), but he empowers each
reader to attempt such rewriting.

Coda: The Narrator

The narrator, a figure who has often been considered a fourth
major character in *Troilus and Criseyde*, must also be discussed,
however briefly, in this chapter, if only to show that he does
not really belong. Although his many comments on the action
provide some justification for linking him with Troilus, Criseyde
and Pandarus, he never becomes a fully developed, independent
human character. He plays no part in the action itself, despite his
emotional involvement, and it is often impossible to distinguish
his statements from those of the poet. The narrator in *Troilus* is
better seen as a flexible literary voice than as a human personality
– a rhetorical element of the text that Chaucer uses to create
a number of different effects. The most important function of
this voice may be to reveal the silences and uncertainties of the
poem and thus encourage the interpretive role of each reader.

Despite the autobiographical claims of Boccaccio's *Filostrato*,
its narrative unfolds with remarkable objectivity, as discussed
in chapter 2. Not so *Troilus and Criseyde*, to which Chaucer has
added an intricate layer of narrative commentary. Substantial
invocations precede each book except the last, and the reader
is frequently addressed in casual asides: after a familiar proverb,

for instance ('This, trowe I, knoweth al this compaignye', I.450), or to mark a change of scene ('Now lat hire slepe, and we oure tales holde/Of Troilus . . .', II.932–3). We are also frequently told about the process of composition: the narrator discusses his source (a certain Lollius), announces his approach (the love-story rather than the war), admits gaps in his information (even when, as in respect to Criseyde's children, *Filostrato* is perfectly clear) and justifies his abridgements. Even more striking are direct expressions of enthusiasm about the progress of the narrative and of the love-affair. The narrator urges on Pandarus' first visit to Criseyde ('Now Janus, god of entree, thow hym gyde!', II.77) and wishes he had experienced such a night of amatory joy ('Why nad I swich oon with my soule ybought', III.1319). Criseyde is an object of special concern; to choose two famous examples among many, the narrator defends her against possible accusations of falling in love too quickly (II.666–79) and is sympathetic even after her betrayal (V.1093–9).

For a long time, when they thought about it at all, critics assumed that such first-person comment, some of which is obviously comic, was in the poet's own voice. Donaldson seems to have been the first to treat the Chaucerian narrator as a separate character. In an influential study of the *Canterbury Tales* ('Chaucer the Pilgrim'), he argued that the portraits in the General Prologue were drawn not by the poet himself but by an independent *persona*, who was enthusiastic, naïve, and not wholly to be trusted. In subsequent articles and in his edition of Chaucer, Donaldson posited an equally independent and unreliable narrator for *Troilus and Criseyde*, whose sentimental opinions, especially in defence of Criseyde, we are meant to question. In order to make this point, Donaldson was forced to posit a fully fictionalized character, who is described in psychological metaphors that endow him with will and emotions. In one article the narrator, whose masculinity Donaldson insists upon, is portrayed as acting 'irritably', 'knowing' something, and wanting the audience to 'share his enthusiasm' ('Masculine', 54–5); in another as experiencing 'one of his tenderest moods' ('Criseida', 71); and in a third as suffering 'internal warfare' that results in 'a kind of nervous breakdown in poetry' ('Ending', 91).

At about the same time Robert Jordan also argued that the narrator in *Troilus* plays a 'role . . . central to the life of the poem' ('Narrator', 237). Jordan's narrator is as fully personalized as Donaldson's and similarly unreliable. A good storyteller, performer, reporter of facts and dispenser of commonplaces, he is finally 'a man of no wisdom': 'Although warm hearted and ingratiating, he is remarkably obtuse, completely imperceptive of the esthetic and moral grandeur of his own creation' (254). In response to the objections of Bertrand Bronson, Jordan later denied that he meant the narrator to be taken as a genuine character of the same order as Troilus, Criseyde and Pandarus (*Shape*, 67), but many subsequent critics have conceived of him in just this way.[14] Often linked with Pandarus, the narrator is treated by some as a disturbed personality suffering from voyeurism or prurience.[15] More positive interpretations also see him as an independent and coherent being. While discussing several different views, Ida Gordon, a critic in the Robertsonian tradition, approvingly cites Muscatine, a decided non-Robertsonian, to support an interpretation of the *Troilus*-narrator 'as a *persona* distinct from the poet' who, like Boethius, is 'brought gradually to a clearer vision as the story proceeds to its inevitable end' (*Double*, 61). Wetherbee also sees *Troilus* as the autobiography of the narrator, and a recent article by Carolyn Dinshaw using the insights of feminism and contemporary theory continues to accept the narrator of *Troilus* as a discrete and consistent consciousness.[16]

Despite the emotions and opinions he expresses, the narrator of *Troilus and Criseyde* is a character or independent *persona* only in a very limited sense. Unlike the narrators of the *Divine Comedy*, *Pearl*, *Piers Plowman* or Chaucer's earlier dream visions, whose experiences truly are central to their respective works, the voice we hear in *Troilus* is never given physical shape and does not participate directly in the events of the poem. He remains, like us, only a reader, isolated in time and space from the genuine characters in the poem, whom he cannot affect and who remain oblivious to him.

A more radical problem with the narrator is the difficulty of defining the extent of his presence in *Troilus*. Is he there only when directly addressing us in the first person or is he responsible for the entire exposition of the poem?[17] William Provost attempts to distinguish five narrative modes in *Troilus* (direct narrative, summary narrative, description, narrator's comment, and invocation), but he is forced to admit that these 'five modes, alas, are not always as distinct as we might wish' (56–8). That is surely the point. How can we hope to distinguish between neutral description and subjective comment in *Troilus*? It is not difficult to identify an unreliable narrator in the various defences of Criseyde, but is the summary of the Trojan War (I.57–98) equally suspect (it contains strong opinions about Calchas) and what about the following portrait of Criseyde that describes her as angelic and heavenly (I.99–105)? It is hard to know where to draw the line. The ending of *Troilus* has been a particular problem in defining narrative presence. Whereas many have seen a retreat into conventional moralizing in the conclusion, and Donaldson imagines the narrator undergoing a nervous breakdown ('Ending'), others hear the voice of the poet himself at last. And there is further disagreement among those who hold this last position: Gordon finds the 'mature, humane poet himself' taking over from the naïve narrator as early as V.1093 (*Double*, 87), whereas Jordan argues that it is not until the last twelve stanzas that Chaucer speaks in his own voice ('Narrator', 253).

Mehl suggests that little is gained, and much lost, by anachronistic attempts to separate clearly poet from naïve narrator ('Audience', 180), a rigid division called 'more convenient than true' by Salter ('Poet', 282), who warns that the identification of an unreliable narrator as the source of the poem's quandaries may fail to recognize 'what may be the poet, making his own statements, tentative as they may sometimes be, about the problematic background to his artistic decisions and procedures' (286). The narrator is certainly not very consistent. He never becomes a familiar companion, like Conrad's Marlow; but, rather, in Payne's phrase, offers a 'multiplicity of perspectives' (*Chaucer*, 85). As Bloomfield first demonstrated ('Distance'), the narrative voice moves between close involvement and historical distance, nowhere more abruptly than in the three formal portraits in book V (799–840); and the voice is much more prominent in the first three books of *Troilus* than in the last two. If the narrator sometimes sounds sentimental and naïve, he can also be authoritative, especially in the proems and in such summary judgements as 'And thus Fortune a tyme ledde in joie/Criseyde and ek this kynges sone' (III.1714–15). Other first-person passages, such as his comment during the consummation that 'Resoun wol nought that I speke of slep,/For it acordeth nought to my matere' (III.1408–9), are comically self-conscious and highly sophisticated.

David Lawton has recently proposed that we regard the narrator of *Troilus* not as a consistent *persona* but as a variable rhetorical device used to emphasize different moments in the text. Even the shift in mood and value at the very end of the poem is not a shift in voice: 'It does what the first-person narratorial voice has done throughout: it responds appropriately to the particular stage of the work's unfolding' (*Narrators*, 82). Lawton rejects the idea that this device is a fourth major character; instead he sees it as the neutral 'voice of performance'': 'almost the voice of the poem itself speaking from the time and continuum of its own performance' (89). Lawton's formulation, which somewhat resembles Wayne Booth's conception of the 'implied author', may minimize the extent to which the narrative commentary complicates as well as supports other aspects of the poem, but he seems quite right to regard the voice as textual rather than personal.

If the narrator never becomes a distinct and coherent character in *Troilus and Criseyde*, the effects of his various comments are important and multiple, especially for the reader. The first-person passages that celebrate the love-affair and empathize with both the joys and sorrows of the lovers increase the emotionalism of Boccaccio's story. These invitations to empathy are a genuine element in the poem, which cannot be dismissed as merely ironic, though ironies of various kinds may also be present. The sympathy extended to Criseyde after she decides not to try to return to Troilus is especially poignant. The regretful pity expressed for one both reviled and miserable is neither naïve nor sentimental, but mixes pathos with tragedy:

> Ne me ne list this sely womman chyde
> Forther than the storye wol devyse.
> Hire name, allas, is publysshed so wide
> That for hire gilt it oughte ynough suffise.
> And if I myghte excuse hire any wise,
> For she so sory was for hire untrouthe,
> Iwis, I wolde excuse hire yet for routhe.
>   (V.1093–9)

In addition to stirring our emotions, the narrative voice also tests our judgement. Its comments force us to question not only the ultimate meaning of the story but also its very telling. Did Criseyde have any children and how closely does the poem follow Lollius? Admissions of ignorance about particular facts and the inability to describe the full joy of the lovers remind us that we are reading a fiction that we must interpret. Recognition of the narrator's unreliability does not make our job any easier. We are right to be suspicious of narrative claims that defend the pace of Criseyde's wooing or that certify the characters' good intentions, but these suspicions do not automatically point to a specific 'right' answer, although this is what critics in the tradition of both Donaldson and Robertson often suggest.[18] The narrative voice in *Troilus* creates openness rather than certainty. No deconstructionist is needed to point out the gaps, subjectivity and contradictions in the text as long as the narrator insists on them himself. Through this voice Chaucer renounces any claims to authorial omniscience and empowers the reader. The central experience of the poem is not the narrator's but ours.

Notes

1 See also Chatman, who remarks on 'how little has been said about the theory of character in literary history and criticism' (107); Bal, who says that no one has yet constructed 'a complete and consistent theory of character' (80); and Rimmon-Kenan, who also asserts that 'the elaboration of a systematic, non-reductive but also non-impressionistic theory of character remains one of the challenges poetics has not yet met' (29).

2 See, for instance, Chatman: 'One [attempt to distinguish kinds of character] that has weathered the hurricanes of literary debate is E. M. Forster's distinction between "round" and "flat" characters' (131–2). Bal calls Forster's distinction 'classical' (81) and Rimmon-Kenan calls it 'pioneering' (40).

3 The believable portrayal of human beings is central to the achievement of contemporary Italian culture, which Chaucer knew better than any other Englishman of his time. In the previous generation Dante became the first medieval poet to portray ordinary contemporaries in serious poetry, and Giotto, whose genius was recognized by Dante, Boccaccio and Petrarch, was quickly and repeatedly praised for his realism in depicting human emotion.

4 For instance, when Criseyde first rejects his advice that she love Troilus and accuses him of deception, Pandarus becomes so angry that he swears by the gods that he meant no villainy and threatens his own death (II.429–46). His response could be read as genuine indignation or as a calculated display to deflect blame.

5 Troilus often calls Pandarus 'friend' or 'brother', but several recent

critics (especially Freiwald and Gaylord) have shown how far the older man's actions fall short of the highest medieval ideal of male friendship, the classical and monastic *amicitia* celebrated by Cicero and Aelred.

6   The rudderless ship was a powerful narrative image in the Middle Ages, as Kolve has shown (ch. 7), and widespread in religious and romance literature.

7   This line is ironically repeated near the end of the poem (V.1540) after Troilus has learned from Cassandra of Criseyde's unfaithfulness and thus realizes that his adventure in love has utterly failed.

8   Spearing calls his offer to win one of his sisters for Pandarus (III.407–13) 'cold-bloodedly immoral' (*Troilus*, 42). Spearing is correct in terms of the conventional morality of chivalry or Christianity, and the reader who depends only on those standards will damn Troilus accordingly, but the prince himself now defines morality entirely by his love, which has its own rules.

9   Troilus has nothing to say here about his own life, but he does defend Criseyde by saying that Cassandra's accusations are the equivalent of libelling Alceste (V.1527). He thus tries to associate his beloved with a positive genre (the lives of illustrious women), though Criseyde's letter from the Greek camp soon indicates that she does not belong in such texts of feminine goodness and self-sacrifice (V.1590–1631).

10   The specific words come from 'Twentieth Century'; but see also Donaldson's *Chaucer's Poetry*, 967–71, and the several articles on Criseyde in his *Speaking of Chaucer*.

11   The fullest argument is by Howard, 'Experience', whose analysis will be discussed in the next chapter. More recently, see Pearsall. John Bayley compares Chaucer's thorough exploration of Criseyde's consciousness with Henry James's method in the first part of *The Golden Bowl* (91).

12   Other examples of the ways in which Chaucer deliberately keeps us at a distance from Criseyde's consciousness will be discussed in the next chapter.

13   For a somewhat different analysis of this scene and of the lack of psychological believability in Chaucer's character, see the important article by Mizener.

14   Almost a decade after Jordan's retraction, Michael Frost claims to be following him in believing that the narrator 'is a full-fledged *dramatis persona*' (35); other proponents of the personalized narrator, not necessarily following Jordan, include Shepherd, who says that it could be claimed that he 'is the only fully-developed character in the poem' ('*Troilus*', 71), and Osberg, who calls him 'a consistent character with a major thematic function' (258).

15 Spearing, *Troilus*, 46–7. An extreme example of giving the narrator a complex, even pathological inner life can be found in the interesting article by Carton; for instance: 'The narrator's disclaimers of control and responsibility, like Pandarus' equivalent self-extrications, are the increasingly desperate evasions of a character who recognizes his deep complicity in a series of events that features seductions and culminates in betrayal' (49).

16 Like others, Dinshaw uses psychological terms to describe the narrator's erotic response to the narrative. Although Dinshaw stresses the act of reading, her dramatic conception of the narrator, which derives directly from Donaldson, makes his reading (not ours) central.

17 Chatman notes how easy it is to confuse the narrator with the implied author, the figure parallel to the implied reader who can be imagined to have invented everything in the narrative, including the narrator (148).

18 For instance, Gordon says that one function of the narrator is 'a vehicle for the wit by which the poet *expresses his own commentary* in the ironic ambiguities' (*Double*, 62; my emphasis). Similarly, Donaldson imagines that Chaucer stands behind the narrator and occasionally 'jogs his elbow' so that the reader will be encouraged 'to see Criseida in a light quite different from [and therefore truer than] the one that the narrator is so earnestly trying to place her in' ('Criseida', 69).

6

Love

Everyone knows that *Troilus and Criseyde* is a poem about love. Exactly what kind of love that might be or how it should be valued, however, has been the subject of intense scholarly debate. Some celebrate *Troilus* as a joyous hymn to human sexuality, others thunder that it is a dire warning of the deadly wages of lust, while most, in the usual academic fashion, adopt some compromise view. The range of these critical differences suggests another position, which I shall argue here: the poem sanctions no single consistent attitude towards the romance between Troilus and Criseyde. Chaucer instead provides a complex literary experience that allows individual readers to find in the love-affair everything from passionate sensuality to divine harmony and from comic cynicism to lyrical idealism. As in no other poem in English, *Troilus and Criseyde* permits us to explore the extraordinary diversity and contradictions of human love.

Some of the most prominent twentieth-century Chaucerians have assumed that they knew exactly what kind of love is practised by Troilus and Criseyde. During the first half of the century, *Troilus* was regularly treated as a poem in praise of 'courtly love', that sensual, quasi-religious, secret system thought to derive from Ovid and the troubadours and to have been codified by Andreas Capellanus.[1] In 1913, William Dodd published his *Courtly Love in Chaucer and Gower*, and two years later Kittredge claimed that the 'sufferings of Troilus are in complete accord with the mediaeval system', a system he variously described as 'courtly love' and 'chivalric love' (*Poetry*, 123, 130–1). The most influential and eloquent advocate of *Troilus* as a poem of courtly love has undoubtedly been C. S. Lewis, whose *Allegory of Love* (1936) dominated discussion of the poem for more than a generation. Although insisting that medieval writers never denied the ultimate truth of Christianity (as seen in the orthodox ending of *Troilus*), Lewis argued for the strong appeal of the rival courtly devotion as the repository of the best qualities of human life. Chaucer's *Troilus and Criseyde* is the culmination of this tradition: 'a great poem in praise of love', whose depiction of amorous passion is 'the crowning achievement' of courtly literature. Lewis insisted that the relationship of the Trojan lovers is 'so nobly conceived' that it reaches the frontiers of Christian marriage (197).

At mid-century, a completely different, but equally powerful, view of love in *Troilus* was offered by D. W. Robertson, Jr. In 'Chaucerian Tragedy' (1952) and again at the conclusion of *A Preface to Chaucer* (1963), Robertson argued with learning and energy that *Troilus and Criseyde* 'is neither a tale of true love . . . nor of courteous love' (*Preface*, 472). Instead, Robertson saw the poem as a profoundly Christian work in the tradition of Boethius' *Consolation of Philosophy*, and he concluded that Troilus' unreasonable passion for the self-seeking and vain Criseyde entangles them both in the snares of Fortune. The religious imagery so often used to describe their love is therefore highly ironic and 'intended to suggest the values from which the hero departs' ('Tragedy', 24), whereas the apparently rapturous consummation is simply 'the deed of darkness', which 'cannot withstand the light of truth and reason' (*Preface*, 492). The prince himself is less a noble lover than a common sinner: 'He is a slave to his desire, a victim of his sin. Like old Januarie in the Merchant's Tale, or like Adam himself, Troilus has made a woman's love the controlling feature in his universe' ('Tragedy', 30). His tragedy 'is, in an extreme form, the tragedy of every mortal sinner' ('Tragedy', 36).[2]

In an essay during the mid-1960s that equals both Lewis and Robertson in intensity and apparent personal commitment, Elizabeth Salter offered a third approach to the Trojan love-story: she advanced the daring thesis that in the course of writing *Troilus* Chaucer rejected orthodox Christian teaching about human sexuality and instead affirmed 'the holiness of the heart's affections' ('Reconsideration', 89). Although claiming to follow Lewis, Salter reads Chaucer's poem not as the culmination of the medieval courtly tradition but as something radically new and subversive. For her, the unique excellence of *Troilus* is neither its creation of character nor rich poetic fabric but 'the growth and release of a poet's imagination', which permitted Chaucer a momentary triumph 'over both his story and his age' (89). Salter sees Chaucer struggling with his inherited material until in book III he confidently asserts the 'goodness and legitimacy' of the lovers'

relationship (100). The poem's religious imagery is neither ironic
nor an indication that the affair resembles Christian marriage, but
a bold granting of 'religious sanction to a love which originally
asked and needed none' (103). Despite the poet's retreat into a
perfunctory orthodoxy at the end, Salter argued that Chaucer was
one of the few medieval artists to 'take full imaginative grasp' of
the complexity of human love, 'to admit its dignity as well as
its vulnerability, and to give serious status to bodily as well as
spiritual compassion' (103–4).[3]

Different as they are, the arguments of Lewis, Robertson and
Salter have each found strong adherents among Chaucerians.
Even today, more than twenty years after the last of these
studies was written, all three have important things to teach
us because each responds to a genuine element in the love-story
– Lewis to its courtliness, Robertson to its self-delusions and
deceit, and Salter to its celebration of physical love – though
each is limited by treating a part of the story as if it were
the whole. The range of interpretations advocated by these
three powerful readings can help us to understand that the
love between Chaucer's Troilus and Criseyde is never simple
and always in question. No single critical approach can explain
it, and thus none is comprehensive.

The multiplicity of the love-affair in *Troilus* was largely added
by Chaucer. Boccaccio's lovers, in contrast, are remarkably alike
and their relationship is clear. Their passion is essentially sensual,
if gracious, from first to last, and the reader always feels that
he understands what each is feeling and doing. That love is
more complex in *Troilus and Criseyde* than in *Filostrato* is a
critical commonplace, but it is not always recognized that the
English poet has altered his source in so many contradictory
ways. To give just a few examples, whereas Chaucer portrays
the lovers as more idealistic, hesitant and attractive than their
Italian originals, he also insinuates a persistent line of moral
criticism that is absent in Boccaccio. Furthermore, Chaucer
adds lyricism and elevated rhetoric to his depiction of love,
but also adds more comedy, sometimes to the point of farce.
Divine love is invoked in *Troilus* to an extent unprecedented
in *Filostrato*, but equally original is imagery that associates
sexual passion with natural patterns of growth and decay. The
English work is, at the same time, more pagan and more
Christian.

Faced with the multiplicity of love in *Troilus*, critics have understandably sought to discover some unifying concept that could define the experience of the lovers. But this is futile. Chaucer keeps forcing us to deal with different values and perspectives. The genre of the love-story, for instance, is never certain. Are we to read it as though it were courtly romance, history, tragedy or moral allegory? Are we expected to respond to the affair as knights and ladies, devout Christians, fellow-lovers, antiquarians or ordinary humans? Support for any and all of these approaches (and many others besides) can be found at particular points in the poem, but none is unchallenged.

Gerald Morgan and Larry D. Benson have recently made convincing cases for two completely different interpretive paradigms by which to understand love in *Troilus and Criseyde*. Using scholastic Christian theology, whose terms he finds echoed in Chaucer's language, Morgan argues that the misery of Troilus and Criseyde is a textbook example of the tragic error of allowing reason to become subject to desire ('Freedom'). Benson, however, offers an alternative, and equally medieval, context that permits us to view the lovers more positively. Although he directly mentions *Troilus* only in passing, Benson argues that by Chaucer's time 'the idea that love was a source of chivalric virtue becomes a commonplace not only in courtly romances and lyrics but even in the "nonfiction" of the time', which non-fiction was both read and acted on by knights and princes (240). The work of these two scholars shows that the poem can persuasively be read as both a scholastic analysis of sin and a chivalric celebration of virtue.

Ian Robinson has called *Troilus and Criseyde* 'Chaucer's great failure', because, although the poet set out to try to 'settle' the question of love 'once and for all', the 'many great parts' of the work 'don't cohere into a great whole' (73). Robinson is right that the presentation of love in *Troilus* is not consistent, but that is evidence of Chaucer's success, not of his failure. Many writers, including Boccaccio in *Filostrato*, offer a single coherent view of love – exploring its variety and contradictions is a task for only the greatest poets.[4]

Chaucer clearly introduces the idea of love's multiplicity in the formal prologues to the first three books of *Troilus and Criseyde*. The prohemium to book I, for instance, after noting both Troilus' 'wo' and 'wele' (I.4), goes on to solicit prayers for

lovers in a number of quite different situations, including those
who 'bathen in gladnesse' despite past 'hevynesse' (I.22–9), those
who share Troilus' fate (I.29–31), those like the narrator who
experience love only from the outside (I.32–5), those who wish
to die because of either despair or gossip (I.36–42), and those who
'ben at ese' and hope so to continue (I.43–6). The prohemium
to book II again announces the principle of multiplicity, as
already noted in Chapter 3. A famous passage in that proem
notes the variety of amorous practices resulting from changes
in time and space: 'Ek for to wynnen love in sondry ages,/In
sondry londes, sondry ben usages' (II.27–8). A later stanza
goes even further to attribute differences in loving to human
nature itself:

> Ek scarsly ben ther in this place thre
> That have in love seid lik, and don, in al;
> For to thi purpos this may liken the,
> And the right nought; yet al is seid or schal;
> Ek som men grave in tree, some in ston wal,
> As it bitit.
>
> (II.43–8)

The most comprehensive theoretical statement of the many
loves that are found in *Troilus and Criseyde*, however, occurs
in the prohemium to book III, which deserves separate treatment.

The Prohemium to Book III

Love is the principal subject of the invocation to Venus that
prefaces book III, the book in which the lovers first meet,
consummate their passion, and enjoy their only happiness. The
seven-stanza proem is based on the first part of a song uttered
by Boccaccio's Troiolo, itself much influenced by Boethius,
that occurs somewhat later in *Filostrato* (3.74–9). Chaucer not
only makes the passage more prominent by locating it at the
beginning of his central book, but he also greatly complicates
its view of love.

The prayer in Boccaccio's work 'is a melding of diverse
conceptions of cosmic love and its powers, emphasizing its

universal power in Neoplatonic terms not incompatible with traditional, Christian interpretations of the love that moves all things' (Gleason, 171). Troiolo invokes Venus as splendid planet and benign goddess (3.74), then notes how extensive is her power over the universe (3.75), how she makes Jove merciful and loving towards humans (3.76), how she ennobles and makes courteous Mars and all others inflamed with her fire (3.77), how she unites kingdoms, families and friends (3.78), and how her laws maintain the universe so that it is futile to oppose her son (3.79). Most of those who have discussed Chaucer's version argue that it is making one of two relatively clear statements: either it describes a continuum between divine and human love or it asserts their clear opposition. Such binary interpretations might possibly fit the original Boccaccian passage, but neither is adequate to Chaucer's prohemium, which stresses the bewildering diversity of love rather than its unity or even duality.

Perhaps the most useful approach to this passage can be found in the first scholarly annotation of *Troilus and Criseyde*, by the seventeenth-century man of letters Francis Kynaston. In the unpublished commentary to his 1635 Latin translation of *Troilus*, which has been preserved in the Bodleian Library (Additional MS C.287), Kynaston declares that the proem to Book III 'includes all kindes of loue', which he goes on to identify as love of God, the 'Platonicke loue' of 'Ideas, vertues & perfeccions', moral love between friends, 'lawfull coniugall loue' and, finally, 'lust, both in men & other creatures' (320). Although we might be tempted to expand this list somewhat (adding courtly and voyeuristic love, for example), Kynaston clearly recognizes the principle of variety in love that Chaucer announced in the prohemium to book III – not one or two kinds of love, but 'all kindes of loue' As we shall soon see, diversity is further emphasized by clashing literary styles in the proem and its lack of a clear hierarchical structure. Even Venus herself, the subject of the invocation, appears in several guises: both pagan deity and astrological influence, the daughter of Jove as well as his master in love, she is simultaneously inspirer of gentle hearts, the force of regeneration in all creatures, a celestial procurer of sexual favours, a worker for social amelioration, and the creator of a Boethian holy bond of cosmic love.

The prohemium to book III opens with grand eloquence:

> O blisful light of which the bemes clere
> Adorneth al the thridde heven faire!
> O sonnes lief, O Joves doughter deere,
> Plesance of love, O goodly debonaire,
> In gentil hertes ay redy to repaire!
> O veray cause of heele and of gladnesse,
> Iheryed be thy myght and thi goodnesse!
>
> (III.1–7)

A noticeable feature of this first stanza is the way that Chaucer imitates and then extends the stilnovistic language he found in Boccaccio. The praise of Venus in *Filostrato*, 'benigna donna d'ogni gentil core' (3.74), becomes 'In gentil hertes ay redy to repaire', making the phrase more like the famous opening line of Guido Guinizelli's poem 'Al cor gentil rempaira sempre amore', which Dante echoes in canto V of *Inferno* and Chaucer may have known from its quotation in the *Convivio* (Windeatt, *Troilus* edition, 249nIII.5). Such courtly vocabulary is appropriate to the long-awaited meeting of the Trojan lovers promised at the end of book II, but it is only the first of many kinds of love evoked in the prohemium.

The next stanza widens our understanding of love in *Troilus* by describing it, first, in Boccaccian phrases derived ultimately from Boethius, as a natural generative force felt in certain seasons by all created things and, second, in a line with no source at all in *Filostrato*, as an emotion experienced and approved of by the Creator himself:

> In hevene and helle, in erthe and salte see
> Is felt thi myght, if that I wel descerne,
> As man, brid, best, fissh, herbe, and grene tree
> Thee fele in tymes with vapour eterne.
> God loveth, and to love wol nought werne,
> And in this world no lyves creature
> Withouten love is worth, or may endure.
>
> (III.8–14)

Elizabeth Salter interprets the last three lines of the stanza as a 'manifesto' that Chaucer will not limit himself to the 'narrower dictates of his age' but will instead demand from his readers 'unqualified sympathy' for the passion of Troilus and Criseyde

('Reconsideration', 97–9). As we have already begun to realize, however, no single attitude towards love is maintained in the proem, which instead insists on the range of Venus' effects. It is true, however, that Chaucer's original and striking reference to God's love, which is echoed by Christian vocabulary added throughout *Troilus*, contributes an additional kind of love (divine) to the courtly and natural varieties already mentioned.

The third stanza further complicates our view of love:

> Ye Joves first to thilke effectes glade,
> Thorugh which that thynges lyven alle and be,
> Comeveden, and amorous him made
> On mortal thyng, and as yow list, ay ye
> Yeve hym in love ese or adversitee,
> And in a thousand formes down hym sente
> For love in erthe, and whom yow liste he hente.
>
> (III.15–21)

In contrast to Boccaccio's Jove, whom Venus is said to make merciful as well as amorous towards humans, Chaucer's Jove is essentially predatory. The deity who in the previous stanza had seemed to resemble the Christian Lord is now revealed as little more than a rapist. Within a few lines Chaucer has developed the possibilities of divine love in two absolutely opposite directions – altruism and force. The violent verb ('hente') that ends the stanza, which is original in the English passage, describes an action far different from the apparently Christ-like love of the previous lines, suggesting the future aggression of Diomede against Criseyde and the rape that brought about the Trojan War itself.

The many possibilities of love identified by Kynaston in his commentary continue to appear in the fourth and fifth stanzas. We are here shown a Venus who can appease the anger of Mars as well as make her other followers 'dreden shame' and 'vices . . . resygne' until they become 'corteys', 'fresshe and begnigne' (III.22–6). After describing this noble chivalric kind of love, which Antigone sings of in book II and which has already been evoked at the beginning of the prohemium, Chaucer in the fifth stanza defines a more disinterested love that is both Boethian and social. In this guise Venus holds 'regne and hous in unitee' and is the 'sothfast cause of frendship' (III.29–30). This love of friends is practised by the Trojan royal family at Deiphebus' house and professed by Pandarus towards both Troilus and Criseyde.

The penultimate stanza of the prohemium introduces a darker picture of love's control:

> Ye folk a lawe han set in universe,
> And this knowe I by hem that lovers be,
> That whoso stryveth with yow hath the werse.
>
> (III.36–8)

The irresistible power of love is, of course, a major theme in *Troilus*. Before concluding with a stanza that requests Calliope's help to tell the 'gladnesse/Of Troilus' (III.47–8), and amidst lines that resemble an address to the Virgin ('Now, lady bryght, for thi benignitee,/At reverence of hem that serven the', III.39–40), the poet describes a further variety of love: his own distant voyeuristic service, which we find expressed throughout the story. The narrator admits that he knows about Venus' law only from those who are lovers, for he is merely their clerk hoping to be taught how to express 'som joye of that is felt in thi servyse' (III.42). Instead of a single view of love or a clear duality, the prohemium to book III provides us with a jumble of all kinds of love – courtly, natural, divine, rapacious, virtuous, social, irresistible and voyeuristic.

The lack of order with which these different kinds of love are presented emphasizes multiplicity. Readers are free to make their own choices and valuations, be they Christian, naturalistic or courtly, but the text establishes no obvious hierarchy or clear preference. Like the portraits in the General Prologue to *The Canterbury Tales*, which the pilgrim teller apologizes for not presenting in accordance with their proper 'degree' (I.743–5), each of the different conceptions of love is unique and of potential value. The thematic variety of the prohemium is further underlined by its many contrasting literary styles. The high rhetoric of the opening lines ('O blisful light of which the bemes clere/Adorneth al the thridde heven faire', III.1–2) soon gives way to the low fabliau-like comedy of Venus inciting Jove to pursue amorous pleasure by going down to earth in disguise to 'hente' his sexual victims (III.20–1). Similarly, the noble declaration of love's positive power at the beginning of the fifth stanza ('Ye holden regne and hous in unitee', III.29) quickly descends to a slangy assertion of Venus' knowledge of who loves whom: 'As whi this fissh, and naught that, comth to were' (III.35). The verse goes from high Boethian rhetoric to colloquial gossip in just seven lines.

The proem also mixes Christian and classical allusions, and an example of the latter suggests in miniature something of its complex view of love. At the beginning of the fourth stanza, we are told that among Venus' powers is the ability to 'fierse Mars apaisen of his ire' (III.22). Undoubtedly, this powerful line refers primarily to medieval allegorical interpretations of the love of Mars and Venus – astrologically as the beneficent power exercised by her planet over his, for example, or philosophically as the harmony of opposites (Root, *Troilus* edition, 465nIII.22). Yet, at the same time, the reader, prompted by the references to Jove's lust in the lines just above, may also be reminded of the comic episode, told by Ovid and Jean de Meun among others, in which the adulterous god and goddess are caught in Vulcan's net during their sexual frolics to the merriment of the other divinities. Both stories – low comedy and high allegory – are available to the reader in this catalogue of the varieties of love.

How Troilus Falls in Love

In the rest of this chapter I will concentrate on the growth of the passion between Troilus and Criseyde, paying particular attention to how Chaucer goes beyond his source to explore the many kinds of love suggested in the prohemium to book III. After comparing the different ways that Troilus and Criseyde fall in love, I shall briefly mention their first meeting and then analyse the consummation of their affair. These scenes are among the most original in *Troilus* and clearly show how thoroughly the English poet transforms and transcends his Italian source.

Boccaccio's Troiolo falls in love quickly, simply and happily. Despite the pain of past affairs, he feels great delight ('diletto sommo') when he chances to gaze on Criseida's face during the festival to Pallas. Ignoring his own advice to his knights against women, he is unaware that Love with his darts ('con li dardi sui') dwells in Criseida's eyes and that an arrow has pieced his heart (1.26–9). Even back in his room, the 'happy youth' ('il giovinetto lieto') has no sense of the woes that are to come (1.35),

for, making plans to attract Criseida, he sings of his love with joy
and hope (1.37).

In *Troilus* the sight of Criseyde is more overwhelming for the
hero and more multi-layered for the reader. Although Chaucer
follows the general outlines of Boccaccio's narrative (his Troilus
is also stricken immediately, and we are allowed full access to
the prince's emotions), the poet deepens his telling with changes
that suggest love's power and variety. One such change is to make
the English Troilus more sexually innocent than his experienced
Italian counterpart. Because he has never been in love before,
Troilus' first speech to his knights against women sets him up
for a harder fall. Chaucer also introduces myth into the scene.
The metaphorical darts and arrow mentioned by Boccaccio are
transformed into a real and angry God of Love, who shows that
'his bowe nas naught broken' when he 'sodeynly' hits the prince
'atte fulle' (I.208–9). This is no cute Cupid, but an irresistible and
hostile deity. The power of love is reinforced by a further change,
Chaucer's first long addition to *Filostrato*, which asserts that Love
conquers all, even the strongest and wisest of men (I.215–66):
'For evere it was, and evere it shal byfalle,/That Love is he that
alle thing may bynde' (I.236–7).

The original description here of the God of Love as a cosmic
power, one of the kinds of love listed in the prohemium to book
III, seems to allow Troilus no escape and no alternative. He
must submit as others have done before. This is certainly one
way of understanding Troilus' experience, but, as so often in
Troilus, Chaucer also offers the reader an alternate perspective
when, immediately after the interpolation on Cupid's power, he
gives an entirely new account of Troilus' first sight of Criseyde
(Jordan, *Shape*, 76–9). This second, independent version of how
Troilus falls in love describes it as a natural and physical process,
another of the kinds of love mentioned in the prohemium of book
III. The God of Love's arrow in the first passage is replaced in
the second passage by the arrow-like vision of Troilus himself:
'His eye percede, and so depe it wente,/Til on Criseyde it smot,
and ther it stente' (I.272–3). Although the process is different,
the earlier intensity remains. 'Smot' and 'stente', especially, tell
us that the prince will never be the same. Instead of attributing
all to an irresistible outside force, Chaucer now explores Troilus'
inner reactions, which are clearly expressed in two original
stanzas (I.274–80 and I.295–301) that detail changes in his

body ('Therwith his herte gan to sprede and rise') and his psyche ('He was tho glad his hornes in to shrinke:/Unnethes wiste he how to loke or wynke'). As Troilus leaves the temple, vivid vocabulary emphasizes the extent of the damage: although 'nat fullich al awhaped' (I.316), Troilus is 'thorugh-shoten and thorugh-darted' (I.325). Not even for a moment is this lover a happy youth.

In addition to providing two separate accounts of Troilus' first sight of Criseyde, Chaucer further complicates our understanding by providing a number of contrasting interpretive contexts. For example, the physical and psychological changes that Troilus feels are classic symptoms of lovesickness, an illness taken seriously by reputable medieval medical treatises, which regard the condition with moral neutrality, as Mary Wack has shown. Yet other elements that Chaucer has added to *Filostrato* allow the reader to interpret Troilus' experience positively. Windeatt notes original references to love as a fellowship and art (*Troilus* edition, 107nI.303); and it is also shown as a faith. Even before Troilus prays to Cupid (I.422–34) or Pandarus declares that his friend will be a noble upholder of his new faith (I.998–1008), the narrator explicitly gives love the status of a religion: 'Blissed be Love, that kan thus folk converte!' (I.308). Chaucer further elevates Troilus' emotion by describing it with language that seems to derive from such delicate French poets as Machaut (Wimsatt, 'Guillaume') and with the most sophisticated piece of rhetoric in the entire first book: Petrarch's sonnet on the paradoxes of love (I.400–20).

The sonnet is a magnificent addition to *Troilus* (whose achievement is even more stunning when we realize that Petrarch's lyrics would not reappear in English poetry for well over a hundred years), but its oxymorons ('O quike deth, O swete harm so queynte') announce that the experience it describes may be taken in radically different ways. Although Chaucer celebrates the depth and sincerity of Troilus' love, as we have just seen, he also adds passages to his source that suggest its deceit, absurdity and pain. The negative aspects of amorous passion implicit in Petrarch's sonnet are made explicit in two speeches, which bracket Troilus' first sight of Criseyde. In these passages the prince himself publicly denounces the foolishness and suffering of loving women (I.190–203, I.330–50).

The comedy that results from having the poem's principal lover attack love is sharpened by making the second condemnation a desperate attempt by Troilus to disguise his own passion. With stinging words only hinted at by Boccaccio, Troilus damns romantic passion as he himself falls under its sway. But, of course, Troilus' love has been linked with deceit from the first. When his heart begins to 'sprede and rise' at the sight of Criseyde, his initial response, in lines original with Chaucer, is to disguise his true feelings: 'And softe sighed, lest men myghte hym here,/And caught ayeyn his firste pleyinge chere' (I.278–80). Soon after, Troilus not only utters his mendacious attack on lovers, but also lies to his companions about 'other besy nedes' (I.355), so that he can be alone to lament his love. His subsequent expressions of grief in his chamber, which are intensified from *Filostrato*, raise still more questions of interpretation. The English poem repeatedly associates Troilus' love with death (I.306) and illness (I.489), and several critics have argued that Troilus' dwelling on Criseyde's image in his room (I.365–7) and his conscious decision to be her man ('Thus took he purpos loves craft to suwe', I.379) closely imitate medieval theological descriptions of the steps by which the human will consents to deadly sin (Morgan, 'Freedom'; Robertson, 'Tragedy').

Chaucer has expanded, complicated and deepened Boccaccio's account of how Troilus falls in love, but interpretation rests with the reader. In fact, interpretation is demanded from the reader. As we have seen, Troilus' passion is attributed in Chaucer's version both to an external divinity and to forces within his own mind and body. His experience can be persuasively seen as a morally neutral sickness, a profound religious devotion, either a courtly or a comic amour, a devastating wound or a serious sin. Of course, even these categories are not simple. Do the several references to love as a religion in this scene, for instance, validate romantic passion or do they invoke Christian standards by which it is to be condemned? Do the images of illness, suffering and death demonstrate the seriousness of Troilus' love or reveal its foolish destructiveness?

The long passage on the power of love that Chaucer adds to his source, which has already been mentioned (I.215–66), suggests that there are no easy answers to these and similar questions. The most obvious import of the lines is to insist on the glories and benefits of love: it has 'worthi folk maad worthier of name,/And causeth moost to dreden vice and shame' (I.251–2) and is 'a thing so vertuous in kynde' (I.254).[5] At the same time, the passage contains darker hints. Patricia Kean notes the association of Love with Fortune ('Stanza'), especially the statement that Troilus has 'clomben on the staire' and now 'he moot descenden' (I.215–16). Like Fortune, Love, for all its virtues, is pictured as an enslaving force (I.231), which must be submitted to because resistance is impossible: 'The yerde is bet that bowen wole and wynde/Than that that brest' (I.257–8). Even worse, Chaucer compares Troilus to an animal. Just as 'proude Bayard' realizes that he must obey 'horses lawe', so this king's son comes to accept that 'may no man fordon the lawe of kynde' (I.218–38).

Some have been tempted to read the Bayard comparison as proof positive that Troilus is simply a slave to pride and bestial sexuality; but, although there is some support for such a judgement, the dominant tone of the passage is not that of Christian moralization. Even the imagery of binding, as Stephen Barney has shown, may refer to the ordered harmony of the universe as well as to the chains of lust (see III.1765–8), and J. D. Burnley demonstrates how carefully Chaucer keeps the lines on Bayard within a 'courtly perspective', thus creating a sophisticated ambiguity that suggests 'the lack of providence in [Troilus'] conduct, without imposing specific condemnation' ('Proude', 152). This first major addition to *Filostrato* allows us to see both the joys and dangers of human love. Throughout the account of how the prince falls in love, Troilus makes us feel the intensity of the experience and, by including a range of implied readers or readings within the text, also suggests the different ways it may be interpreted.

How Criseyde Falls in Love

The manner in which Criseyde falls in love is also transformed by Chaucer, but to other, if equally complex, effects. Boccaccio's Troiolo and Criseida are quite similar lovers, but the English poet changes his two principal characters in exactly opposite directions. Whereas Troilus is more quickly and completely overwhelmed than his original in *Filostrato*, Criseyde comes to accept love much more slowly and as the result of many different influences. In contrast to traditional gender stereotypes, Chaucer's Troilus feels, his Criseyde thinks. Less swept away by sexual desire than Troilus or her model in *Filostrato*, and

more wary, Chaucer's Criseyde is not tortured by life and
death oxymorons, but tries to satisfy the desires of others
while preserving her safety, independence and honour. It is not
certain if she ever surrenders herself fully to love. In contrast
to the passion of Troilus, which we are allowed to see clearly,
Criseyde's falling in love is deliberately kept hidden from the
reader.

In *Filostrato*, Criseida, like Troiolo, is inflamed by desire almost
from the start, and Boccaccio leaves us in no doubt about what
she is feeling. Despite some brief criticism of Pandaro for trying
to make her follow the rules of love, Criseida's initial objection
to Troiolo is no deeper than the fear that his passion will last
only a few days (2.50). Given such meagre resistance, Pandaro's
practical *carpe diem* argument that she should act before time
steals her youth and beauty ('Non perder tempo, pensa che
vecchiezza/o morte torrà via la tua bellezza') is immediately
accepted by Criseyde and prompts her to ask if she indeed
might achieve the 'solace and joy of love' ('d'amor sollazzo e
gioco', 2.54–5). When she retires to consider her position in
an extended soliloquy, Criseida cannot get the prince's hand-
some image ('il bel viso') out of her mind (2.78), and her
dominant thoughts are bold and willing: she wonders why she
should not have an affair like everyone else and decides that
the joy of hidden love is greater than that of married love,
just as stolen water is sweeter than wine in abundance (2.74).
Criseyde's response to seeing Troiolo after she knows of his
interest is as passionate as was his first sight of her: 'and so
suddenly was she captured ('sì subitamente presa fue') that she
desired him more than any other good, and she greatly regret-
ted the lost time when she had not known his love' (2.83).

Boccaccio's Criseida is ready to love once she is convinced that
it is safe; Chaucer's Criseyde has to be convinced that she should
want to love at all. When she first writes to Troiolo, Boccaccio's
Criseida says that she would be willing to please him if the world
allowed it (2.124–5), but even at this late date Chaucer's Criseyde
offers nothing more than a sister's love (II.1221–5). Criseyde is
more passive than her model, and the insistent manipulations
of Pandarus are crucial in getting her to act. His *carpe diem*
argument, which was decisive in *Filostrato* (II.393–406), is not
nearly enough to convince the English heroine. When she first
consents to look kindly on Troilus, it is not, she insists, out of

any pleasure, but only to protect herself in case Pandarus' threat that he and Troilus will kill themselves is true: 'I shal myn herte *ayeins* my lust constreyne' (II.476, my emphasis). Whether or not we believe Criseyde here, she is never shown as the object of Cupid's flaming arrows.

Criseyde undoubtedly falls in love more carefully and less passionately than either Troilus or Boccaccio's heroine, but the actual process remains obscure because, as was shown in the previous chapter, Chaucer does not allow us to see as much of her mind and heart as we do of Troilus'. Criseyde's crucial private soliloquy in book II (687–812), during which she considers at length whether to accept Troilus' love, is certainly more intricate and believable than its source in *Filostrato*, but its effect is to introduce questions in the reader about the heroine's real experience of love because the topics she considers remain so detached from her feelings. Alone in her chamber after Pandarus' first visit, Criseyde weighs the social consequences of different actions, such as the advantages and disadvantages of being loved by a member of the Trojan royal family (II.703–14), without addressing her own personal desires. The simple opposition in the debate of Boccaccio's Criseyde between the pleasures of hidden sensuality and the difficulties of keeping the affair alive and secret (2.68–78) becomes in Chaucer's reshaping a tangle of conflicting motives and forces open to a variety of interpretations by individual readers.

The deliberate uncertainty that I am claiming is not the generally accepted view of how Criseyde falls in love. In an influential essay, Donald Howard argued that during this section of *Troilus* 'the reader is allowed to participate in Criseyde's mental life', and that during the soliloquy itself 'we are able to *feel* her feeling just as we are able to think her thoughts' ('Experience', 174, 178). His conclusion is that 'for a space of some four hundred or more lines in Book II, I have *been* Criseyde, have experienced the world as she experienced it, have had my mind and being subsumed in her' (191). Howard's view that we intimately share Criseyde's consciousness has been frequently repeated by others.[6] In contrast, I would argue that Chaucer's opaque characterization of Criseyde, already discussed in the previous chapter, keeps us at a distance from her heart and mind while she falls in love, as is not true with Troilus, so that individual readers are themselves forced to create the psychic being that is only suggested in the text. During her private soliloquy in book II we are given little more than the sporadic illusion of sharing Criseyde's experience. We simply do not know what she truly feels and must ourselves decide what her response is to the various possibilities she considers. Howard's explanation of Criseyde's consciousness is in such a reading, but only one of the many allowed by Chaucer's elusive text.

In her soliloquy, Criseyde first declares that she ought not to grant Troilus her love (II.703–4), and then goes on to consider the possible trouble if she angered the king's son (II.704–14), the need for moderation (II.715–21), the prince's virtues (II.722–8), the impossibility of stopping others from thinking what they will about a love-affair (II.729–35), the honour (well deserved, she thinks) of having been chosen over all other women in Troy (II.736–49), and her freedom to do what she likes in love (II.750–63). Then, negative thoughts occurring to her (II.764–70), she considers the danger to her freedom that love poses (II.771–84), the treachery of lovers (II.785–98) and the malice of gossips (II.799–804). What Criseyde never says during this remarkable speech is whether she actually loves Troilus. Her arguments remain hypothetical and detached. Although declaring that she has the right to love 'in cas if that me leste' (II.758), we never learn if that is indeed what she does wish. For all our exposure to her calculations, Criseyde's deepest thoughts and emotions remain open to multiple interpretation.

At other crucial stages in the wooing, Chaucer is deliberately silent about what Criseyde feels about love. Boccaccio's Criseida reads Troiolo's ardent first letter eagerly and with delight, vowing to find a time and a place to 'quench this fire' ('spegner questo foco', 2.114–15). In contrast, Chaucer's account is almost impudent in its refusal to tell us anything important about his heroine's response:

> Avysed word by word in every lyne,
> And fond no lak, she thoughte he koude good,
> And up it putte, and wente hire in to dyne.
> (II.1177–9)

We assume that Criseyde is here feeling many things in addition to approval of Troilus' epistolary style, but we are not allowed to know what these other feelings are.

The subtlety of the process by which Criseyde, in contrast to Troilus, falls in love, and the way that Chaucer keeps much of the process hidden, while provoking our interpretation, are demonstrated by an original episode just before Criseyde's soliloquy. After Pandarus tells his niece that she is loved by Troilus, she retires to her room and presently sees the prince himself ride by under her window (II.610–86). In contrast to the full account of Troilus' first sight of Criseyde, Chaucer makes it more difficult than is usually recognized to understand what his heroine is thinking and feeling at a parallel moment in her experience. We know that she has been affected in some way, but must ourselves decide precisely how and why. The scene deserves to be examined carefully.

The first stanza of the episode deliberately moves the narrative focus from Criseyde ('But as she sat allone and thoughte thus,/Ascry aros at scarmuch al withoute', II.610–11) down into the street to report the voice of Trojan citizens as they notice Troilus' return from battle: 'Se, Troilus/Hath right now put to flighte the Grekes route!' (II.612–13). The narrative remains objective and distant from Criseyde in the next stanza (II.617–23). We hear the conclusion of the townspeople's speech, and then, in the voice of the narrator, a factual description of Troilus' ride and a general statement ('men seyn') about the inevitability of necessity. The third stanza (II.624–30), which describes Troilus' appearance more particularly, remains in the third person, though the previous objectivity gives way to strong approval: 'But swich a knyghtly sighte trewely/As was on hym, was nought, withouten faille,/To loke on Mars, that god is of bataille' (II.628–30). Despite the introduction of a definite point of view, it remains unclear who it is that is supposed to be looking at this 'sighte'. Presumably it is the townspeople, whose observation of the prince has been previously emphasized, or perhaps it is the narrator himself, though his observation could only be an act of the imagination.

The most serious difficulties with perspective begin in the following stanza (II.631–7). Admiration for Troilus becomes much warmer, and the suggestive phrase 'For bothe he hadde a body and a myght/To don that thing, as wel as hardynesse' (II.633–4) has been understood as Criseyde's admiration for Troilus' potential prowess as a lover, apparently on the principle that whenever a word or phrase is ambiguous in English ('to don that thing') it must be sexual. Certainly many modern readers, perhaps most, assume that the next statement, which can also be taken erotically, is Criseyde's (Donaldson, 'Cresseid False', 70–1): 'So fressh, so yong, so weldy semed he,/It was an heven upon hym for to see' (II.636–7). These lines *might* indeed describe what the heroine is thinking (their special intensity is an argument in favour), but nothing identifies them as such. The text signals no return to Criseyde, though some have assumed that the whole scene is meant to be seen through her eyes (Taylor, 123). The only voices that have been definitely established within the lines, as we have seen, are those of the narrator and the townspeople, either of whom might be imagined to have such thoughts about Troilus, especially if the words are not read sexually, which they need not be. In fact, both perspectives are reaffirmed in the very next stanza (II.638–44), which provides an objective description of what Troilus has suffered in battle ('His helm tohewen was in twenty places . . .', II.638) and then reports more speech from the people in the street: 'Here cometh oure joye,/And, next his brother, holder up of Troye!' (II.643–4). The text hints that the sight of Troilus' wounded but physically powerful body might have been one of the forces that impelled Criseyde to accept his love, but we cannot be certain that this is what she feels. The scene is deliberately constructed to leave the experience open to multiple interpretations by its readers.

Before Criseyde is ever mentioned again, attention switches briefly to Troilus, as he blushes in response to the townspeople's praise (II.645–6), and then we again are told of a definite but unidentified viewer: 'That to byholde it was a noble game/How sobrelich he caste down his yen' (II.647–8). When the narration finally returns to Criseyde, we are shown her consciousness, as usual, only opaquely:

> Criseÿda gan al his chere aspien,
> And leet it so softe in hire herte synke,
> That to hireself she seyde, 'Who yaf me drynke?'
>   (II.649–51)

Although the focus is now definitely on Criseyde, we are not much wiser. Something has happened to her, but what exactly? We are told that she sees Troilus' blushing face and that she lets that sight, which is not further analysed, slip into a heart that remains hidden. What we are left with is her magnificently enigmatic question, 'Who yaf me drynke?'

Despite the drama in these words, which are among the most memorable in *Troilus*, they remain no more than an exterior expression of Criseyde's response, similar to the public speech of the townspeople except that they demand interpretation. Chaucer forces us to imagine exactly what drink she has been given. Is it a powerful poison, strong liquor, or just a little white wine? Older editors glossed 'drynke' as 'love-potion', but the recent (and wiser because less prescriptive) practice has been to take it as 'any intoxicating beverage' (*Riverside Chaucer*, 1033n651). Although Criseyde's words will immediately suggest to most readers the irresistible love-potions of medieval romance (which may be the way Criseyde wishes to explain the experience to herself), the context of *Troilus* makes us aware, as John Bayley notes (93), that, whatever the apparent similarities, Criseyde's experience is fundamentally *different* from that of lovers like Tristan and Isolde, even as their sudden overwhelming passions are evoked. For Criseyde there is no fatal potion, no one irrevocable moment when love becomes an absolute, as there is for Isolde, for heroines like Lavinia in the Old French *Eneas* (Muscatine, *French*, 154–5), or, indeed, for Troilus.

Although Criseyde blushes and withdraws her head from the window after seeing Troilus ride by, she appears less moved by passion than by self-regard and pity. Her next words note that this is the man her uncle said would die without her mercy (II.653–5), and the narrator declares that, although she ponders his 'prowesse', 'estat', 'renown', 'wit', 'shap', and 'gentilesse', she favours him most because 'his distresse/Was al for hire' (II.659–64). The narrator then disputes those who would accuse Criseyde of having 'so lightly loved Troilus' at 'firste syghte'; on the contrary, he insists that she only 'gan enclyne/To like hym first', after which Troilus' own good service began to undermine ('myne') her resistance, helped by the favourable influence of the planet Venus (II.666–86). Some modern critics read this statement as Chaucer's clever way of raising questions about Criseyde's motives while claiming to defend her, but Jill Mann persuasively resists such a cynical reductive interpretation ('Swoon', 323; cf. Salter, 'Poet', 287–8).

The narrator's remarks accurately define how Criseyde falls in love. It is a long, contingent, mysterious process. Many different forces, in addition to the sight of Troilus and the stars, bring Criseyde to accept love, including Pandarus' incessant arguments and threats, her own deliberations, Antigone's lovely idealistic song in praise of love (II.827–75), and the haunting dream of the eagle painlessly snatching her heart away (II.925–31). All make their contribution; but, despite the attempts of different critics to see one or another of these moments as decisive, Chaucer does not himself define the relative importance of each as Criseyde falls in love. After Antigone's song, the text tells us nothing more positive than that it made her fear love less ('lasse for t'agaste') and began to make her able to convert (II.901–3), whereas after the dream it offers no interpretation at all.

Specific evidence that Criseyde has fallen in love appears only much later, when, in bed with Troilus and in response to his declaration that she is caught, she replies: 'Ne hadde I er now, my swete herte deere,/Ben yolde, ywis, I were now nought heere!' (III.1210–11). Yet even here Chaucer makes us decide about the nature of Criseyde's passion for Troilus. As before, our knowledge of the heroine is wholly external; we hear her intriguing spoken words but are kept from her inner thoughts. Although she assures Troilus that she had previously fallen in love with him, we are not allowed to know when this decisive moment actually occurred, as Spearing shrewdly notes (*Troilus*, 19), nor are we told exactly why or how. Later still, as the lovers are about to part, Criseyde insists that she loved Troilus only because of his 'moral vertu' (IV.1667–73). We need not assume that Criseyde is deliberately lying to recognize this as one more public and partial explanation for a private experience beyond our comprehension.

As we saw in the previous chapter, the traditional mystery and otherness of women, which is one of the results of their political marginalization in patriarchal societies, is used by Chaucer to produce a Criseyde who challenges every reader to rewrite her unresolved text. Like most medieval literature, *Troilus* exists within a male aesthetic that can only gaze on women from afar, but it is Chaucer's particular achievement to accept and use, rather than attempt to deny, this limitation. His is the only version of the story in the Middle Ages that refuses to draw a lesson (always negative, of course) about the heroine. It is the openness of Chaucer's Criseyde that makes her such a central symbol of the multiplicity of *Troilus*. Chaucer understands that

it would be just as futile to legislate the final meaning of Criseyde
as to attempt that for the poem as a whole: his function as author
is to use his poetic skills to entice individual readers to become
engaged with the many possibilities of both texts so that they,
as collaborators, will complete each for themselves.

The Consummation

Boccaccio's lovers are essentially alike, but Chaucer shows us
the different paths by which Criseyde and Troilus come into
each other's arms. The English pair are more reserved and
delicate than their Italian originals, and they consummate their
passion only after many hesitations and delays. Although Troilus
falls in love immediately, he, like the more reluctant Criseyde,
needs Pandarus' help to resolve the affair, a process during
which Chaucer invents two original scenes: the party given by
Deiphebus at which the couple first meet and talk, and the
dinner given by Pandarus after which they finally go to bed
together. During this section of *Troilus and Criseyde* (roughly
from the last third of book II to the middle of book III) Chaucer
abandons Boccaccio's material for a longer period than in any
other part of the poem. Nothing like the two scenes is necessary
in *Filostrato* because neither Troiolo nor Criseida has any doubt
what should be done about their mutual attraction. Each falls in
love upon seeing the other, and at the first opportunity Criseida
summons Troiolo to her house where they quickly embrace and
soon mount the stairs to satisfy their urgent desires.

The various narrative elements, values and perspectives that
Chaucer has woven into the scene at Deiphebus' house have
already been discussed in Chapter 3, and we need note briefly
only that the portrayal of love here is equally multi-layered –
mixing the good, the bad and the comic. The first meeting of
Troilus and Criseyde certainly affirms the courtliness of their
relationship. Amidst the 'love of friends' so generously practised
by the Trojan royal family, Troilus' cry to Criseyde for mercy
and his offer of service, the sincerity of which is underscored by
his embarrassed agony (III.82–94), reveal a depth of feeling and
courtesy to which she responds with a tentative acceptance and
kiss. Pandarus has reason to fall to his knees and call their meeting
a 'merveille' (III.189), for it suggests the ideal love celebrated by

Antigone's song – mutual, noble, gracious and even physical. At the same time, Chaucer also introduces other, negative elements into the scene. Troilus' pretended illness, which brings about the private meeting, activates images of sickness and death that have been associated with the affair from the start. Pandarus' manipulations further qualify the purity of the love-affair, and Troilus himself is far from innocent. For all his sincerity, the prince is delighted with his friend's deceptions and willingly lies to family as well as to Criseyde. Moreover, Chaucer further complicates our response with comedy. It is difficult not to laugh at Troilus as he lies stunned, blushing and tongue-tied before his beloved, just as the wit and energy of Pandarus' endless schemes (and claims of marvels) are as delightful as they are shameless.

The multiplicity of love that Chaucer explores throughout *Troilus* is nowhere more evident than in the events that lead to the lovers' consummation. As usual, the couple are passive and Pandarus the instigator: he invites Criseyde to his house for dinner and, having manoeuvred her into agreeing to spend the night, he brings Troilus secretly into her bedchamber by means of an invented story about the prince's jealousy of a certain Horaste. The stylistic complexity of the consummation scene has been brilliantly explored by Charles Muscatine, who demonstrates the tension between its courtliness and comedy: 'The poem's stretch between the idealized and the practical in sentiment and action is drawn to its farthest limit in this sequence' (*French*, 148–53, 153). On one side we have Criseyde's 'semilyric, semiphilosophic' speech on jealousy, the narrator's sympathy with love, and Troilus' earnest nobility; on the other we have Pandarus playing the clown to such a degree that he becomes the first go-between in medieval literature who 'must go so far as actually to pick up the hero and throw him into the lady's bed' (151–2). Robert Frank wittily defines a similar contrast in the hero when he asserts that the consummation scene 'gives us Troilus' finest and funniest hours, exalted lover and mouse's heart, now in a rapture, now in a dead faint' (163).[7]

But even the duality of courtliness and comedy so well analysed by Muscatine and Frank, important as it is, does not tell us all. Chaucer has once again developed *Filostrato* in a number of very different directions at once. At one moment frankly carnal, at another reaching for the divine, while constantly punctuated by buffoonery, the consummation of the love of Troilus and Criseyde can be variously seen as sensual, courtly, comic, lyrical, transitory, ideal, manipulative and mutual. Although most readings stress only one or two of these elements, all must be recognized and their contradictions accepted to appreciate Chaucer's achievement.

If previous criticism rarely acknowledges the full range of the different elements in the central love-scene, most such studies contain important individual insights. For instance, those who downplay the comic elements of the consummation are right to insist that at the core of the episode is a powerful sensuality that the narrator works to make his readers feel and envy. Lewis observed that book III of *Troilus* contains 'some of the greatest erotic poetry of the world' (*Allegory*, 196), and Charles Owen has demonstrated how the rising and falling rhythms of the narration parallel the struggles of Troilus and Criseyde to achieve complete sexual fulfilment ('Mimetic'; cf. Howard, 'Literature', 448). The night at Pandarus' house has elements that are directly carnal (Richard F. Green notes that the setting 'reminds one more of a fabliau than an "old romance" ', 215), though this physicality is lyrically celebrated, as when Troilus strokes Criseyde's body:

> Hire armes smale, hire streghte bak and softe,
> Hire sydes longe, flesshly, smothe, and white
> He gan to stroke, and good thrift bad ful ofte
> Hire snowissh throte, hire brestes rounde and lite,
> Thus in this hevene he gan hym to delite,
> And therwithal a thousand tyme hire kiste,
> That what to don, for joie unnethe he wiste.
>
> (III.1247–53)

Eroticism is an important element in Chaucer's account of the consummation, but it is only one of the many elements the text offers its readers. The courtliness of the consummation is certainly emphasized by Chaucer (his lovers are less driven by pure appetite than Boccaccio's), but he also uses the scene to suggest the possibility of equality between men and women in love (Mann, 'Swoon', 320, 329–30; Aers, *Chaucer*, 97) – an ideal which occurs throughout his poetry, as in the famous opening of 'The Franklin's Tale'. As a result of their sexual union, the lovers are able to heal one another and overcome their deepest fears: Criseyde gives up her characteristic timidity ('al quyt from every drede and tene', III.1226) and comes to trust Troilus ('Opned hire herte and tolde hym hire entente', III.1239); whereas the prince, for his part, escapes from his deep-seated morbidity into hope: 'right as he that seth his deth yshapen/. . . And from his deth is brought in sykernesse' (III.1240–3). While the lovers are in bed together, they are able to forget the encircling war and create a private world of love. The exchange of rings in this scene, among other things, has led some to suggest that Troilus and Criseyde may have contracted a genuine, if clandestine, marriage (Kelly, 230–42; Maguire). Although the evidence for their being man and wife is slight, they do pledge their truth to one another. Troilus' vows are frequent, but even the elusive Criseyde finally declares her devotion in words that begin to match her beloved's in beauty and emotional commitment:

> O herte deere,
> The game, ywys, so ferforth now is gon
> That first shal Phebus fallen fro his spere,
> And everich egle ben the dowves feere,
> And everich roche out of his place sterte,
> Er Troilus oute of Criseydes herte.
>
> (III.1493–8)

Criseyde's lines are lovely and moving, but we need not hear the Pandarian echo in 'game' or wait for her eventual betrayal to realize that they express only one element of the episode. As moralistic critics have helped us to see, Chaucer supplements the idealism, courtliness, physical satisfaction, and even comedy of the consummation with darker, more ominous perspectives. Troilus' supposed jealousy of Horaste (though a fiction) foreshadows Diomede's future conquest, and the several mythological love-stories that the prince rapidly invokes before he enters his beloved's bedroom describe love as destruction and rape (III.715–35). The route by which the prince is said to reach his beloved is similarly unromantic, for it includes a 'goter, by a pryve wente [way]' (III.787), a 'stuwe' (which might suggest a brothel) in which he waits (III.698) and a 'secre trappe-dore' (III.759). As with the first meeting at Deiphebus' house, the union of lovers happens only because of the schemes of Pandarus. He invites Criseyde to dinner, hides Troilus and invents the rival. Yet, if Pandarus is the main culprit, Troilus and Criseyde are willing accessories in deceit. Troilus is again happy to go along with Pandarus' fabrications, and at a crucial moment Criseyde grants her uncle control: 'So werketh now in so discret a wise/That I honour may have, and he plesaunce:/For I am here al in youre governaunce' (III.943–5). In addition to the manner of Pandarus' involvement, it is its extent that undermines any purely courtly reading of the affair. We are not even sure that on the night of the consummation he ever leaves the lovers' bedroom. His voyeurism, which the reader is made to share to some degree, has been emphasized in many recent studies and reaches its peak the next morning when Pandarus leeringly jokes with Criseyde about the activities of the night that has just passed (III.1555–78).

Like the courtliness and comedy of the consummation, its voyeurism and deceit are only parts of an intricate whole. A completely different element of the episode links the passion of Troilus and Criseyde with divine love. Before he leads the prince into his niece's bedchamber, Pandarus assures his friend that 'thow shalt into hevene blisse wende' (III.704), the same 'hevene blisse' that the narrator later says he cannot describe (III.1322). Immediately after the erotic description of Criseyde's body, and before his pledge of chivalric service, Troilus speaks in a new key, launching into a hymn ('O Love, O Charite!') which draws on Boethius and St Bernard's prayer to the Blessed Virgin in Dante's *Paradiso* to extol 'Benigne Love, thow holy bond of thynges' (III.1254–74). Later the joyful Troilus utters his magnificent Boethian song on the power of love in the universe (III.1744–71), which Chaucer substitutes for Troiolo's original song in *Filostrato* already used for the proem to book III. These exalted lines on the 'hosom [wholesome] alliaunce' and 'acord' that love creates between heaven and earth are in sharp contrast to the prince's Petrarchan song in book I on the pain and paradoxes of love. Troilus' assertion of love as positive, unifying and cosmic has been much commented on and variously interpreted. Is he sadly deluded about the nature of his love for Criseyde or does the intensity of his devotion approach the divine? My purpose here is not to answer this question, but to note the variety of elements, images and tones in the consummation scene that have been added to *Filostrato*.

One further aspect of this episode in *Troilus* (though others might also be identified and discussed) is the suggestion that the love between Troilus and Criseyde, however potentially exalted, is part of the temporal contingent world. Faced with Pandarus' manufactured claim that Troilus is jealous of Horaste, even Criseyde, who generally takes things as she finds them, launches into a quasi-philosophical speech on the instability of earthly happiness:

> 'O God,' quod she, 'so worldly selynesse,
> Which clerkes callen fals felicitee,
> Imedled is with many a bitternesse!'
>
> (III.813–15)

The transitoriness of love in this world is also emphasized by the many natural images added to Boccaccio's account, such as the comparison of Criseyde to an aspen leaf (III.1200) and to a nightingale (III.1233) or of both lovers to a lark and hawk (III.1191–2) and to woodbine encircling a tree (III.1230–2). The limits of earthly existence are seen in the pain it causes Troilus and Criseyde to part even briefly, just as their cursing the approach of 'cruel day' (III.1695–1701) sharply contrasts with the ordered succession of day and night praised by Troilus in his Boethian song (III.1751–7). Even though joy is repeatedly evoked during the consummation scene, other lines remind the reader of love's brevity and fragility.

The multiplicity of love revealed during the consummation scene continues to be explored throughout the rest of *Troilus and Criseyde*. Near the end of book III there occurs a description of achieved and mutual love with few equals in literature:

> For ech of hem gan otheres lust obeye.
> Felicite, which that thise clerkes wise
> Comenden so, ne may nought here suffise;
> This joie may nought writen be with inke;
> This passeth al that herte may bythynke.
>
> (III.1690–4)

But other, less perfect kinds of love appear in the last two books of *Troilus*, which continue to demonstrate the irreducible complexity of human life, as we shall see in the following chapters. We are presented with Calchas' expression of paternal affection, however belated; Diomede's cynical rapacity; the promise of courtly romance at Sarpedon's party; Criseyde's 'slydynge of corage' (V.825), regret, and hopes for the future; Pandarus' proposal that Troilus find another woman and then anger over Criseyde's betrayal; and Troilus' immutable loyalty in love. If the one best answer for Chaucer and his contemporaries was the unfeigned and uncircumscribed love of God so powerfully urged at the end of the poem, even that transcendent truth did not remove the attractions and interest of earthly love from the mind of the fourteenth century, as the works of Dante and Petrarch also testify. In the love of Troilus and Criseyde, we find a tangle of noble aspiration and sensual desire, delicacy and absurdity, promise and delusion – all of which Chaucer, as no other poet in English, has allowed us to experience and variously interpret.

Notes

1   Gaston Paris is credited with popularizing the elusive term 'amour courtois' in 1883, although the word had some currency in the Middle Ages (see Larry Benson, 239). At least ten years earlier H. A. Taine had already declared that for Chaucer, and for his audience, love not only had the 'force of law', but was also 'inscribed in a code' that drew on Christianity to form 'a sacrament of love' (119; for a history of scholarship on courtly love, see Boase). Despite a few early sceptics, most Chaucerians for more than a generation accepted courtly love as central to *Troilus and Criseyde*, the most exhaustive study being by T. A. Kirby. A fundamental problem with any belief in a systematic 'code' of courtly love, however, is that a clear formulation seems to be found only in Andreas's treatise, a puzzling work whose sincerity has been questioned by two scholars (Robertson, 'Courtly'; Donaldson, 'Myth') who agree on little else. Spearing is probably right to conclude that it is misleading to describe 'Chaucer's poem as being "about courtly love" in any more specific sense than that it is about the love of courtly people' (*Troilus*, 28). Medieval literature reveals a new interest in romantic love between noble men and women, sometimes called 'fyn amor' (Kane; Reiss, '*Fin*' amors'), but its expressions are too individualistic to be explained by any monolithic system.

2   This view has been applied relentlessly by Gill and Wood, *Elements*. Although Gordon (*Double*) shares the same general approach, her subtle analysis responds to the sympathy for the lovers in *Troilus*, which is noted but rarely practised by Robertson, as well as to the poem's *sentence*.

3   Alfred David offers a more nuanced, if similar, argument that the praise of love in the first three books of *Troilus* is not ironic, because, whatever Christian lessons he claims to teach, Chaucer 'was of Criseyde's party without knowing it' (*Strumpet*, 29; see also David, 'Comedy'). David relies on the appealing, but

somewhat unmedieval argument that we esteem the love of Troilus and Criseyde all the more because it is transitory: 'The brevity and fragility of love of kynde [natural love] enhance its value for us' (*Strumpet*, 33). Aers also sees the poem as a celebration of human love, which functions as a counter to social oppression.

4 Even the ambiguities of love in *Troilus and Criseyde* that have been so skilfully analysed by such as Charles Muscatine in *Chaucer and the French Tradition* tend to resolve themselves into binary oppositions (romance versus fabliau) that do not grant the poem its true plurality. Love in *Troilus* is less stable than even the most sophisticated readings are willing to allow. Robert Frank, noting the clash of different value-systems in the poem, calls it an oxymoron in which opposite ideas of love are stated but never resolved (170), and David Lawton also finds the poem 'oxymoronic' because it contains both a troubled religious view of love and one that is amoral and ludic ('Irony', 105). Useful as these formulations are (and true as far as they go), they still understate the full complexity of love in *Troilus and Criseyde*, whose contradictions and permutations resist even the most subtle critical formulation.

5 These are real virtues, though virtues of civilization rather than of religion, and not 'vices masquerading as virtues' as claimed by Robertson (*Preface*, 477). See Larry Benson's article, already mentioned, which discusses the widespread chivalric belief that love indeed produced virtue.

6 Mann, *Estates*, 199; Aers, *Chaucer*, 97; see Pearsall for a recent and quite subtle reading of Criseyde in the Howard mode; for an opposite argument that is nevertheless different from mine, see apRoberts, 'Growth'.

7 The comedy of the consummation in book III has bothered some Chaucerians, who attempt to minimize its presence. C. S. Lewis largely ignores the buffoonery before the consummation, explaining it away as a technique of literary inoculation, a way of forestalling inappropriate laughter from the audience by locating it within the poem itself (*Allegory*, 171–3), an idea that is further developed by Howard ('Literature', 449–51). Great love-poetry does not usually also try to make us laugh, but the blissful union of the lovers in *Troilus* is immediately preceded by extended, sometimes slapstick comedy. For instance, we are treated to the farce of Troilus' slow-motion swoon when he thinks the story of Horaste has lost him his lady's love, followed by what might be called the amatory first-aid of Pandarus and Criseyde: the uncle removes the inert prince's clothing and puts him in a warm bed (Criseyde's), where the niece provides a kind of mouth to mouth resuscitation – 'and ofte tyme hym keste' (III.1129).

7

Fortune

Book III of *Troilus and Criseyde* concludes with a picture of fully achieved love. Despite past difficulties, Troilus now dwells 'in lust' (that is, pleasure) and 'in quiete' with Criseyde 'his owen herte swete' (III.1819–20). But the end of this contentment is announced from the very first words of book IV: 'But al to litel, weylaway the whyle,/Lasteth swich joie, ythonked be Fortune' (IV.1–2). The happiness of Troilus and Criseyde is destroyed by a particular stroke of bad Fortune. From the Greek camp the traitor Calchas demands the return of his daughter, thus reintroducing the world of war and social obligations from which the lovers had escaped to enjoy their passion. Although Fortune is mentioned throughout *Troilus and Criseyde*, the goddess is especially dominant during the last two books, which tell of the coming destruction of Troy and of the loss by Troilus 'of lyf and love yfeere' (IV.27).

The prominence of Fortune in *Troilus* reveals an added layer of philosophical material only briefly present in Boccaccio's less intellectual narrative. Many of these philosophical themes derive from Boethius' influential *Consolation of Philosophy*, but to identify their source is not to explain their function. *Troilus* is not the *Consolation* in English verse, for it neither reproduces Boethius' complete arguments nor endorses his conclusions. Chaucer is a poet not a philosopher, and he uses pieces of the *Consolation* in unexpected ways to ask questions rather than to provide answers. Perhaps Chaucer's biggest debt to Boethius is the figure of Fortune. Fortune is not only one of the central elements – along with setting, characterization and love – that make up the multiplicity of *Troilus*, but, as we have seen with respect to these other aspects of the poem, it is also complex within itself. Fortune appears in many guises in *Troilus* (serious, comic, decorative, hostile and benign) and is capable of various interpretations. It can be understood as simply a metaphor for

the ways things are, as a function of the human will, or as
the expression of an implacable destiny. Throughout Chaucer's
poem, Fortune expresses a human, pagan view of the world, and
the different responses by the two lovers to its blows define the
heroism and pathos of their individual tragedies.

Fortune as Philosophy

In his use of Fortune, Chaucer has once again taken a minor
element in Boccaccio's *Filostrato* and developed it fully and in
diverse ways. *Filostrato* contains brief and scattered references
to 'fortuna', but the term is only rarely personified and usually
represents little more than a synonym for chance or luck.[1]
In *Troilus* these casual allusions are increased in number and
expanded in scope until Fortune becomes a well-developed and
significant figure. The proem to book IV, which announces the
special prominence of Fortune in the final movement of the
story, is based on a passage at the end of part 3 of *Filostrato*,
in which Boccaccio blames Troiolo's coming unhappiness on
'Fortuna invidiosa':

> But for a short time lasted such happiness
> because of envious Fortune, who in this world
> allows nothing to remain stable. She turned towards him
> her angry face by means of a new event that occurred,
> and, turning everything upside down, took from him
> Criseida and his sweet pleasures and turned his happy
> love into sad griefs. (3.94)

Although this is one of Boccaccio's most extensive descriptions of Fortune, Chaucer, in keeping with his greater emphasis on the goddess and her powers throughout *Troilus*, not
only sets the portrait at the beginning of book IV as a formal prologue, but also makes it more vivid and detailed:

> But al to litel, weylaway the whyle,
> Lasteth swich joie, ythonked be Fortune,
> That semeth trewest whan she wol bygyle
> And kan to fooles so hire song entune
> That she hem hent and blent, traitour comune!

And whan a wight is from hire whiel ythrowe,
Than laugheth she, and maketh hym the mowe.

From Troilus she gan hire brighte face
Awey to writhe, and tok of hym non heede,
But caste hym clene out of his lady grace,
And on hire whiel she sette up Diomede. . . .
(IV.1–11)

This new and shocking vision of Fortune's malevolent power is more than the familiar pessimism of Murphy's law: the common view that anything that can go wrong will go wrong. The mention of Fortune's song, her victims' blindness, and especially the repeated mention of her wheel point to the specific source for this expansion of *Filostrato*. Like many other medieval authors, Chaucer obtained his information about Fortune largely from Boethius' early sixth-century *Consolation of Philosophy*, which he translated as *Liber Boecii de Consolacione Philosophie* (*Boece*) at about the same time that he was composing *Troilus*. The literary form of the work (dialogue in Latin verse and prose), its classical learning (much of it unavailable elsewhere in the Middle Ages) and the personal intensity of the *Consolation* made it especially appealing to sophisticated vernacular poets such as Jean de Meun, Dante and Chaucer.[2] In the shadow of political ruin and death, Boethius represents himself as turning to the methods of philosophy to assert central Christian truths, including the primacy of human choice and the contrast between the partial goods of this world and the eternal *summum bonum*. Although Boethius differs from the technical philosophy of late-medieval scholasticism,· his *Consolation* was still being commented upon by major scholars in the fourteenth century (Minnis, 'Aspects'), and his ideas on Fortune and the related concepts of Providence, free will, fate and determinism remained central to contemporary philosophical speculation.[3]

As we have already seen, *Filostrato* itself contains a few passages that derive from Boethius, such as Troiolo's song to love (3.74–9); but Chaucer, following his usual manner of developing the potential of his source, adds many more. For instance, after transforming Troiolo's song into the prohemium to book III, he gives a magnificent new *canticus* to the prince taken from elsewhere in the *Consolation* (III.1744–71), and he even allows Criseyde a somewhat unexpected Boethian speech

on the vanity of earthly happiness (III.813–40). The longest
such addition is Troilus' speech on predestination in book IV,
which extends to fully 120 lines (IV.958–1078). The *Consolation*
supplied more lines to Chaucer's poem than any other single
source except *Filostrato* itself, and the extraordinary mixture of a
worldly amorous romance with transcendent Christian philosophy
describes one of the central tensions of *Troilus and Criseyde*.
Indeed, the poem may be read on one level as a constant struggle
between Boccaccio and Boethius.

Although some readers have questioned the artistic judgement
of including serious philosophical matter in a courtly tale, its
presence tells us that, among his other roles in *Troilus*, Chaucer
saw himself, in C. S. Lewis's words, 'as a poet of *doctryne* and
sentence' ('What Chaucer', 62). As a more recent study notes, the
'philosophical dimension is indeed the most distinctive feature of
Chaucer's version of the Troilus story' (Reichl, 135). The poet's
earliest followers, such as Hoccleve and Usk, well understood this
aspect of his achievement, the latter going so far, in reference
to *Troilus*, as to call Chaucer 'the noble philosophical poete in
Englissh'.[4]

The philosophical matter derived from Boethius' *Consolation*
makes a major contribution to the multiplicity of *Troilus*, but it
does not give us the single key that will unlock the meaning of
the whole. Those who read *Troilus* as a mechanical restatement of
Boethius' orthodox and other-worldly message underestimate the
literary and thematic complexity of Chaucer's poem, which can
be seen if we return to the prohemium to book IV.[5] The account
of Fortune given there echoes the initial mistaken views that
Boethius ascribes to himself, not the authoritative redefinition
of the goddess provided by Lady Philosophy. In the first two
books of the *Consolation*, Boethius depicts himself as complaining
that he has been the victim of an all-powerful Fortune who has
ruined him unjustly, but Lady Philosophy answers that he is
misguided in expecting honesty from that blind goddess, whose
very nature is change, as symbolized by the ceaseless turning of
her wheel. Because of their unreliability, the temporal gifts that
Fortune grants in this world are finally worthless: 'in whiche
ther nys nothyng to ben desired, ne that hath in hymselve naturel
bownte, as it es ful wel yseene' (*Boece*, II.pr 6.122–4). No voice
in *Troilus*, however, ever utters such a complete and convincing
rejection of Fortune and her gifts.

Later in the *Consolation*, Fortune is linked to the more profound concepts of Providence and Destiny in ways that may
help us to understand its complex use in *Troilus*.[6] Boethius
asks Philosophy whether the seeming arbitrariness of human
fortune (in which good things often happen to the wicked
and bad things to the just) means that events in this world
are merely the result of chance, 'the hap of fortune' (IV.pr
5.38). Philosophy answers this by making a crucial distinction
between Destiny and Providence (IV.pr 6). What we see as
the random unjust actions of Fortune or as the hostility of
Fate is no more than the human inability to comprehend the
divine order of the universe. God's eternal plan for the world
is Providence, but the working-out of the same plan in time
is Destiny or Fate: 'lat the unfoldynge of temporel ordenaunce,
assembled amd oonyd in the lokynge of the devyne thought, be
cleped purveaunce, and thilke same assemblynge and oonynge,
devyded and unfolden by tymes, lat that ben called destyne'
(IV.pr 6.73–8). The difference is a matter of perspective. From
a divine perspective, capable of comprehending the unity of all
things and outside of time, the particular events of earthly fortune
take their place as part of God's Providential plan. From a limited,
human, temporal perspective (our perspective), however, these
same events can be understood only partially and thus appear
to be the result of an unknowable chance or irresistible fatality.
Lady Philosophy insists that human beings are not subject to
either chance or fate as long as they exercise their free will to rise
above the perishable gifts and continual shocks of Fortune ('the
unfoldynge of temporal ordenaunce') and seek the providence of
God's eternal truth.

Boethius' ideas about Fortune, Providence and Destiny are
echoed in *Troilus*, but they appear in the service of a variety of
literary purposes. Chaucer's poem is set in this world and by no
means simply endorses Lady Philosophy's transcendent views. As
the teller of 'The Nun's Priest's Tale' humorously notes about
the related Boethian question of whether God's foreknowledge
controls human action, 'in scole is greet altercacioun/In this
mateere, and greet disputisoun,/And hath been of an hundred
thousand men' (VII.3237–9). Modern Chaucerians, if somewhat
less numerous, have engaged in equally fierce debate over the
function of Fortune in *Troilus*. Two schools in particular assert
that Chaucer gives the goddess a clear role in his poem, but they

come to precisely opposite conclusions about what that role is. One group argues that the account in the proem to book IV of hostile Fortune as irresistible destiny is meant seriously; the other argues that it is deeply ironic and that the audience is meant to supply Lady Philosophy's 'correct' answer that Fortune's powers are limited and can be resisted by the human will. The consequences of these contradictory positions, which still divide critics today, are represented by two distinguished Chaucerians of an earlier generation: Walter Clyde Curry, who called *Troilus* a 'deterministic tragedy' in which 'an absolutely inescapable necessity governs the progress of the story' (165, 152), and Howard Rollin Patch, who fixed responsibility for the tragic outcome on the characters themselves – 'Troilus and Criseyde become responsible for their own doom' ('Predestination', 411n38; see also Patch, 'Determinism').[7] Both interpretations have won learned adherents and have real justification in Chaucer's text; but, because each looks at only one aspect of Fortune in *Troilus*, each underestimates the poem's multiplicity.

Curry's position has been held by some of Chaucer's most sensitive readers, who assert that *Troilus and Criseyde* endorses the importance of fate and destiny in human affairs. Kittredge declares that 'Fate dominates in the Troilus' (*Poetry*, 112), Bloomfield stresses the 'crucial importance of the concept of predestination in the poem' ('Distance', 22), and Geoffrey Shepherd articulates the understanding of many others: 'From the beginning of the poem we are conscious that the whole action is under the grip of a larger control' ('*Troilus*', 73). Strong textual support for this view can be found in both the prohemium to Fortune to book IV and throughout *Troilus*. Fortune's malevolence is stressed in the first stanza of the proem: she 'hent and blent' foolish humans and is nothing less than 'traitour comune' (IV.4–5). Her overwhelming power in throwing humans from her wheel is underlined by association with the Furies, who 'compleignen evere in pyne', as well as 'cruel Mars' (IV.22–5) and is later reinforced by the mention of 'fatal destyne' and the Fates themselves at the beginning of book V (1–4).

The narrative of *Troilus* often supports this sense of doom. Although Boethius' *Consolation*, as we have seen, ultimately mocks the power of the goddess Fortune and regards Fate as nothing more than our human inability to perceive the larger designs of Providence, such destinal forces are regularly identified by the characters and by the narrator as determining the main action in *Troilus*. For instance, the prince declares that it is his 'destine' to love (I.520), the planets are said to be favourable to the lovers (II.680–6), and we are told that Fortune wills that Troilus see Criseyde again soon after the consummation (III.1667–70), just as it later prevents the prince and Diomede from killing one another (V.1763–4). Finally, it is 'Fortune, which that permutacioun/Of thynges hath', that is said to bring about the general destruction of Troy, in the course of which 'fate' (twice mentioned) wills the death of Hector (V.1541–52).

Although good evidence exists in the text to believe that Fortune as fate and destiny determines the course of action in *Troilus*, other critics have reason to support Patch's contrary insistence that these forces lack ultimate power and that whatever happens is the personal responsibility of the characters (for example: Bolton, 261; Gordon, 'Processes', 130; Kean, *Making*, 139–41). A recent group of moralistic scholars reads *Troilus* as a direct endorsement of Lady Philosophy's condemnation of Fortune and her assertion of the freedom of the human will. Thus John McCall declares that Chaucer's poem 'is primarily a historical tragedy, one that dramatizes a man's systematic subjection to Fortune and the awesome consequences of that subjection' ('Five-Book', 308); and the leader of this school, D. W. Robertson, Jr, insists that Troilus is a victim not of destiny but of his own sins ('Tragedy'), and elsewhere argues that 'Fortune is, as Boethius explains, no menace to the virtuous, but only to those who subject themselves to it by setting their hearts on a mutable rather than an immutable good', as Troilus has done in loving Criseyde (*Preface*, 473).

The proem to book IV also contains evidence that supports this second, less respectful view of Fortune. The goddess seems less terrifying than comic when, having thrown a person from her wheel, she laughs and 'maketh hym the mowe' (IV.6–7). The proem also raises questions about the extent of Fortune's authority and power (Bishop, 48–9). The first stanza implies that she deceives only those silly enough to allow themselves to be snared ('fooles'), and whereas the fall of Troilus and rise of Diomede are at one moment attributed directly to the agency of Fortune (she 'caste [Troilus] clene out of his lady grace,/And on hire whiel she sette up Diomede', IV.10–11) at another they are seen as a result of a character's choice: 'For how Criseyde Troilus forsook' (IV.15).[8]

Similar human choices are seen to motivate events throughout *Troilus*. Troilus deliberately decides to love Criseyde ('Thus took he purpos loves craft to suwe', I.379), and she debates about the merits of loving him in a long inner soliloquy, as we saw in the previous chapter. Although Troilus gives a long speech asserting the power of predestination in book IV, Charles Owen shrewdly comments that the 'irony of Troilus' coming to a decision through a train of thought that rejects freedom of the will was perhaps no small part of the passage's appeal to Chaucer' ('Significance', 4). Moreover, Troilus' speech is followed by long discussions between Troilus and Pandarus and, especially, Troilus and Criseyde during which they discuss various courses of action to take in response to their coming separation. Criseyde decides that she will be able to trick her father and return to Troy, and Troilus agrees not to abduct her by force. Although both lovers prefer to avoid taking direct responsibility for their actions (Criseyde often blames Pandarus for causing events and Troilus claims to be constrained by such outside forces as fate, love and honour), each is constantly seen making choices about what he or she will do.

Fortune as Literature

The intricate dialectic of these two contrasting concepts of Fortune in *Troilus* (Fortune as the result of destiny and Fortune as the result of choice) is often ignored by Chaucerians, who regularly insist that one view is dominant in the poem and expresses the author's own intention. Yet even acknowledgement of a double attitude towards Fortune in *Troilus*, which is found in some critics (Spearing, *Troilus*, 60–1), does not go far enough. Chaucer once again transcends binary opposition, however intense, and instead offers a variety of approaches to interpretation. As imaginative fiction, *Troilus and Criseyde* has no obligation to provide a coherent didactic answer to the question of Fortune. Although philosophy contributes to the multiplicity of *Troilus and Criseyde*, the experience of the poem cannot be reduced to specific intellectual positions.

In his *Boece* Chaucer faithfully translated the *Consolation*, but in *Troilus* he repeatedly adapts the same material for dramatic rather than philosophical ends. As we have seen, a Boethian hymn celebrating the love that binds the universe (II.m 8) becomes Troilus' praise of sexual fulfilment (III.1744–71), just as some of Lady Philosophy's loftiest words (II.pr 4) are used by Criseyde in her criticism of amorous jealousy (III.813–40). A central example of such dramatic appropriation of the *Consolation* is the longest and to many the most obtrusive Boethian addition in *Troilus*: the prince's speech on destiny in book IV. After the Trojan parliament decides to return Criseyde to her father, Troilus first blames Fortune (IV.260, IV.274, IV.324) and then later, alone in a temple, he utters a long lament on predestination during which he rehearses all the bleak doubts of the character Boethius about free will with none of Lady Philosophy's reassurances (IV.953–1078). Despite the theoretical speculations of 'grete clerkes many oon' (IV.968) about the relationship of fate and free will, and despite the subtle distinctions made between simple and conditional necessity, Troilus knows only that he is trapped and helpless: 'For al that comth, comth by necessitee:/Thus to ben lorn, it is my destinee' (IV.958–9). For him, intellectual argument is no remedy for the real misery of having been thrown from Fortune's wheel.

Troilus' lament has been interpreted by some critics as further proof of the control of destiny in the poem, and by others as deliberately raising questions whose orthodox Christian answers, as given by Lady Philosophy, are meant to be supplied by the reader. As with the tensions in the proem to book IV, both readings of Troilus' speech have some justification, though if his words are taken only as a philosophical statement, whether direct or ironic, we may well understand why so many, including most beginning readers, have regarded the lines as an artistic blemish. In Lanham's uncharitable assessment, the argument of the passage is 'so long, so involved, and so boring' ('Opaque', 175). Whatever its didactic effect, the artistic effect of Troilus' determinist speech is to remind us that the events of the poem unfold in a world of change and decay. *Troilus* is a story told from the point of view of its characters, who, as the prince forcefully declares in the temple, feel subject to the whims of powerful and unknowable forces. Chaucer's narrative repeatedly represents this world to be under the sway of Fortune (as even Lady Philosophy would agree, which is why she urges transcendence), while largely ignoring the over-arching order of divine Providence. Whether or not we accept its despairing conclusion, Troilus' speech effectively expresses the helpless lack of control that is so often the human condition: 'the confusion and ambiguity which necessarily surround all earthly motives and events' (Moorman, 71; cf. Knight, 57). Fortune is thus 'an emblem of the world' (Wimsatt, 'Medieval', 212).

The reader of *Troilus* also exists in the sublunary realm of Fortune. Because the outcome of the love-story is announced at the beginning, some critics have suggested that we achieve the divine perspective described by Boethius: 'the reader knows from the outset that Troy is to fall, Aeneas to escape, the West to be founded' (Howard, *Temptations*, 140; cf. Bloomfield, 'Distance', 22; Mann, 'Chance', 81). Although readers occupy a position of privilege, our point of view is more that of a historian than that of God. As explained in the *Consolation*, God not only sees everything that ever has or will happen simultaneously in an eternal present, but, more important, He also understands how the individual events of fortune fit into a Providential plan. What the reader of *Troilus and Criseyde* perceives is much more limited. Even the facts of the story are not always certain. In the proem to book IV, Chaucer directly states that 'Criseyde Troilus forsook', though even this is immediately softened by 'Or at the leeste, how that she was unkynde' (IV.15–16), and a few lines later it is suggested that the traditional story of her faithlessness might possibly be false: 'And if they on hire lye,/Iwis, hemself sholde han the vilanye' (IV.20–1). Such statements remind us how un-Godlike our knowledge really is. Although the general shape of the plot is clear to us from the beginning, we remain ignorant about motives and about the final destiny of both Troilus and Criseyde. Where does Mercury assign him to dwell? Is she true to Diomede?

The reader of *Troilus* is restricted to a human perspective. Even if some believe that a Providential plan exists in the heavens, the poem nevertheless forces all to experience the distance from God felt by Troilus and many fourteenth-century nominalist theologians. The narrative keeps us located in this life amidst the vagaries of Fortune and the poignancy of completed, if imperfectly understood, history. Unlike God, there is little we can do except to look on and weep. In the proem to book IV, the poet's response to Troilus' fall from Fortune's wheel is neither despair nor superior moral scorn but human sympathy:

> For which myn herte right now gynneth blede,
> And now my penne, allas, with which I write,
> Quaketh for drede of that I moste endite.
>
> (IV.12–14)

Fortune in *Troilus* often represents the basic condition of human life on this earth – an unredeemed natural world of ceaseless motion with no Lady Philosophy in sight. In Chaucer's short ballad 'Fortune,' the goddess defends herself:

> Why sholdestow my realtee oppresse?
> The see may ebbe and flowen more or lesse;
> The welkne hath might to shyne, reyne, or hayle;
> Right so mot I kythen my brotelnesse.
> In general, this reule may nat fayle.
>
> (60–4)

As the nature imagery of the ballad suggests, Fortune is Troilus' foe only in the sense that he must suffer the consequences of her inevitable 'brotelnesse'. In contrast to the transcendence of earthly things advocated by Boethius (and by his modern followers), Troilus and Criseyde are entirely caught up in the joys and bound by the constraints of this world. The lovers exist in time and space, which permit them the deep pleasures of a fully realized physical love. During their consummation, Troilus and Criseyde are said to embrace one another 'as aboute a tree, with many a twiste,/Bytrent and writh the swote wodebynde' (III.1230–1). But, of course, such attractive natural imagery, similar to that in the ballad, carries within itself the assurance of change and decay.

After Troilus hears that Criseyde will be sent over to the Greeks, he is compared to a very different tree in a passage modelled on one in the *Inferno* but made even bleaker by Chaucer:

> And as in wynter leves ben biraft,
> Ech after other, til the tree be bare,
> So that ther nys but bark and braunche ilaft,
> Lith Troilus, byraft of ech welfare,
> I bounden in the blake bark of care.
>
> (IV.225–9)

In contrast to the perpetual cycles of Fortune's wheel or of Nature, the love of Troilus and Criseyde, like human life itself, must eventually come to an end. Fortune in *Troilus* is temporal existence in all its flux and chaos. Both good and bad, it randomly brings both happiness and sorrow. It is never fair or reliable.

In addition to establishing a firm earthly perspective for the poem in contrast to the divine perspective continually urged in the *Consolation*, Fortune serves other literary functions. The concept is sometimes used playfully and sometimes reminds us of the nature of narrative. As an example of the former, the fullest and most direct expression of Boethius' conception of Fortune occurs within a context that forces us to question its seriousness. After her dinner with Pandarus in book III, Criseyde appears about to frustrate his secret plan to bring her together with Troilus as she starts to return home: 'She took hire leve, and nedes wolde wende' (III.616). Suddenly, the narrator speaks in his most rhetorically elevated mode:

> But O Fortune, executrice of wierdes,
> O influences of thise hevenes hye!
> Soth is, that under God ye ben oure hierdes,
> Though to us bestes ben the causez wrie.
> This mene I now: for she gan homward hye,
> But execut was al bisyde hire leve
> The goddes wil, for which she moste bleve.
> (III.617–23)

These lines are the most orthodox Christian statement about Fortune in the entire *Troilus*. They echo one of Boethius' central conceptions, which is repeated by Dante in *Inferno* 7.78–80. Fortune rightly understood, as Lady Philosophy and Dante's Virgil carefully explain, is no blind goddess of chance, but the earthly agent of Providence ('executrice of wierdes'), as ordained by the Deity ('under God'), even though we mortals remain ignorant of the divine plan: 'to us bestes ben the causez wrie'.

Although this passage is sometimes cited to prove that Chaucer fully endorses Boethius' views of Fortune, the comic context ought to prevent any such simple interpretation. The grandiloquent 'influences of thise hevenes hye' actually manifest themselves in nothing more celestial than the 'smoky reyn' (III.628) that prevents Criseyde, not altogether unwillingly, from returning home, just as the 'goddes wil' seems to refer only to the sexual union of the lovers. The powerful stanza makes its contribution to the multiplicity of Fortune in *Troilus and Criseyde* and might have reminded some contemporary readers of the goddess's place in the Christian scheme of things, but its effect goes beyond direct philosophical statement. Indeed, the tension in this passage between exalted rhetoric and amorous event is more reminiscent of *The Rape of the Lock* (or 'The Nun's Priest's Tale') than the *Consolation of Philosophy*.

Furthermore, for all their apparent differences, the two critical interpretations of Fortune in *Troilus* discussed above are more similar, and therefore more limited, than they might first appear. Whether the goddess is seen as an overwhelming destinal force or as capable of being resistible by the human will, both schools regard her as purely negative. From a philosophical standpoint such a conclusion may be inevitable, but for those primarily interested in the pleasures of poetry Fortune is not necessarily a bad thing. As Boethius, Dante and Chaucer repeatedly emphasize, the essence of Fortune is change: at the end of *Troilus* she is identified as 'Fortune, which that permutacioun/Of thynges hath' (V.1541–2), just as Pandarus had previously noted that 'if hire whiel stynte any thyng to torne,/Than cessed she Fortune anon to be' (I.848–9). Such ceaseless change is devastating, even fatal, for those realms and individuals who are its victims, but the result is quite different for those of us who instead read about such events. The constant change effected by Fortune produces the delight and excitement of narrative. If humans never ascended on the Wheel of Fortune or never descended, but always remained in the same condition, there would be no stories. From a moralistic perspective, it may be a sin that Troilus commits himself to the mutable world of Fortune by loving Criseyde, as some assert, but which reader is not in fact glad that he did so? Had he not, Chaucer would have had nothing to write about and we would have nothing to read. The Wheel of Fortune may be horrifying for those it spins about, but its giddy motions are the engines of story-telling. Chaucer's interests as a producer of poetry (and ours as consumers) are different from those of a philosopher.

The Changing Faces of Fortune

Change is the essence of Fortune, and it is therefore appropriate that her role develops in the course of *Troilus and Criseyde*. As the poem unfolds, the goddess becomes more powerful and more malignant. In the first three books, the reader is allowed to believe that she is generally unthreatening to human beings and capable of being managed. Once, as we have seen, she even appears as the agent of Providence, albeit in the comic context of a rainstorm. The scattered suggestions in this section that Fortune may have darker, more ominous consequences are discounted (usually by Pandarus) or remain submerged, leaving only a shadow of unease that will not be fully exploited until the last two books. Although mentioned more often and in greater detail by Chaucer than by Boccaccio, Fortune in the early part of the English narrative, as throughout the Italian, is virtually synonymous with such familiar concepts as chance and luck.

Fortune is first mentioned in *Troilus* when we are told that some days on the battlefield the Greeks had the upper hand and some days the Trojans:

> and thus Fortune on lofte
> And under eft gan hem to whielen bothe
> Aftir hir course, ay whil that thei were wrothe.
> (I.138–40)

Despite the personification of the goddess and the explicit reference to her wheel, both of which are added by Chaucer, 'Fortune' is little more than a metaphor here for the varying accidents of war, which appear to have achieved an equilibrium.

The second mention of Fortune in the poem (I.837–54), which is part of a long original addition to the dialogue between Troilus and Pandarus on love, is potentially more worrying. Troilus melodramatically tells his friend that 'Fortune is my fo' and claims that no man can withstand her 'cruel whiel' because, as she wills, 'she pleyeth with free and bonde' (I.837–40). This is an unsettling view of hostile destiny, which Troilus will come to again in his later speech on predestination, but for now Pandarus successfully discounts it. With his common-sense humanism, he sees nothing vindictive about Fortune.

In language modelled on the *Consolation*, Pandarus notes that the goddess is 'commune' to everyone and that if her wheel stopped she would cease to be herself. The sanguine conclusion he draws from this is that, because Fortune is forever changing, Troilus' sorrow must eventually pass, and her 'mutabilite' may even now be on the verge of giving the prince 'cause for to synge' (I.841–54). Taking a practical optimistic view of things, Pandarus sees the revolutions of Fortune's wheel not as a threat but as an opportunity. He therefore urges Troilus to reveal the name of his beloved so that they can plan how to take advantage of circumstances. When his friend blushes, Pandarus replies: 'Here bygynneth game' (I.868). Instead of Fortune cruelly 'playing' with human beings, as Troilus feared, she has been redefined as merely part of a pleasant amorous 'game'.

Fortune appears in this relatively innocent guise, susceptible to some human control, during most of the rest of the first three books of *Troilus*. In a passage modelled on *Filostrato*, Pandarus urges Criseyde to take advantage of the good luck of Troilus' love, assuring her that failure to seize the opportunity will not be the fault of 'cas ne fortune', but of her own 'slouthe and wrecchednesse' (II.285–6). Shortly thereafter, Pandarus uses 'fortune' in a fatal context, but the word itself is innocent enough. He tells his niece that, if she rejects Troilus, the prince will seek death (presumably in battle), 'if his fortune assente' (II.335). In two later references with no source in *Filostrato*, the narrator casually mentions Fortune to explain what happens in the story without any sense of an inevitable or hostile fate. Soon after the consummation, 'for that Fortune it wolde' (III.1667), Troilus learns that he will be with Criseyde again, and a few lines later we are told that the lovers now meet often: 'And thus Fortune a tyme ledde in joie/Criseyde and ek this kynges sone of Troie' (III.1714–15). Despite the potential ominousness of 'a tyme' here, Fortune remains a vague and generally benign force in the first three books of *Troilus*. At worst, she stands for the ordinary vicissitudes of the world; at best, she seems to offer some hope for the lovers. Most often she is just a literary personification for the way things occur in time.

Fortune becomes a much more frightening figure in the last two books of *Troilus*. Instead of a metaphor for the inevitable ups and downs of life (or an agent of Christian Providence), the goddess now represents the inexorable doom of fate – a threatening power indifferent to justice or human suffering. Her destructive potential, only hinted at in earlier appearances, is now dominant, for she offers no opportunity except death and ruin. Fortune comes to represent those superhuman forces that overwhelm the city of Troy and crush the private world of the lovers. If she is the way of the world, it is a frightening and hopeless world in which humans can do little to affect their fatal destiny and in which hopeful dreams are replaced by nightmares.

The treachery of Fortune announced in the prohemium to book IV immediately manifests itself on the battlefield. The encircling war is virtually ignored during the amorous delights of book III, but it suddenly reappears. In contrast to the balance of success and failure granted by Fortune to each army at the beginning of the poem (I.134–40), things now go badly for Troy and, for the first time, we are told that the defenders have lost a battle (IV.47–9). In the opening three books the war had seemed no immediate threat; instead, it provided an opportunity for Hector and Troilus to display their prowess and a subject for Pandarus to joke about when visiting both Troilus (I.548) and Criseyde, despite her genuine fear (II.127–8). Now, however, the triumphant Greeks have seized one of the chief warriors of the city: 'So that, for harm, that day the folk of Troie/Dredden to lese a gret part of hire joie' (IV.55–6). It is indeed the beginning of the end, as the rhyme suggests, for Antenor will be the agent through whom both Troy and Troilus lose their joy absolutely.

Not only does the full malignant potential of Fortune, previously discounted, begin to reveal itself, but the flux previously associated with the goddess in the text also hardens into an unavoidable fate. At the moment of Troy's military defeat, the traitor Calchas reappears and speaks directly to us for the first time. He insists on Troy's bloody destiny ('ybrend and beten down to grownde', IV.77) and unintentionally (for even sages are not in control of this world) dooms the lovers by requesting the return of his daughter. Although Criseyde later suggests that the gods might have spoken to her father 'in amphibologies' (IV.1406), there is no doubting the authority of his prophecy for the city:

'On peril of my lif, I shal nat lye;
Appollo hath me told it feithfully;
I have ek founde it be astronomye,
By sort, and by augurye ek, trewely,
And dar wel say, the tyme is faste by
That fire and flaumbe on al the town shal sprede,
And thus shal Troie torne to asshen dede. . . .'
(IV.113–19)

Henceforth, the doom of Troy is a constant theme. In the last
book, Troilus dreams that 'he was amonges alle/His enemys, and
in hire hondes falle' (V.251–2), and Diomede frightens Criseyde
with the totality of the revenge that the Greeks will take on their
defeated foe: 'Ther shal nat oon to mercy gon on-lyve,/Al were he
lord of worldes twës fyve!' (V.888–9). In a passage that is original
with Chaucer, Calchas reveals that even mythological powers are
arrayed against the city: because Phoebus and Neptune were not
paid by Priam's father for building the walls of Troy they are
'so wrothe/That they wol brynge it to confusioun' (IV.122–3).

The fall of Troy from Fortune's wheel fractures the human
affection that had distinguished the private life of the city. Rather
than protecting Criseyde, Troy now trades her as though she
were a prisoner. In contrast to the first half of the poem, the
last two books show us nothing of the pleasures of Trojan family
life. Calchas's belated assertion of his paternal rights brings only
misery, and Helen's sympathy for Troilus at the end of book II is
replaced by Cassandra's heartless truth-telling about Criseyde in
book V. In an uncharacteristic reduction of his source, Chaucer
eliminates a scene between Troilus and his siblings in which they
show their concern for his sorrow. Even Sarpedon's courtly party,
full of wine, women and song (V.400–504), can offer no comfort
to Troilus, for the focus of the action is now elsewhere, especially
in arenas such as parliament and the battlefield where Fortune is
dominant. The lovers simply cannot operate effectively in this
public world. Despite his passionate laments back in his room,
Troilus is mute during the parliamentary debate about returning
Criseyde. At the exchange itself, Criseyde is much more passive
than her Boccaccian original (compare V.57–60 with 5.6–9 in
Filostrato), and Troilus, despite his anger and self-reproach, is
helpless to do anything but appear the decorative knight: with
'hauk on honde' and 'an huge route', he rides out towards the

Greek tents with Criseyde and then must ride back without her
(V.64–70).

The human actors become increasingly incapable of dealing
with the blows of Fortune. After he learns that Criseyde will
be exchanged, Troilus restates his earlier view, which had been
dismissed by Pandarus, that Fortune is his foe:

> 'Fortune, allas the while!
> What have I don? What have I thus agylt?
> How myghtestow for rowthe me bygile?
> Is ther no grace, and shal I thus be spilt?
> Shal thus Creiseyde awey, for that thow wilt?
> Allas, how maistow in thyn herte fynde
> To ben to me thus cruwel and unkynde?
>
> 'Have I the nought honoured al my lyve,
> As thow wel woost, above the goddes alle?
> Whi wiltow me fro joie thus deprive?'
>
> (IV.260–9)

Troilus' words suggest that even now he retains some of Pandarus'
optimism, for he addresses Fortune as if she were a rational being
capable of feelings and of being persuaded. Wondering if his sins
('agylt') may be at fault, he seems to expect 'rowthe' and 'grace', as
though the goddess were a Christian figure or even human. After
appealing for mercy, he then looks for justice. How could she be so
'cruwel and unkynde' when he has always honoured her above all
other gods? Of course, such logical arguments are futile. Fortune
is neither friend nor foe. Although her active hostility to mortals
is suggested in passing by two original lines in *Troilus* (V.468 and
V.1134), the real terror of the forces she represents is their absolute
indifference to human concerns. Despite frequent personifications
of Fortune, *Troilus* never shows her to have anything like the
consciousness or heart that Troilus here attributes to her. Fortune
is not really a goddess at all; instead she represents those social,
natural and historical forces that indifferently doom the best plans
and hopes of human beings and produce the despair of Troilus'
speech on predestination.

Because change is the essence of Chaucer's conception of Fortune, and given the multiplicity of her representations in *Troilus*,
it is not surprising that near the end of the poem we are again
offered a potentially positive view of the goddess. In an addition to

Filostrato, the narrator again echoes Boethius (and Dante's *Inferno*, 7) in describing her as a Providential agent:

> Fortune, which that permutacioun
> Of thynges hath, as it is hire comitted
> Thorugh purveyaunce and disposicioun
> Of heighe Jove, as regnes shal be flitted
> Fro folk in folk, or when they shal be smytted,
> Gan pulle awey the fetheres brighte of Troie
> Fro day to day, til they ben bare of joie.
>
> (V.1541–7)

The passage is hardly an unambiguous affirmation of celestial transcendence, however, for the mention of 'heighe Jove' suggests a pagan context, and the next stanza firmly re-establishes the limited human perspective that we have noted throughout the poem. For Hector, whose end 'gan aprochen wonder blyve', as for the other citizens of Troy, Fortune manifests herself not as Providence but as remorseless Fate, 'Ayeyns which fate hym helpeth nat to stryve' (V.1548–54). Once again the only response to the blows of Fortune offered by the narrator is the reader's human sympathy:

> For which me thynketh every manere wight
> That haunteth armes oughte to biwaille
> The deth of hym that was so noble a knyght.
>
> (V.1555–7)

Until the very end of *Troilus*, its characters increasingly seem to be victims of superhuman but sublunary powers beyond their control (see Stevens, 'Winds', 285). In book V, the prince, like the Duke of Dorset in Beerbohm's *Zuleika Dobson*, realizes that he will soon die because he has heard the shriek of 'The owle ek, which that hette Escaphilo' (V.319). Dreams are a prime example of the extrarational manifestations of Fortune that more and more seem to determine the course of the action in the poem. Pandarus, of course, scorns their importance: 'A straw for alle swevenes significaunce!' (V.362). He is a practical humanist, who, in lines much expanded from Boccaccio, believes in the dignity of mankind: 'Allas, allas, so noble a creature/As is a man shal dreden swich ordure!' (V.384–5). But there are forces at work in the world of *Troilus* not dreamt of in Pandarus' rational philosophy, forces which reduce even this most active and inventive character at last to helpless silence.

Along with war, nature and Fortune herself, dreams in *Troilus and Criseyde* become more threatening as the story comes to an end. Criseyde's early vision of love, in which violence is sublimated in the image of an eagle painlessly exchanging hearts with her (II.925–32), is replaced at the conclusion of the poem by Troilus' much uglier, more directly sexual dream of a quite different animal: the boar with great tusks beside whom 'faste in his armes folde,/Lay kyssyng ay, his lady bryght, Criseyde' (V.1240–1). In *Filostrato*, Troilus himself interprets his vision, but Chaucer gives this role to Cassandra, whom he calls 'Sibille' (V.1450). Like Calchas, who also has access to divine knowledge, Cassandra's message is about the doom of Fortune. She says that if her brother wishes to know the truth of his dream he must 'a fewe of olde stories heere,/To purpos how that Fortune overthrowe/Hath lordes olde' (V.1459–61).

In her account of those overthrown by Fortune, Cassandra tells the mythological history of Thebes, stressing the death and destruction it contains. The story of the siege and fall of Thebes, which Criseyde and her women were reading for pleasure in book II, now reappears (complete with mention of Amphiorax's fall into the underworld – compare II.105 with V.1499), reinforced with a summary of the narrative in Latin verse that appears in almost all manuscripts. At the prompting of Pandarus, Criseyde had put away her Theban book, but the episode returns with a vengeance. History once again impinges on the private world of the lovers. Not only will Troy's fate soon equal that of Thebes, but also Criseyde has been wooed and conquered by Diomede, the son of one of the Theban warriors whose story had previously entertained her. The vicissitudes of Fortune at the end of *Troilus* are not merely inconvenient or confined to a book, but have become real and fatal. Cassandra shows how Fortune brings about the tragedy of the lovers.

Fortune as Tragedy

As we have seen, the multiplicity of *Troilus and Criseyde* also extends to genre. The poem has been plausibly labelled by critics as romance, Christian comedy, epic, drama and novel, and it certainly contains elements of lyric, philosophy and farce. The genre that is identified at the end of the text itself, however, is tragedy:

> Go, litel bok, go, litel myn tragedye,
> Ther God thi makere yet, er that he dye,
> So sende mygh to make in som comedye!
> But litel book, no makyng thow n'envie,
> But subgit be to alle poesye;
> And kis the steppes where as thow seest pace
> Virgile, Ovide, Omer, Lucan, and Stace.
>
> (V.1786–92)

What exactly is meant by this modest description of the poem ('*litel* bok . . . *litel* myn tragedye') and somewhat regretful mood (the speaker seems to wish he had written a comedy) is, however, unclear. Although modern critics generally agree that *Troilus* is a tragedy, there is little agreement about what kind (Clough, 226n26). The most common form in the late Middle Ages was *de casibus* tragedy, involving the calamitous and often unmotivated fall of great men from Fortune's wheel, as in Boccaccio's famous *De Casibus Virorum Illustrium* and such English imitations as Lydgate's *Fall of Princes* and *The Mirror for Magistrates*. Chaucer's knowledge of this sort of tragedy is evident from a gloss in *Boece* ('Tragedye is to seyn a dite of a prosperite for a tyme, that endeth in wrecchidnesse', II.pr 2.70–2) and from the statement of the Monk in the *Canterbury Tales*:

> I wol biwaille in manere of tragedie
> The harm of hem that stoode in heigh degree,
> And fillen so that ther nas no remedie
> To brynge hem out of hir adversitee.
> For certein, whan that Fortune list to flee,
> Ther may no man the cours of hire withholde.
>
> (VII.1991–6)

The plot outlined in the first stanza of *Troilus* suggests *de casibus* tragedy ('Fro wo to wele, and after out of joie', I.4), as does Cassandra's mention of a 'fewe of olde stories' about lords overthrown by Fortune (V.1459–61). Nevertheless, Monica McAlpine and John Norton-Smith are undoubtedly

correct that Chaucer moved beyond any such mechanistic tragedy into something more complex and profound.[9] Other critics, especially D. W. Robertson, see *Troilus* as a Christian
tragedy of sin, believing that the lovers are wholly responsible for their own fate (Robertson, 'Tragedy'; Morgan, 'Freedom'; Wood, *Elements*). As we have seen, the characters do
exercise their free will in the course of the narrative; but,
being limited mortals, they are also victims of larger forces
beyond their control. Moreover, as noted by Joseph Gallagher,
'no reference to sin ever accompanies the repeated references
to Fortune' (60). Andrea Clough has identified several distinct categories of tragedy in the fourteenth century, including Ovidian tales of deserted women, and she suggests that
Chaucer created a new, hybrid form, which she calls 'romance
tragedy' (213).

As the list of classical poets that Chaucer urges his little tragic
book to honour implies, the medieval understanding of tragedy is wider than many ancient and modern conceptions. Paul
Strohm quotes a representative definition from the thirteenth-
century *Catholicon* of Johannes Januensis, which 'distinguishes
between tragedy and comedy on the basis of the persons they treat,
the levels of their styles, and the upward or downward movements
of their plots' (356). According to Johannes, comedy deals with
the acts of private individuals, tragedy with those of kings and
other great men; comedy is written in a humble style, tragedy
in a high style; comedy begins in sadness but ends in happiness,
tragedy reverses the direction. This definition begins to explain
why both Virgil and Ovid were regarded as tragic poets in the
Middle Ages (Robertson, *Preface*, 473). Although *Troilus and
Criseyde* seems quite different from the Greek or Shakespearian
plays that shape modern ideas of tragedy (though we should note
a slight resemblance to *Romeo and Juliet*), it fits Johannes' three
criteria quite well, not only because of the woeful course of its
action, but also because of the dignity of its style (despite comic
elements) and nobility of its persons. Genuine tragedy can only
exist within the limits of this world, which is one of the reasons
why Dante called his transcendent poem of divine justice and love
a comedy.

Fortune brings about the dual tragedies of the lovers in *Troilus*,
which are as different as was their falling in love. Troilus defines
himself as a conventional tragic figure during his lament to Fortune

in book IV. His declaration, 'O Troilus, what may men now the
calle/But wrecche of wrecches, out of honour falle/Into miserie?'
(IV.270–2), recalls the *de casibus* formula of a fall from prosperity
and is especially close to the Monk's definition. More unusual and
profound is Troilus' identification with Oedipus, the supreme
classical exemplar of tragedy. Troilus' first allusion is indirect,
an account of himself as 'I, combre-world, that may of nothyng
serve,/But evere dye and nevere fulli sterve' (IV.279–80), which
may echo Statius' description of Oedipus' living death in *Thebaïd*
(especially, 1.46–8 and 11.698). The comparison becomes explicit
a few lines later:

> 'What shal I don? I shal, while I may dure
> On lyve in torment and in cruwel peyne
> This infortune or this disaventure,
> Allone as I was born, iwys, compleyne;
> Ne nevere wol I seen it shyne or reyne,
> But ende I wol, as Edippe, in derknesse
> My sorwful lif, and dyen in distresse. . . .'
>
> (IV.295–301)

Although Chaucer could not, of course, have known Sophocles
directly, his hero does suffer something of the heroic agony of the
Theban king.

The action of book IV is in many ways a replay of book
I, but Troilus has grown. In the face of the utter loss of
Criseyde and of real, not metaphorical, death for himself and
his city, his loyalty in love takes on a new kind of nobility.
No longer merely a lovesick boy consumed with self-pity,
Troilus endures to the end the torment that Fortune gives
him. His adventure has become a 'disaventure'. If the sudden
snatching-away of Criseyde suggests the unexpected calamities
of *de casibus* tragedy, his capacity to endure pain recalls the
protagonists of Greek and Shakespearian drama. Although he
cannot rescue Criseyde or himself, his response to misfortune
turns pathos into tragedy.

The growing heroism of Troilus stands in contrast to the decid-
edly non-tragic Pandarus. When he finally reaches the prince's
bedroom after the parliament, Pandarus responds to the imminent
loss of Criseyde by criticizing Fortune in words that at first seem
to echo Troilus'. He, too, is unable to believe what has happened:

'Who wolde have wend that in so litel a throwe/Fortune oure joie wold han overthrowe?' (IV.384–5). He further sounds like Troilus in criticizing the goddess: 'Swich is this world! Forthi I thus diffyne:/Ne trust no wight to fynden in Fortune/Ay propretee; hire yiftes ben comune' (IV.390–2). But there are important differences between the two men. Pandarus had already in book I told Troilus that Fortune's gifts were 'comune', and here as there he is not especially dismayed by the realization that 'swich is this world'. Pandarus takes the world as he finds it and tries to make the best of it. Troilus' extreme grief makes no sense to Pandarus, for, after all, the prince has had more than his fair share of good fortune: 'Whi listow in this wise,/Syn thi desir al holly hastow had,/So that, by right, it oughte ynough suffice?' (IV.394–6). Pandarus' view of Fortune is, as always, pragmatic rather than tragic. Although supposedly offered only 'for the nones' (IV.428), his advice to Troilus is to accept the changeableness of Fortune and find another woman: 'If she be lost, we shal recovere an other' (IV.406). When Troilus utterly rejects this, Pandarus then advises direct action: the prince should be a man and defy the town by stealing Criseyde away – 'Go ravysshe here!' (IV.530).

Pandarus' approach to the turning of Fortune's wheel is that of a practical rationalist; he deals as well as he can with things as they are. Despite the gathering doom, he remains optimistic about the manageability of Fortune: 'Thenk ek Fortune . . ./Helpeth hardy man unto his enprise' (IV.600-1). We can imagine that he would have advised Oedipus to separate quietly from Jocasta and pay off the messenger. Had Troilus listened to Pandarus, there would be no tragedy, only the accommodations that characterize most human relations. Troilus would have found another woman to enjoy (at least until the fall of Troy), or he would have taken Criseyde away by force as Paris did Helen. Pandarus' ways are the ways of the world, but Troilus' refusal so to act shows the distance he has come. No longer simply following his friend's advice, Troilus' devotion to Criseyde's love has made him the kind of tragic hero that Pandarus could never be.

The last *canticus* that Troilus sings in *Troilus* is a single stanza that replaces a long song adapted from Cino da Pistola in *Filostrato*:

> 'O sterre, of which I lost have al the light,
> With herte soor wel oughte I to biwaille

That evere derk in torment, nyght by nyght,
Toward my deth with wynd in steere I saille;
For which the tenthe nyght, if that I faille
The gydyng of thi bemes bright an houre,
My ship and me Caribdis wol devoure."
                                    (V.638–44)

Even though his guiding star no longer gives light and he suspects the promised reunion on the tenth day will not occur, Troilus continues on his tragic journey. He seems to know that he has sailed too far, into darkness and death, so that his quest, like Ulysses' mad flight in Dante's *Inferno* 26, will end by his being devoured by a whirlpool. Such behaviour is not sensible, and certainly not Christian, but there is a heroism in it. Prevented from the romantic tragedy of lovers such as Romeo and Pyramus when Criseyde regains consciousness in book IV, Troilus goes on to a deeper tragedy of suffering. As Bradley notes in discussing Hegel: 'the noble endurance of pain that rends the heart is the source of much that is best worth having in tragedy' (82).

In the last book of *Troilus*, the prince bears the full weight of Fortune's blows. Unlike Boccaccio's Troiolo, he does not propose going to Sarpedon's for courtly diversion (Pandarus does) nor does he any longer attempt suicide (though he expects to find death in battle). Troilus accepts his tragic situation and allows the wheel of Fortune to become a wheel of fire. His suffering should be recognized for what it is: he neither abandons his adventure of love when it becomes excruciating nor does he transcend it. In his last direct speech, Troilus laments his beloved's unfaithfulness and says that his birth was cursed; but, even though he assumes that Criseyde has forgotten him, he remains committed to her: 'I ne kan nor may,/For all this world, withinne myn herte fyne/To unloved yow a quarter of a day!' (V.1696–8). The tragedy of Troilus is a tragedy of faithfulness. He refuses to imitate the changeableness of Fortune even though she holds sway in the world as he knows it.

Criseyde also suffers a tragic descent on Fortune's wheel, although her fate is more pathetic (and more universal) than Troilus'.[10] When Criseyde learns that she will be traded to the Greeks, her first response is dread and fear. Like Troilus, she imagines that existence can now be only a living death, and the sincerity of her love is suggested by her thinking as much about his suffering as about her own:

> 'How shal he don, and ich also?
> How sholde I lyve if that I from hym twynne?
> O deere herte eke, that I love so,
> Who shal that sorwe slen that ye ben inne?'
>   (IV.757–60)

But Criseyde is also her uncle's niece, and is soon planning to counter this stroke of Fortune with a number of schemes that will allow her to return to Troy. Only later, trapped in the Greek camp and about to succumb to Diomede, with her pleasure and joy 'torned into galle' (V.732), does she realize that she has made the wrong decision:

> 'To late is now to speke of that matere.
> Prudence, allas, oon of thyne eyen thre
> Me lakked alwey, er that I come here!
> On tyme ypassed wel remembred me,
> And present tyme ek koud ich wel ise,
> But future tyme, er I was in the snare,
> Koude I nat sen; that causeth now my care.'
>   (V.743–49)

Burnley sees an implied moral criticism of Criseyde here, though one that is not necessarily Christian, because she has chosen such a foolish course when 'a more penetrating review of her circumstances would have rejected this affair in pursuit of more lasting secular happiness' (*Language*, 61). The lines may indeed yield this bracing lesson for some readers, but they also define the poignancy of Criseyde's tragedy, which each of us shares to some extent. How can we feel superior to Criseyde unless we have the ability to see the future? And which of us knows how to achieve lasting secular happiness? In her bafflement and undoubted weakness (for she does betray Troilus), Criseyde lacks Troilus' heroism, but her tragedy is therefore more universal. It is nothing less than the tragedy of the human condition. Like her, none of us can see far enough.

The inescapable ignorance of human beings in this world is a major theme throughout *Troilus and Criseyde*. In his first significant addition to Boccaccio, Chaucer develops a brief allusion into a major discussion of the inability of even the wisest and proudest to anticipate what their future will bring, especially in matters of love: 'O blynde world, O blynde entencioun!' (I.211). Such blindness is not confined to lovers alone, however. In another addition at a comparable position in book IV, Chaucer makes explicit the unwitting folly of the Trojan parliament in exchanging Criseyde for Antenor:

> O Juvenal, lord, trewe is thy sentence,
> That litel wyten folk what is to yerne,
> That they ne fynde in hire desir offence;
> For cloude of errour let hem to discerne
> What best is. And lo, here ensample as yerne:
> This folk desiren now, deliveraunce
> Of Antenor, that brought hem to meschaunce,
>
> For he was after traitour to the town
> Of Troye. Allas, they quytte hym out to rathe!
> O nyce world, lo, thy discrecioun!
>
> (IV.197–206)

In using Criseyde to ransom Antenor the Trojans are hardly guilty of mortal sin (despite their arrogant indifference to Criseyde's desire) or even lack of consideration; they make what they think is a shrewd political decision to trade a mere woman for one of their chief warriors. What they do not know, what perhaps even Antenor himself does not yet know, is that their well-considered scheme will hasten their destruction. Instead of defending Troy, Antenor will be one of its betrayers. The world we live in is inevitably 'blynde' and 'nyce', subject to the whims of Fortune, regardless of our best efforts to be wise and discreet, for mortals inevitably live in a 'cloude of errour'. Although she is the most poignant example, Criseyde is not the only one whose prudence does not extend far enough. Everyone has trouble with the future in the poem, including the Greeks, who know they will conquer Troy but seem unaware of the trials in store for them on their return home.

Critics sometimes hold the characters in *Troilus* to an impossibly high standard of responsibility. One, for instance, says that readers come to see 'that providence gives even to pagans the freedom to choose their destiny: Troy will fall, but its people make it deserving of its fate; the Trojan parliament ratifies the plan to exchange the prisoners' (Economou, 41; cf. Patch, *Goddess*, 31; Gordon, 'Processes', 130). Chaucer's characters make choices all the time in the poem, but how free and meaningful can such choices be when they are based on faulty premises and their consequences remain unknown? Rather than the moral superiority that the story provokes in some, Dieter Mehl urges on us 'a kind of superior compassion', which the narrator often expresses, as we 'watch the pathetic ignorance of the actors and their vain efforts to look for alternative courses' (*Introduction*, 94).

The problem with human free will in *Troilus* is demonstrated by its strongest advocate – Pandarus. He refuses to recognize the power of necessity and instead argues that humans have the ability to shape their own destiny. As we have seen, he tells both Troilus (I.841–65) and Criseyde (II.281–7) to take advantage of Fortune, for he is certain that the goddess helps those who help themselves (IV.600-1). Pandarus is a practical man of action rather than a philosopher, but he resembles Boethius in asserting the freedom of the human will and in scorning the power of destinal influences such as dreams and fate. But Pandarus is finally too optimistic. Fortune increasingly has her way in the natural world of Troy, until Pandarus has been made irrelevant and finally admits he can neither say nor do anything more.[11] Criseyde takes over Pandarus' role in book IV when she treats the proposed separation as a practical problem that her ingenuity can solve with 'an heep of weyes' (IV.1281). As soon becomes apparent, however, Criseyde's ability to control her fate is even less successful than Pandarus'. Although she proclaims to Troilus that reason and patience can make one 'lord' of Fortune (IV.1587), in the Greek camp she learns that she is a helpless victim of forces beyond her control.

The tragic vision of *Troilus and Criseyde* demonstrates the limitations of human effort and reason. Many critics are like Pandarus, however, and believe that there is something that could have been done: 'Troilus is a noble young man who comes to disaster because of a limited vision which leads him to place his faith in earthly love and beauty, and to see it as an end in itself rather than as a reflection or an image of a spiritual beauty and love that is immutable' (Toole, 25). Such interpretations, which are common, have a certain plausibility, and undoubtedly have always given comfort to some readers, but they do not answer the narrative situation. Troilus could hardly have escaped disaster even if he had done precisely what these critics want. Earthly love and beauty are the best that are available to him in a world in which limited vision is inescapable.

Chaucer chose to tell a tale about pagans, and the fatal result is inevitable: secular life offers no happy endings, only death. George Steiner makes a pertinent distinction between the biblical and classical view of earthly disaster: 'the fall of Jericho or Jerusalem is merely just, whereas the fall of Troy is the first great metaphor of tragedy' (5). Jewish thought interprets events as the clear working-out of providential justice, whereas pagan thought explores the vulnerability and ignorance of human life: 'The Judaic vision sees in disaster a specific moral fault or failure of understanding. The Greek tragic poets assert that the forces which shape or destroy our lives lie outside the governance of reason or justice' (6–7). Concrete moral lessons, following the Judaic vision, were often drawn from the ruin of Troy and its lovers in the Middle Ages (about pride and lust, for example), which have been echoed by some modern Chaucerians. The reader may indeed learn such things from *Troilus* if he or she chooses, as we shall see in the next chapter, but this has nothing to do with the Trojan characters' inability to save themselves in this world, which is where the story remains until the last few stanzas.

Troilus is not primarily a work of philosophical instruction. Although it does make a profound Boethian point about the unsatisfactoriness of the sublunary realm of Fortune, it largely ignores the *Consolation*'s insistence on our ability to transcend this world. The poem remains on earth and expresses the tears of things. Like Malory's Fellowship of the Round Table, the love of Troilus and Criseyde is glorious but contains the seeds of its own destruction. *Troilus* explores the frustration of human hopes and plans, even when they seem most noble or reasonable, and the inevitable tragedy of the unredeemed world.

Notes

1 The few exceptional places in *Filostrato* when *fortuna* is clearly personified, she nevertheless remains a relatively vague figure (see 3.94 and 4.30–2); most of the references to this concept are brief and undeveloped – for example, 2.44, 2.51, 2.77, 2.132, 3.45, 3.64, 4.45, 4.56, 4.73, 4.104, 4.113, 4.121, 4.154, 4.166, 5.6, 5.23, 5.66. Boccaccio also uses other terms for the concept, such as 'ventura' and 'destino'.

2 See Patch, *Goddess*; for a recent collection of essays on Boethius, see Gibson.

3 Shepherd calls the question of free will and determinism 'the obsession of the century' ('Religion', 281).

4 For Usk and Hoccleve, see Brewer, *Critical*, 1.42 and 1.63 respectively. The philosophical matter in *Troilus*, and especially Troilus' long soliloquy on fate and predestination in book IV, has been judged prolix and irrelevant: in the early nineteenth century Godwin called the soliloquy 'offensive to true taste' (1.84), later in the century Lounsbury found it 'an intrusion of the worst kind' and in 'bad taste' (3.374–5), and more recently Baum concluded that 'artistically it is a blemish' (148).

5 The view of *Troilus* as a Boethian poem has been expressed most forcefully by D. W. Robertson. He and his followers have identified an important element in the poem, though it exists with other, competing elements, as I have tried to indicate throughout this study. The Robertsonian view has been discussed throughout, especially in the chapters on Troy and Love, and will be confronted most directly in the next and last chapter.

6 The following discussion is much indebted to Mann, 'Chance', 78–90.

7 Some critics have seen greater complexity in this issue; for example, Elbow argues that the speeches on Fortune should be read on three different levels; Bartholomew notes that Fortune is at once an irrational goddess and a providential agent (37); and Spearing notes in *Troilus* both a strong sense of predestination and a powerful sense of free will (*Troilus*, 60–1).

8 Elbow notes that there are many events in *Troilus* attributed to Fortune that are fully explained, on the information supplied by the text, by human choice (89–90).

9 Norton-Smith, 192–212; McAlpine. Nevertheless McAlpine's argument that the poem contains both the Boethian comedy of Troilus, because he makes 'morally enhancing choices', and the Boethian tragedy of Criseyde, because she makes 'a morally degrading choice' (33), is too neatly schematic, despite its appeal, and excessively moralistic in its own fashion.

10 Lawlor sees pathetic tragedy in *Troilus* as a whole (72); Spearing says that the 'dominant effect of Chaucer's poem is perhaps pathos rather than tragedy' (*Troilus*, 59).

11 Mann notes that, whereas in the middle of the poem with his powers at their height Pandarus is described (III.533, 521) as though he were 'a kind of mini-providence', his appearance of all-embracing control in the face of Fortune is finally revealed as 'a pathetic sham' as we realize the 'limitations of human control' ('Chance', 87).

8

Christianity

Of the many different kinds of material that Chaucer added to *Filostrato*, perhaps the most troubling to the modern reader is that drawn from Christian belief and practice. Earlier versions of the love-story, from Benoît's *Roman* to Boccaccio's *Filostrato*, treat it as a thoroughly secular tale, whose only moral is the untrustworthiness of women. Chaucer is the first to give a significant religious dimension to the story: in addition to nominal expressions of faith by the narrator of *Troilus*, its Trojan characters, while remaining believably pagan, introduce images, concepts and oaths that we, but not they, recognize as derived from medieval Catholicism. Such Christian phrases and concepts occur throughout *Troilus*, but they never dominate until the very end of the poem, when the narrator or (as some believe) Chaucer, at last speaking in his own voice, describes Troilus' ascent to the heavens, harshly rejects paganism and all its works, recommends the love of Christ and celebrates the Trinity (V.1807–69).

Whereas the Christian material in *Troilus* is dismissed as irrelevant and merely conventional by some critics, others believe it expresses the clear meaning of the poem. Both positions simplify what Chaucer has done. To ignore the Christianity of *Troilus* is to diminish the whole, for it is a significant, if often submerged and never unalloyed, part of the poem's texture; yet, at the same time, that Christian element is multiple and therefore provides no simple key to meaning. Medieval Catholicism was far from a monolithic system of belief, and Chaucer reproduces this diversity in *Troilus*, which contains a range of possible Christian attitudes towards the story, from lofty contempt of the world to deep human sympathy. As he does with other aspects of *Troilus*, Chaucer here creates a dramatic and highly complex experience that encourages the reader to be aware of various layers and responses. This is especially true at the poem's conclusion, where the Christian challenge to the reader is most demanding.

The Christianity of *Troilus* does not derive from Boccaccio. Just as *Filostrato* has only the most superficial pagan colouring, it also contains very little that reflects post-classical religious practice. The narrator never presents himself as a Christian: he opens the poem with mention of Jove, Apollo and the Muses, and draws a wholly secular moral about the need for young men to take care when choosing their lovers (8.29–33). The characters in *Filostrato* casually evoke God ('Dio' and 'Iddio') with no particular suggestion of the Deity of Abraham or Paul. In common with other medieval French and Italian poets, Boccaccio does use metaphorical religious language in his account of the love of Troiolo and Criseida (it being the most available vocabulary to describe the extremes of bliss and suffering), but the phrases he employs are so general that their debt to medieval Christianity is usually only nominal. For example, Criseida's beauty is described as both 'angelica' (1.11) and 'celestiale' (1.27). More specific to Christianity (and Dante) is Troiolo's assertion that his love has led him from 'inferno' to 'paradiso' (3.16, 3.56) and the comparison of Criseida's face to 'paradiso' (4.100, 7.69), but even these comparisons are brief and relatively infrequent. The discourse of *Filostrato* is sensual and courtly rather than religious.

In characteristic fashion, *Troilus and Criseyde* greatly expands and complicates Boccaccio's use of religious language to describe romantic passion (Howard, 'Literature', 451). Chaucer follows his source in calling Criseyde's beauty 'aungelik' and then goes further to present her as a 'hevenyssh perfit creature' sent down in scorn of Nature (I.102–5). Chaucer's God of Love is a fully realized (and rather terrible) deity, instead of the more metaphorical figure in *Filostrato*, and the bliss of love in *Troilus* is more often associated with heaven (I.31, II.895, III.704, III.1204, III.1251, III.1322, III.1599, III.1657, IV.712). In addition to increasing the frequency and intensity of such religious usage, Chaucer also makes it more specifically Christian. As early as the prologue to book I, the narrator describes himself, in words modelled on a papal title ('servant of the servants of God'), as one who 'God of Loves servantz serve' (I.15). He then proceeds to offer prayers for various classes of lover in imitation of the 'bidding prayer' of the Mass (I.29–46) and declares that he hopes his 'sowle best avaunce' by praying for and writing about lovers and living 'in charite' (I.47–9).

Medieval Christian terms are consistently added to Chaucer's version of the love-story, though they are rarely prominent (Dodd, 189–208). Slaughter notes the frequency and complexity with which the word 'grace' is used throughout the poem, and the concepts of conversion and penance are emphasized early. The narrator celebrates Troilus' passionate response to the sight of Criseyde with 'Blissed be Love, that kan thus folk converte!' (I.308), and Pandarus somewhat later predicts that Troilus, 'converted out of wikkednesse' by the goodness of the God of Love, will be a powerful upholder of Love's 'lay' just as renegade clerks 'converted from hire wikked werkes/Thorugh grace of God' become strongest and most orthodox in the faith (I.998–1008). Once he falls in love, Troilus is described as 'repentynge' that he ever scorned lovers (I.319), later Pandarus urges him to 'bet thi brest' and tell the God of Love that 'I me repente,/If I mysspak, for now myself I love' (I.932–4), and still later Pandarus reports overhearing Troilus saying to the God of Love, 'Now, *mea culpa*, lord, I me repente' (II.525) and going through a form of the three stages of Catholic penance: contrition (II.525), confession (II.528) and satisfaction (II.529). In bed with Criseyde, Troilus sees himself as an example of the central Christian doctrine that 'mercy passeth right' (III.1282), whereas Antigone compares the soundness of judgements about the 'parfit blisse of love' to the knowledge 'seyntes' have of 'hevene' and 'fendes' have of 'helle' (II.890–6).

Troilus, in contrast to *Filostrato*, also contains many original passages dependent on Christianity that have nothing directly to do with love. Pandarus' first words in the poem, which are designed to provoke Troilus, are surprisingly theological. He professes to attribute the prince's distress to 'som remors of conscience' and 'som devocioun' that makes him lament 'thi synne and thin offence', if only imperfectly ('attricioun'); and he marvels that the Greeks are able to bring 'oure lusty folk to holynesse!' (I.554–60). Less technical, but equally Catholic, is Criseyde's reply to Pandarus' later suggestion that she put away her book and dance in observance of May: 'It satte me wel bet ay in a cave/To bidde and rede on holy seyntes lyves' (II.117–18). Also notable is the greatly increased use of God's name by both the narrator and the characters. Elliott comments that the 'almost constant invocations of God add an unmistakable religious dimension to narrative and dialogue which may seem out of keeping with the classical setting and the poignant love story' (249). These evocations are frequently more specific than Boccaccio's simple 'Dio' or 'Iddio' and include such familiar Christian phrases as 'love of God' (I.571, I.612, II.225, II.246, II.290, II.577, II.1131, II.1476, II.1565, II.1676, III.73, III.118, III.416, III.755, III.941, III.1048, III.1138, III.1224, III.1289, III.1301, IV.69, IV.109, IV.895, IV.1286, IV.1600, V.144, V.159, V.656, V.1392), 'God me (us) blesse' (I.436, V.1212), 'grace of God' (I.1005, II.243; other formulations at III.1349, III.1456, V.1631, V.1702), 'God spede' (I.1041, II.744), 'almyghty God' (IV.693, V.1742), 'God so my soule save' (III.102; other formulations of 'God save' at II.114, II.163, II.978, II.1713, III.1378, III.1501) and 'God so wys be my savacioun' (II.381, II.563). As Dunning observes, these and other evocations of the divine include both casual oaths and those 'which are manifestly in earnest and reflect belief in a Creator and in His government of the universe' (169).

Pagan Story and Christian Narrator

Troilus and Criseyde lacks the overt moralism of so many Middle English romances like *Havelok* or *Le Bone Florence*; instead, its introduction of Christian elements is subtle and discreet. As we saw in Chapter 3, Chaucer creates a believable Trojan world through the addition of ancient myth and history, and his characters do not commit gross anachronisms. Even their mention of such things as saints (so obviously medieval to us) would almost certainly have been accepted by a fourteenth-century audience as part of a pre-Christian vocabulary, just as knighthood was thought to have flourished among the Greeks and Romans. Chaucer never goes too far. Pandarus may refer to 'Seynt Idiot' (I.910), and Troilus, in many manuscripts, to 'Seynt Venus' (III.705, III.712), but no character calls on Saint John or Saint Thomas. Although some oaths to God in *Troilus* may remind the reader of Christian formulations, none depends on the characters' knowledge of Revelation whereas there are many explicitly pagan oaths to such as Mars and Jove. The casual expressions that we recognize today as specific to medieval Christianity, such as Pandarus' telling Criseyde that he has 'plat to yow myn herte *shryven*' (II.579, my emphasis), would probably not have been noticed as such by Chaucer's original audience or indeed by the poet himself, any more than our acceptance of historical films is necessarily undermined by actors who use modern pronunciation and vocabulary.

We begin to understand the absence of explicit Christianity in *Troilus and Criseyde* when we realize that none of the characters feels any sense of sin or religious guilt about the love-affair or, indeed, about anything else. Pandarus' initial charge that Troilus' suffering results from 'som remors of conscience' concerning 'thi synne and thin offence' (I.554–7) is nothing but a ploy, and he never uses such specifically religious language to discuss personal faults again. His own later admission of potential blame for having won Criseyde for Troilus is sharpened and expanded from *Filostrato* but remains wholly secular (III.239–343). He admits that 'shame' might result from his part in this 'game' (III.249–50) and recognizes that, as Criseyde's uncle, he would be called 'traitour' (III.273, III.278) were his actions to be exposed, but he apparently does not feel actual guilt about any of this because he assures Troilus that all will be well as long as secrecy is preserved. As far as he is concerned, the most serious vice in such dealings is 'coveitise', from which he absolves himself (III.260–3), or being a 'labbe' (III.300), for he asserts that the 'firste vertu is to kepe tonge' (III.294). Despite the religious associations (for us) of some of the terms he uses, Pandarus himself appeals to no standard beyond that of this world.

The values of the characters in *Troilus and Criseyde* are consistently social and practical rather than Christian. Like her uncle, Criseyde worries more about her name than about the actual morality of her actions because virtue in her world is defined by reputation. She never cites divine prohibitions to counter Pandarus' insistence that she accept Troilus and never says that it would be a sin to love, only that it might affect her honour. In her inner debate she asserts that she may love if she wants to because 'I am naught religious' (II.759), by which she apparently means she has made no formal vow of celibacy such as that of a Vestal Virgin. Hers is a pagan perspective; for a medieval Christian, of course, sexual relations outside marriage would have been illicit for lay and religious alike. When the narrator imagines criticism of Criseyde's falling in love, he does not mention religious objections but only the possible complaint that she may be proceeding too quickly (II.666–79).

Chaucer's Troy is not particularly pious even in respect to its own beliefs. The pagan gods often seem far away in *Troilus* and their worship, as at the opening feast of Pallas with the knights and ladies 'ful wel arayed . . ./Ye, bothe for the seson and the feste' (I.167–68), is personal and civic rather than devout. In an original passage, Pandarus says that he has heard that every human is susceptible 'to suffren loves hete,/Celestial, or elles love of kynde' (I.978–9) and then quickly finds the first inappropriate for Criseyde. Her beauty and youth argue for knightly rather than celestial love, he says, and unless she acts accordingly 'I holde it for a vice' (III.987). The most powerful deity in *Troilus*, except for Fortune whom he resembles (IV.1189), is the God of Love; and Antigone, like Pandarus, uses the Christian vocabulary of vice and virtue to praise, rather than to condemn, sexual passion. In her beautiful song, she declares that the life of a true lover banishes 'alle manere vice and synne' (compare I.252) and that those who consider it a vice are envious or ignorant (II.851–60).[1]

In contrast to the paganism of the story and its characters, the narrator of *Troilus* is clearly Christian, yet until the end of the poem we understand this largely by implication. His oaths are rarely more obviously doctrinal than those of his characters: compare, for instance, the narrator's 'God leve hym werken as he kan devyse!' (III.56) with Pandarus' 'God do boot on alle syke!' (III.61), Troilus' 'Wher me be wo, O myghty God, thow woost!' (III.66), and Criseyde's 'O for the love of God, do ye nought so/To me' (III.73). Although the narrator in the opening prologue calls himself by a version of a papal title (I.15), imitates a Catholic liturgical prayer (I.29–46), and vows to live in prayer and 'charite' (I.48–9), the devotion he expresses is in fact to the God of Love rather than to the Christian Lord. One of the few direct references to Christian belief in the narrative is made problematic by its context. When Pandarus leeringly appears at his niece's bedside the morning after the consummation, the narrator blandly dismisses the implications of this charged scene ('I passe al that which chargeth nought to seye') and then declares: 'What! God foryaf his deth, and she al so/Foryaf, and with here uncle gan to pleye' (III.1576–8). This astonishing comparison, in which God's forgiveness for those who crucified Him is likened to Criseyde's forgiving her uncle for his pimping, forcibly reminds us (whatever else its does) that, whereas the narrator has a knowledge of the Incarnation and the Crucifixion denied to his pagan characters, he almost never seriously addresses Christian questions or explains the story in terms of Christian values. He defers any overt Christian advocacy until the final stanzas, and even then what he says is neither direct nor simple. Christian phrases and concepts are used unconsciously by the characters and consciously by the narrator throughout *Troilus and Criseyde*, but they do not dominate in the telling of the poem.

Christian Presence

Because the Christian element added by Chaucer rarely appears directly or unalloyed, its importance to *Troilus* has been variously assessed. Some critics discount these Christian additions as largely irrelevant or superficial. Such allusions as do occur are taken to be playful, even potentially subversive, rather than devout, as with the comparison between Criseyde and Christ on the cross just mentioned. Or they are discounted as mechanical reflections of contemporary religious discourse. In this view, Chaucer uses specific terms like 'saint' and larger concepts like repentance, but the theological meaning behind the borrowings does not engage his intellectual interests or poetic sensibility. Noting Chaucer's courtly audience, Shepherd argues that the poet wears his morality lightly, conscious of the need 'to satisfy a whole range of worldliness which appreciates display, luxury, leisure and the solid reassurance of wealth and power and rank' (*'Troilus'*, 74). In the judgement of other critics, however, the Christian additions in *Troilus* (however limited in number) are more than adequate to provoke a strict doctrinal response to the story in medieval readers. Each critical position has its strengths and limitations. Sceptical readings can be helpful in pointing out the lack of overt Christian analysis in the poem, though they tend to flatter modern secular tastes by suggesting that Chaucer's real values must be similar to ours. More pious readings quite properly call attention to the Christian cultural context in which the poem was written, though they then go too far in demanding that we read *Troilus* (along with all other medieval secular literature) by means of a rigid and ironic Augustinian template. If both approaches have merit in the hands of skilful critics, each tends to underestimate Chaucer's achievement. Neither dismissal nor moralistic irony is adequate to the subtle absence and presence of Christian discourse in the poem.[2]

The Christian element in *Troilus* is difficult to evaluate properly because it appears so elusively and in combination with pagan and secular material. Often it is difficult to tell whether it is really there or not. As suggested above, many references to the divine in *Troilus*, while not anachronistic in fact, are so phrased that they may suggest the Christian God. For example, in assuring Troilus that she will return from the Greek camp, Criseyde claims that she loves him more than all the world – 'Or ellis se ich nevere Joves face!' (IV.1337). The citation of Jove is clearly pagan, but the words, which are original in *Troilus*, echo such biblical passages as Christ's promise in the Sermon on the Mount that the clean of heart are blessed because they 'shall see God' (Matthew, 5.8), St. Paul's famous formulation that whereas on earth we see through a glass darkly later we shall see 'face to face' (1 Corinthians, 13.12), and John's vision that the residents of the new Jerusalem 'shall see [God's] face' (Apocrypha, 22.4).

In his transformation of Boccaccio, Chaucer often makes *Troilus* simultaneously more Christian and more pagan. A simple reference in *Filostrato* by Pandaro to 'Dio' (2.21) becomes 'for Joves name in hevene' (I.878), which adds not only a pagan reference (Jove again) but also Christian phrasing, as we recognize when we remember the frequency with which some form of 'God's name' is used as an asseveration by characters in the *Canterbury Tales*. Evidence that Chaucer is deliberately playing with the absence and presence of Christianity in such additions can be found in an invocation by Pandarus when Troilus and Criseyde first meet at Deiphebus' house: ' "Immortal god," quod he, "that mayst nought deyen,/Cupide I mene" ' (III.185–6). The delayed naming of Cupid underlines by its unexpectedness, even as it ostensibly removes, the suggestion of the Christian Deity.[3] For some medieval (and modern) readers, Christian sentiments may be heard even in apparent silence. The joyous spring festival that the Trojans hold in honour of Pallas might suggest Easter to some just as Apollo's prediction of Troy's doom might suggest Christ's contrasting mercy for humankind. For such readers, absence itself creates presence.

The shadowy presence of Christianity in *Troilus* demands an active reader: first to identify such allusions and then to give them meaning. Because such material is usually presented indirectly, both recognition and interpretation are subject to individual judgement. Many examples, such as Pandarus' use of 'shryven' (II.579) or passing references to saints, are probably without much significance and simply represent an unavoidable Christian element in medieval accounts of the past. No anachronism or religious implication seems intended in such cases, although the modern reader (as was perhaps also true for medieval readers) can never be certain. Other passages, however, such as Cupid's being called 'immortal god' (III.185), are clearly self-conscious and provocative. There is no doubt here that Chaucer is deliberately playing with Christian discourse. In between these two categories, which are themselves far from distinct, fall the vast majority of Christian additions whose exact number will differ with each reader.

Identification of a phrase, passage or concept as influenced by Christianity is, however, only the first step towards interpretation. Even those passages most obviously dependent on medieval Catholic practice, such as Pandarus' attribution of Troilus' suffering to remorse for sin (I.554–60) or the prince's supposed confession to the God of Love and imitation of the three stages of penance (II.523–32), occur in markedly non-Christian contexts that make their relationship to faith and doctrine highly problematic. To choose only two possible readings of a single incident, does Troilus' confession to Love dignify his passion by describing it as a religious devotion or does it subject it to criticism by suggesting its distance from worship of the true God? Different readers, modern and medieval, have responded differently. The Christian element so subtly added by Chaucer to his poem increases the challenge of interpretation rather than making it easier.

Even if we are willing to concede that *Troilus and Criseyde* is indeed a Christian poem, we still need to ask what kind of Christianity it contains. The Christian material added by Chaucer is as various as the other aspects of the poem we have examined and equally open to multiple readings, although this is not always recognized. Critics both sympathetic and unsympathetic often assume that a 'Christian' reading of *Troilus and Criseyde* can come to only one conclusion: the poem is a systematic denunciation of the wages of cupidity whose purpose is to show that the lovers have sinned in following their passions rather than the dictates of reason. Even those who most vigorously insist that *Troilus* means something other, and more, often meekly accept that this, and only this, is the *Christian* reading of the poem. It is no wonder, then, that many prefer to ignore the religious element in *Troilus* altogether rather than adopt such narrow conclusions. The most influential Christian reading in the past generation, which is identified with D. W. Robertson, Jr, undoubtedly identifies a genuine Boethian dimension that Chaucer has added to his source, as we saw in the previous chapter, but it ignores other elements in the work and assumes a monolithic, dogmatic understanding of faith that predetermines all interpretation.

In the Middle Ages, few readers or writers seem to have adopted the Robertsonian position;[4] instead, both before and after Chaucer, the love of Troilus and Criseyde is regularly treated as a secular event. When an explicit lesson is drawn from the story by Benoît, Guido and Boccaccio, and later by such as Lydgate in his *Troy Book* and Wynkyn de Worde in his 1517 edition of *Troilus*, that lesson invariably condemns only the faithlessness of Criseyde towards her noble knight rather than the immorality of the love-affair itself. In *The Legend of Good Women* Chaucer himself makes a similar defence of his practice in *Troilus*: the true lover ought not to blame him because his 'entente' in the poem was 'to forthren trouthe in love' and to warn against 'falsnesse' (F 471–3).

In fact, the strictest moral reading of *Troilus* in the Middle Ages would not be that the story condemns vice, as the Robertsonians claim, but that the telling of such a story ought itself to be condemned. This is the position of the 'Retraction' at the end of the *Canterbury Tales*, in which Chaucer 'revoke[s]' the 'book of Troilus' along with other 'worldly vanitees' (X.1084–5). The same view is echoed more than a century later in Sir Thomas Elyot's dialogue *Pasquyll the Playne* (1533), in which Pasquyll encounters someone holding a New Testament to screen a hidden copy of *Troilus* and comments: 'Lorde what discorde is bytwene these two bokes' (4ª). Although such distrust of secular literature was frequently heard in the Middle Ages, medieval Christianity is anything but monolithic. A belief system with personal salvation as its goal, it offered many possible routes by which that might be achieved. It is catholic as well as Catholic. Charlemagne, St Francis, Urban VIII, Dante, Thomas Beckett and Bede, to name just a few, were all regarded in this period as defenders and exemplars of the faith, despite the deep differences between them. The moralism of the Robertsonians is one Christian reading of *Troilus*, but only one.

A different but equally valid Christian reading of the poem, for instance, would look past clichés about the evil of cupidity and the goodness of *caritas* (of which there could hardly be any dispute) and instead examine Chaucer's subtle account of the virtues and limitations of the pagan past. Despite its lack of faith, the pre-Christian world continued to be honoured in the Middle Ages for its human and moral achievements. Aristotle and Plato were considered supreme thinkers; Homer, Virgil and Ovid were imitated as the greatest poets, and Hector, Alexander and Caesar were included among the Nine Worthies. Although he assigns both Aristotle and Virgil to Hell, Dante hails the former as the 'master of those who know' and the latter as the source of his own poetic achievement.

Fourteenth-century English intellectuals and theologians were especially fascinated by pagan life and thought, as Beryl Smalley and Alastair Minnis (*Pagan*) have shown, and this interest also appears in both Chaucer and his contemporary Gower. A Christian reader alive to this tradition could learn from the account of the ancient world in *Troilus* without feeling any threat to his or her own faith. He would see differences in customs and beliefs ('Ecch contree hath his lawes', II.42) with no need either to reject or accept the pagan world as a whole. In addition to satisfying his intellectual curiosity about the past, such a reader might also recognize the attractiveness of this civilization as well as its dangers. Genuine virtues such as Troilus' bravery and Deiphebus' generosity would be seen to be mixed with negatives such as the characters' ignorance of the true God and their hopeless fatalism. In short, a serious Christian might read *Troilus* as a complex portrait of a society without Revelation.

One could imagine a number of other Christian readings of *Troilus* (the ways in which Trojan and Catholic conceptions of love overlap and diverge could produce several), but I want to discuss briefly only one further aspect: the deep sympathy *Troilus* expresses for its characters and especially for Criseyde even as she betrays Troilus. Although this sympathy has been taken too sentimentally by some, the greater current danger is from those readers, both moralizers and their opponents, who find only irony in the narrator's concern, thus ignoring a unique and central quality of the poem. G. K. Chesterton, who has some authority as a Christian reader, declared that the 'charity of Chaucer toward Cressida is one of the most beautiful things in human literature; but its particular blend belongs entirely to Christian literature' (144). He finds Chaucer's delicate mixture of adoration, pity and condemnation unparalleled in ancient poetry, and equalled perhaps only by Dante, the supreme Christian poet. Even Shakespeare and Boccaccio are merciless towards their hero-ine in contrast to Chaucer. But, as Robert Henryson so powerfully dramatized in his *Testament*, harsh and unforgiving condemnation of human weakness is not a specifically Christian attitude; on the contrary, it is most appropriate to those purely natural forces represented by the pagan gods who so severely punish Cresseid in the Scots poem. A more Christian response to the ruin of Troy and its lovers might echo the narrator's human sympathy and go on to acknowledge human frailty and its need for God's mercy.

The potential Christian readings of *Troilus* so briefly sketched above – the moralistic, the antiquarian and the sympathetic – are not mutually exclusive. Each responds to a genuine aspect of the poem, and therefore a supple and inclusive interpretation would acknowledge all. Of course, it is perfectly possible to read *Troilus* with pleasure and profit while ignoring its religious element altogether. Christianity is not at the centre of *Troilus*, as it is at the centre of other great medieval poems like the *Divine Comedy* and *Piers Plowman*; rather, the poem is so designed that it may be viewed from the pagan perspective of the characters themselves. Many good critics have done exactly this and approached *Troilus* as an essentially modern work. The insights of such readings are often illuminating, but the final effect, as with the Robertsonian position, is to close off some of the possibilities of this intricate and open poem. The Christianity of *Troilus* need not be taken as either irrelevant or determining. Whatever its importance to some of its original readers (or even to Chaucer), Christianity remains one aspect of the poem's multiplicity: it contributes to the variety of voices in *Troilus* but it does not either silence or dominate the others.

The Multiplicity of the Ending

The Christian element of *Troilus and Criseyde* is most insistent in the last few stanzas of the poem. After telling of Troilus' ascent to the heavens and scorn of the world, the narrator urges his readers to choose the love of Christ over deceptive worldly affection, damns pagan practices, and concludes with a prayer that calls on the protection of the Trinity and the mercy of Christ. Yet despite the appearance of such orthodox sentiments the conclusion of *Troilus* is no simple didactic lesson. In these last few stanzas both the multiplicity of *Troilus* and the need for the reader's response are undeniable. Spearing has noted that we tend to give special attention to the end of a long work because 'it is expected somehow to complete or sum up the meaning of the whole' (*Readings*, 109); an expectation expressed by Pandarus when he notes that, however intricately men tell their stories, their 'tale is al for som conclusioun' because 'th'ende is every tales strengthe' (II.259–60). Pandarus' words well describe *Troilus*, but not quite in the way he means them. Here the end has a special strength precisely because it does not achieve a single conclusion. Rather than bring the meaning of the poem to a close, the end of *Troilus* asserts openness.

The conclusion to *Filostrato* contains some interpretive play of its own, for Boccaccio immediately follows a denunciation of young women in part 8 with a commendation of his book and himself to his own 'donna gentil' in part 9. Whether or not he was inspired by this apparent contradiction in his source, Chaucer develops an intricate series of tensions at the end of his poem. Avoiding both *Filostrato*'s conventional anti-feminism as well as its address to a particular lady, Chaucer adds significant material from Dante's *Commedia* and Boccaccio's own *Teseida* along with original addresses to a wide variety of readers. Because it is transformed in so many different directions at once, the end of *Troilus* is a paradigm of the multiplicity of the poem as a whole.

A strong indication of the complexity of the ending of *Troilus* is that critics cannot agree on its duration or on what to call it. Because Chaucer did not set off the conclusion to his poem in any formal way, in contrast to the prologues at the beginning of the first four books, once popular critical terms such as 'palinode', 'epilogue' or 'envoi' are not really appropriate. The vaguer terms 'ending' or 'conclusion', which I shall use here, more accurately describe the elusiveness of Chaucer's practice: the narrative fades away rather than clearly stopping, and the narrator offers no clear or consistent comment on what has occurred. Indeed, the events of the story are not completely over at the poem's conclusion: we do not know what happens between Criseyde and Diomede (a gap Henryson filled with brilliant results) nor are we shown the ultimate fate of either Troilus or Troy. The poem could be said to begin to end at many points. It is forecast in the very opening stanza, as Spearing notes (*Readings*, 117), made inevitable by the change of Fortune in the prohemium to book IV, and underlined by the mood of elegy throughout book V. All agree that some more definite closure is attempted by the narrator in the last few stanzas, but few agree on the precise moment when this occurs.[5]

The complexity and contradictions of the ending have long been recognized, as in Lowes's statement: 'I know nothing quite like the tumultuous hitherings and thitherings of mood and matter in the last dozen stanzas of the poem' (153). Likewise Bronson refers to the 'kaleidoscopic conclusion' (21), an image that superbly well captures the rapid shifts of material, style and tone that both disorient and dazzle the reader. In addition to the subdivisions identified by Meech, Malone, Tatlock and Wetherbee, other critics recognize that Chaucer concludes *Troilus* with 'a set of multiple endings' (McAlpine, 239) or 'a number of discrete sections' (Spearing, *Readings*, 122). Undoubtedly the most brilliant and influential such exposition is by E. Talbot Donaldson, who deftly analyses the contradictions, twists and turns, starts and stops, sublimity and farce offered by Chaucer in the last eighteen stanzas of the poem ('Ending').

Although Donaldson's essay remains the most satisfactory account of literary variety at the end of *Troilus*, he is careful to pull back from fully endorsing the disunity implicit in his reading; instead, he attributes the apparent contradictions he discovers (disgust for the world immediately followed by deep appreciation of its loveliness, for example) to a single identifiable source – the narrator. As in his account of the pilgrim narrator in the *Canterbury Tales*, Donaldson insists that Chaucer creates multiple effects through the agency of a coherent persona. Neither the poet nor the poem is in any serious disarray, in this view, but only the narrator, whose 'internal warfare' results in 'a kind of nervous breakdown in poetry' ('Ending', 91). Donaldson's argument that the ending of *Troilus*, and implicitly the poem as a whole, is best understood as a psychodrama of an inept narrator attempting to come to terms with the difficulties of his material is widely accepted today by critics who agree on little else.[6] Objections to this approach are similar to those made against the 'dramatic principle' of reading *The Canterbury Tales* as expressions of their individual tellers, which I have dealt with at length elsewhere (*Drama*). In rejecting 'a stable and fully characterized "persona" clearly distinguishable from the poet', Spearing notes that such arguments simply transfer the notion of 'organic unity', rightly questioned by modern literary criticism, from tale to teller (*Readings*, 122).

The anarchic ending so well described by Donaldson and others is more radically multiple than usually recognized. It cannot be contained by a single narrator, however psychologically complex; but, like other elements in *Troilus*, is capable of a variety of contradictory readings. That the reader is the key to the ending of the poem is indicated by the text itself, as Evans has recently suggested. Lines V.1744–71, which many identify as the beginning of the end, speak to an audience whose presence is recognized (see especially V.1750, V.1753, V.1765 ff.) but whose precise nature remains largely undefined. As the poem moves into its final lines, however, the audience begins to be separated into specific groups, though general statements also continue to be made (V.1828–34, V.1849–55). Diverse and contradictory classes of reader are addressed one after the other, often with explicit apostrophes that suggest Chaucer's anxiety about the ways his text will be understood. First, 'every lady bright of hewe' and 'every gentil womman' (V.1772–3) are beseeched not to take offence; then the 'litel bok' (V.1786) itself is formally dismissed and told to reverence its betters; then, after Troilus' ascent, 'O yonge, fresshe folkes, he or she' are addressed (V.1835); then 'O moral Gower' and 'philosophical Strode' (V.1856–7) are asked for their corrections; and finally the Trinity (V.1863) and Jesus (V.1868) are prayed to and their help sought. The text's insistence on its various audiences is not narrative breakdown, but the clearest statement yet that the meaning of the ending of *Troilus* is the responsibility of its many different readers.

The moral at the end of Boccaccio's *Filostrato* is the anti-feminist lesson drawn in almost every other version of the story: 'Giovane donna, e mobile e vogliosa/è negli amanti molti' ('a young woman is fickle and desirous of many lovers', 8.30). Chaucer presents no such condemnation but instead offers an apology to women and a warning that it is they who should beware of men (V.1772–85). In contrast to the secular lesson of *Filostrato*, *Troilus* concludes with a series of passages (addresses to various readers, Troilus' ascent, condemnations of pagan practices, and prayers) that introduce explicit Christian material and whose relationship to the poem as a whole has been the subject of intense critical debate. Two of the most popular interpretations of what Chaucer means by these additions appear to be utterly irreconcilable, though, as we shall see, they are more similar than they first seem. One group of critics reads the ending as the culmination of the Christian message implied throughout the work, whereas another finds it utterly opposed to the human values of the story just told.

The view that the ending is radically different from the rest of *Troilus* expresses itself in two ways. Although rarely argued today, the position of some critics has been that the ending is a formal retraction of the love-story, a product of the so-called 'double truth', in which a philosophical system might be taken seriously on its own terms during the Middle Ages despite its conflict with orthodox Christian doctrine (Denomy). According to this argument, Chaucer treats courtly love as a worthy rival religion during the narrative itself, but at the end he must finally acknowledge the higher truth of Christianity. The most famous expression of this position is by C. S. Lewis, who invents a striking metaphor to describe the ending of *Troilus* as a genuine palinode, like the poet's 'Retraction' to the *Canterbury Tales*: 'We hear the bell clang; and the children, suddenly hushed and grave, and a little frightened, troop back to their master' (*Allegory*, 43; cf. Kittredge, *Poetry*, 143).

A second group of critics who regard the ending of *Troilus* as disjunctive treat it as a pietistic betrayal or, at best, an irrelevance. Curry insists that 'dramatically' it is 'a sorry performance': 'Here in the Epilog the poet, without having given the slightest hint of warning, suddenly denies and contradicts everything that has gone before in the poem' (165). Although taken by itself the 'Epilog is a poem of great beauty', Curry concludes that it expresses the conventional religious sentiments of Chaucer the man, which Chaucer the artist had courageously suppressed during the narrative itself in order to tell his tragedy of love. As a result, the ending is 'not a part of the whole and is detachable at will' (168). Although this argument is apparently less popular than it once was, it can still be seen in David Aers' dismissal of the style and thought of the ending, especially its questioning of human love, as 'incoherent', 'inadequate,' 'superficial', and not 'serious' (*Chaucer*, 140; cf. Aers, 'Women', 200n31) – a general position that is also found in more subtle analyses of the ending by Elizabeth Salter ('Reconsideration') and Alfred David (*Strumpet*, 27–36).

In contrast to those critics who believe that the end contradicts the spirit of the narrative are those who believe that it fulfils it. This is the position of Robertson, who asserts that the final suggestion in *Troilus* to turn to Christ rather than to 'feyned' loves 'is what Chaucer has to tell us about love, not only here but in *The Canterbury Tales* and in the major allegories as well' (*Preface*, 501). Earlier in this century Root claimed that the final Christian lesson about the limits of this world was 'no mere tacked-on moral' but 'implicit in the whole poem' (*Troilus* edition, l; see also Shanley); and, more recently, Gerald Morgan also declares that the ending 'contains the essential meaning that the poem as a whole seeks to convey' ('Ending', 258), which is that 'the limited and imperfect love of man receives its true value only when united to its divine source' (260). Steadman finds the ending harmonious within and without: 'Not only have the various sections of Chaucer's conclusion been linked together by common themes but they also share the same Boethian frame of reference in common with the rest of the poem' (152).

Despite their apparent opposition to one other, all the arguments just summarized share a fundamental assumption. Each accepts that the final stanzas of *Troilus* offer a coherent statement of Christian doctrine. Whether the critics see it as unfortunately imposed by contemporary ideology or nobly expressing the underlying logic of the poem, whether they find it detachable or organic, all agree that the poem's end contains a straightforward lesson about the need to choose divine love over that of this world. Even Donaldson, who has most successfully emphasized the literary variety of the poem, says that the *moralitee* of the poem is transparent (human love, like everything else human, is 'unstable and illusory'), though he insists that the 'meaning' of *Troilus* is 'a complex qualification of the moral' ('Ending', 92). I would suggest that the Christianity of the ending is more problematic than even Donaldson acknowledges, certainly for a modern audience but also for a medieval one. The moral that so many find obvious is never expressed directly or unambiguously by the poet, who once again depends on the reader to create meaning. The end of *Troilus* is not so much a dogmatic Christian lesson as a variety of different statements, events and prayers addressed to a Christian audience.

The initial prayers to God in these final stanzas are not particularly religious at all. After requesting that ladies not be angry with him for telling of Criseyde's untruth, the narrator mentions the betrayal of women by 'false folk', villains whom he curses like the poet of a popular English romance – 'God yeve hem sorwe, amen!' (V.1781). The deity is invoked again in the author's formal dismissal of his book that immediately follows. After identifying his present work as a tragedy, he expresses a hope for different inspiration: 'Ther God thi makere yet, er that he dye,/So sende myght to make in som comedye!' (V.1787–8). In the next stanza he calls on God twice for help to ensure that the poem be correctly written and understood: 'So prey I God that non myswrite the' (V.1795) and 'That thow be understonde, God I biseche!' (V.1798).

These several prayers may imply a religion shared by narrator and audience (presumably Christianity, though the phrases are imprecise), but the sentiments expressed are far from devout and offer no lesson about the renunciation of this world. On the contrary, each requests practical action: sorrow to be visited upon the false, a new poem to be produced, and the present work to be written and understood correctly – all concerns that are more secular than spiritual. In fact, *Troilus* itself is put in pagan company when the narrator orders literary reverence from his little tragedy: 'kis the steppes where as thow seest pace/Virgile, Ovide, Omer, Lucan, and Stace' (V.1791–2). Although God is repeatedly invoked in the lines we have just discussed, Chaucer avoids any clear or profound Christian statement.

Troilus' ascent to the eighth sphere, which soon follows, would seem to offer a more promising Christian lesson (V.1807–27). The episode, borrowed from Arcita's journey in Boccaccio's *Teseida*, is Chaucer's longest and most dramatic addition to the final stanzas and has seemed to many to supply a spiritual ending to the poem. Looking back to 'this litel spot of erthe', Troilus 'gan despise/This wretcched world' and contrasted its 'vanite' to 'the pleyn felicite' of heaven. Laughing at those mourning his death, he 'dampned al oure werk that foloweth so/The blynde lust, the which that may nat laste,/And sholden al oure herte on heven caste'. The language here is certainly moral enough, and for many critics the scene is conclusive. Some assert that it shows that human love may win divine sanction (for example: Heidtmann, 246–7; Dronke, 'Conclusion', 49; Kirby, 282; Leyerle, 124). Others, responding more to the prince's severe words than to his heavenly elevation, argue that Chaucer is directly condemning this world and human affection. Gill says that Troilus expresses a divinely comic perspective of heaven and earth (100-2; cf. Robertson, *Preface*, 500-1), and Steadman, who claims that Troilus 'achieves a philosopher's insight into true and false felicity' (137), says that 'the hero's ascent and freshly attained insight could serve as commentary on the entire poem' because it stresses the 'opposition between the unstable felicity of the world and the changeless beatitude of heaven' (121–2).

As indicated by their opposition to one another, both the sentimental and moralistic readings of Troilus' ascent are far from inevitable. The sentimental view assumes that there is no real conflict between sexual and divine love, though its proponents have trouble finding any other medieval examples in which heaven is achieved in just this way. Indeed, Troilus' rapid ascent and distant vision may seem to emphasize the contrast between this world and the divine rather than their unity. Moreover, Troilus' reward is not as certain as is sometimes assumed. The scene concludes with the statement that Troilus went forth 'ther as Mercurye sorted hym to dwelle' (V.1827). His final destination is left unspecified, and the pagan guide would argue against a Christian location (Conlee).

Moralistic interpretations of the ascent are equally limited. Troilus' damnation of the world and all its works, as McAlpine suggests, is reminiscent of the dream of Scipio in *The Parliament of Foules*, and it therefore represents 'the highest vision of *pagan* wisdom' rather than Christian truth (179; cf. Reiss, 'Failure'). Although *contemptus mundi* is a genuine medieval position, it is, at best, only a partial Christian view. Bishop notes that the scene is impersonal, with no mention of other humans or of love, the ultimate Christian virtue (95–6). Troilus has finally escaped the world of Fortune, but what has he learned? His scorn for those mourning his death can hardly be taken as ideal: it is reminiscent of the harsh natural justice given Cresseid by the planetary gods in Henryson's *Testament* and utterly contradicts the human sympathy that is one of the distinctively Christian elements of *Troilus*, especially in the final book. Perhaps Troilus has not changed that much. Without ignoring that we are told that Troilus' soul rose 'ful blisfully' to an experience of the 'armonye' of 'hevenysshe melodie' (V.1812–13), is there not an echo here of the prince's callow laughter towards lovers in book I?

My point is not to offer a definitive reading of this significant addition, but rather to suggest that the passage offers no sure grounds for any such thing. To many critics Troilus' ascent validates one or another Christian meaning of the poem: either it proves that sexual love loyally pursued can win divine favour or it proves the utter worthlessness of this world. In fact, Chaucer has so constructed the scene that it cannot be taken as an authoritative statement of either position. It is one element in a complex conclusion, and its own significance is far from clear. Troilus makes a peculiar spokesman for Christianity: we cannot be sure of his reward and cannot trust his judgement. His ascent gives him an external point of view of events that may not be any better than that of the reader. From the eighth sphere he looks back at the story and tries to make sense of it, as we do. Although his divine perspective raises the possibility of a Christian interpretation of the poem, he is an inadequate vehicle to supply it. Rather than the ultimate voice of the poem so many seek, he is but one interpreter of the story among many others.

Those critics who want Chaucer (or at least the narrator) to speak directly in his own person at the end of *Troilus* and give us the true meaning of the work misunderstand the poet's own sense of his function. The supposed Christian ending of *Troilus* is both repeatedly deferred and made complex, so that even those stanzas that seem most harshly didactic are more problematic than they first appear. For instance, immediately after Troilus' ascent, a preaching voice is suddenly heard:

> Swich fyn hath, lo, this Troilus for love!
> Swich fyn hath al his grete worthynesse!
> Swich fyn hath his estat real above!
> Swich fyn his lust, swich fyn hath his noblesse!
> Swich fyn hath false worldes brotelnesse!
> And thus bigan this lovynge of Criseyde,
> As I have told, and in this wise he deyde.
>
> (V.1828–34)

Despite the moralistic tone of the passage, the sentiments expressed are not especially Christian (there is nothing here of faith, hope or charity); rather, as in Troilus' vision, what we hear is much more appropriate to stoic philosophy. Moreover, the lines are imprecise. The repeated phrase 'swich fyn' seems to promise the announcement of a particular result (the reward Troilus has earned from his behaviour); but, as already noted, uncertainty remains about just what 'fyn' Troilus did achieve (except death) and where Mercury has him dwell. The lines are therefore as much of a question as they are a statement because we cannot be certain of Troilus' end. That he (like all men) must die is hardly a surprising idea for either Christians or non-Christians, then or now; the more important point, however, is left to individual readers: what is the appropriate response to such inevitable mutability?

An equally severe stanza of repetitive denunciations three stanzas later also does not supply a clear meaning for the poem:

> Lo here, of payens corsed olde rites!
> Lo here, what alle hire goddes may availle!
> Lo here, thise wrecched worldes appetites!
> Lo here, the fyn and guerdon for travaille
> Of Jove, Appollo, of Mars, of swich rascaille!
> Lo here, the forme of olde clerkis speche
> In poetrie, if ye hire bokes seche.
>
> (V.1849–55)

The apparent lesson here (a denunciation of the Gentile gods) is somewhat irrelevant. No conceivable medieval or modern audience of the poem has ever needed to be warned against the pagan gods. Jove, Apollo, Mars and other such rascals were not seriously worshipped during the fourteenth century or during the 600 years since *Troilus* was written, and therefore the fervid denunciation of 'payens corsed olde rites' can hardly be the purpose of Chaucer's poem.

The two moralistic stanzas just discussed themselves suggest their lack of absolute authority. For all their bluster, neither is consistently harsh; but, as Markland and others have observed, the final couplet of each produces 'anticlimax' ('Inviolability', 157; see also McAlpine, 241–2). After five lines of 'swich fyn', the final couplet of the first stanza 'traces the arc of Troilus' experience with no hint of condemnation' (Wetherbee, 236), and the concluding mention of 'the forme of olde clerkis speche/In poetrie, if ye hire bokes seche' (V.1854–5) in the second stanza seems more a concession than further condemnation. The couplet evokes the great poets whose artistic and even moral value was repeatedly reaffirmed by medieval Catholic thought and who had been so lavishly praised just nine stanzas earlier by the narrator himself (Dean, 180). Neither stanza offers a lesson that is fully confident or fully Christian, but each is so framed that it 'reserves final judgment to the audience' (Wheeler, 116). The repeated words 'swich' and 'here' cause us to ask 'which' and 'where'. Rather than closing off meaning, they force us to return to the text in search of it.

Between these two harsh passages are two very different stanzas, which are sweeter in tone and more affirmative in their explicit Christianity:

> So yonge, fresshe folkes, he or she,
> In which that love up groweth with youre age,
> Repeyreth hom fro worldly vanyte,
> And of youre herte up casteth the visage
> To thilke God that after his ymage
> Yow made, and thynketh al nys but a faire,
> This world that passeth soone as floures faire.
>
> And loveth hym the which that right for love
> Upon a crois, oure soules for to beye,
> First starf, and roos, and sit in hevene above;
> For he nyl falsen no wight, dar I seye,
> That wol his herte al holly on hym leye.
> And syn that he best to love is, and most meke,
> What nedeth feynede loves for to seke?
>
> (V.1835–48)

The loveliness and human sympathy in these lines have been much commented on, particularly by Donaldson ('Ending', 98), and certainly the transformation from Boccaccio is extraordinary. The corresponding passage in *Filostrato* warns young men ('giovinetti') in whom there grows amorous desire ('l'amoroso disio') not to trust women, especially young women who are fickle, promiscuous and as changeable as a leaf in the wind (8.29–30). In contrast to these standard anti-feminist sentiments, Chaucer's lines are tender and include both sexes ('he or she'). But the beauty and generosity of these lines should not lead us to assume that even they offer a conclusive Christian lesson.

Robertson cites these two stanzas without analysis as the summation of 'what Chaucer has to tell us about love' in *Troilus* and elsewhere. It is, he claims, the 'message' expected by the medieval reader, and 'to say that an author intends it is simply to say that he is a Christian' (*Preface*, 501–2). Although the Christianity of the passage is undeniable, its particular message is far from simple. Donaldson and others have noted the love of the fair world that also haunts these lines. Moreover, the reminder that humans are made in God's image qualifies the rejection of the world elsewhere in the ending, and the address to 'yonge, fresshe folkes' echoes the description of Troilus, 'so fressh, so yong, so weldy semed he' (II.636), as he rides under Criseyde's window and intoxicates her.

The mention of Christ's meek love for human beings expresses orthodox Catholic doctrine and there is no reason to doubt that it expresses Chaucer's own personal belief and that of most of his readers, but it does not therefore follow that this is therefore the 'message' of the poem. The recommendation of Christ is offered humbly ('dar I seye') for the reader's consideration. Rather than the 'exhortations' claimed by some (Steadman, 153), these two stanzas, as Anthony Farnham has so shrewdly observed, end in a question. Young people are not ordered to choose Christ over 'feynede loves', though the lines could have been written that way, but asked why they do not do so. A Christian answer is suggested (although note that it is specifically addressed to only one segment of the audience, young people), but it is deferred. Once again the burden of choice and action is put on the reader. What the narrator asks is not merely a rhetorical question, as McAlpine assumes, which 'backfires when, for some readers at least, it turns into a genuine question' (242). It has always been a genuine question: for many modern readers, of course, but also for the most orthodox medieval reader, who is left to decide precisely what 'feynede loves' are. If all human loves are false and to the same degree, what, then, becomes of the Christian injunction to love one another (Wheeler, 115–16)? The relationship between what Jesus calls the two great commandments (to love God and to love one's neighbour, Matthew 22.37–40) is certainly raised during these two stanzas, but it is not answered. As one of the central challenges of Christian life, whose exploration has occupied the greatest spiritual writers, how could the question be adequately addressed in such a context?

The last address to a specific human audience during the ending of *Troilus* is a kind of dedication:

> O moral Gower, this book I directe
> To the and to the, philosophical Strode,
> To vouchen sauf, ther nede is, to correcte,
> Of youre benignites and zeles goode.
> (V.1856–9)

These few lines are especially interesting because, in addition to being Chaucer's tribute to valued poetic and intellectual contemporaries, who were probably his friends, they suggest how we might approach *Troilus* by once again stressing the importance of the reader. In the particular terms that he chooses to describe Gower and Strode, Chaucer seems to acknowledge that his poem may have moral or philosophical lessons; but, at the same time, he suggests that any such lesson must be drawn by others. His job is to produce an exciting poem: to involve us with the characters and incidents of the story and complicate our response by adding a variety of contrasting elements to the narrative he inherited from Boccaccio. The job of finding meaning, however, must be left to the poem's readers, whose prototypes are Gower and Strode. Unlike some modern critics, Chaucer does not deny that his work may be used to produce morality and philosophy, but in order for either to have validity they must be the work of those who read the poem. The 'correction' of readers from Gower and Strode to the present, as well as our goodwill and zeal, are necessary to make *Troilus* a complete work. Nor does Chaucer suggest that there is any one meaning, any single moral or philosophy. He cites two, presumably different readers (Gower and Strode), just as earlier he had beseeched God that his poem might be understood wherever it be 'red . . . or elles songe' (V.1797), suggesting a range of performances and receptions.

The poem concludes with a direct address to the Trinity, whose beginning is closely modelled on *Paradiso* 14:28–30, which the narrator, in a personal introduction, says is ever his heartfelt prayer (V.1860–2):

> Thow oon, and two, and thre, eterne on lyve,
> That regnest ay in thre, and two, and oon,
> Uncircumscript, and al maist circumscrive,
> Us from visible and invisible foon

Defende, and to thy mercy, everichon,
So make us, Jesus, for thi mercy, digne,
For love of mayde and moder thyn benigne. Amen.
(V.1863–9)

The profundity of this Christian moment, which offers a vision
of love and protection beyond the flux of Fortune, is undeniable,
yet its significance remains as complex as the verse itself. One
effect of these lines is surely to display Chaucer's own literary
prowess by demonstrating that, in his hands at least, English
could be made to equal the most accomplished Christian poetry
ever written. Yet even here the poem refuses to preach. It offers
not a proscriptive lesson but a prayer for God's mercy. Instead
of a reasoned argument, verse is employed to suggest some of the
central mysteries of Christianity, including the three persons in
one God, a God who is also fully human, and the maiden who is
also a mother (Wheeler, 118). These mysteries are good emblems
for *Troilus* itself, whose experience, as we have seen, Chaucer
continually makes complex, contradictory and elusive.

The presence of Christianity at end of the *Troilus* is modest
rather than triumphant. It is found in questions, suggestions,
prayer, and mysteries that present no final conclusions. *Troilus*
is so designed that, just as one reader may draw a narrow moral
from its experience, so may another dismiss its Christian element
as largely irrelevant. Those who take either approach are still left
with a great poem, though one less rich than if they had responded
to the full range of its various qualities. Christianity is one part of
Troilus, for some perhaps its deepest part, but a part that, like the
poem as a whole, offers wide freedom to medieval and modern
readers. The poem ends with prayers for salvation rather than
a statement of doctrinal orthodoxy, with the love of Christ and
the protection of the Trinity rather than with lessons and rules,
and even these are gently recommended rather than mandated.
In contrast to the omnipotent Trinity at the beginning of the last
stanza, the final figure in the poem is Mary, 'mayde and moder',
the most human of those without sin and the final word, except
for 'amen', is 'benigne'.

Notes

1 The pagan setting of *Troilus* seems to absolve its characters from the strictest medieval judgement because they lack the option of Christianity. Readers who are Christian may be able to recognize the moral errors in the narrative (and might even learn from them), but the characters themselves have some excuse for their blindness. There is no reason not to think that Troilus and Criseyde are both damned, but this is deliberately left unclear by Chaucer: in contrast to Dante, he does not allow us to know the final disposition of either lover and is apparently not much interested in resolving the question.

2 The terms 'absence' and 'presence' are here used in their common, literal sense rather than in the way they are used in deconstructionist criticism.

3 This is continued with Pandarus' wonder that Venus has caused the bells to sound by themselves, a miracle common in romance and saints' lives (cf. Windeatt, *Troilus* edition, 257nIII.189).

4 See Patterson for an account of an actual fifteenth-century moralistic reading of *Troilus* (or at least of part of *Troilus*) that is far from Robertsonian.

5 Meech identifies a double ending beginning twenty-seven stanzas from the end (129–38); Malone (128) and Wheeler (105) along with many others argue for an ending of eighteen stanzas, which Malone divides into two parts; Steadman, though aware of the problems of precise definition (149–50), notes the mixture of incident and *envoi* in the last fifteen stanzas (143), the point at which Windeatt (*Troilus* edition, 557nV.1765–99) also identifies the poem as ending; Wetherbee locates the narrator's 'first attempt to conclude his poem' fourteen stanzas from the end (224), but also finds a significant new perspective in the last six stanzas, made up of two triads (235); Tatlock defines an *envoi* of twelve stanzas in six parts ('Epilog', 113–14) and Curry one of nine stanzas (165).

6 See, for instance, Markland ('Inviolability'), who argues that the disorder of the ending is both real and intentional, but who sees this as a function of the narrator. Wetherbee also reads *Troilus* as the experience of the narrator, whom he imagines 'sputtering' (225) at the end of the poem until he finally achieves a new Christian perspective (231). Note also the centrality of the narrator's experience in the challenging criticism of Carolyn Dinshaw, even though this has the effect of controlling meaning in the poem despite her professed desire to accomplish the opposite. I have tried to suggest that the reader is a better source of multiple meaning than the narrator.

Bibliography

Ad C. Herennium, ed. and trans. Harry Caplan, Loeb Classical Library (Cambridge, Mass.: Harvard University Press, 1954).

Aers, David, *Chaucer* (Brighton: Harvester, 1986).

Aers, David, 'Criseyde: woman in medieval society', *Chaucer Review*, vol. 13 (1979), pp.177–200; reprinted with some changes in *Chaucer, Langland, and the Creative Imagination* (London: Routledge, 1980).

Anderson, David, 'Theban history in Chaucer's *Troilus*', *Studies in the Age of Chaucer*, vol. 4 (1982), pp. 109–33.

apRoberts, Robert, 'The growth of Criseyde's love', in Wolf-Dietrich Bald and Horst Weinstock (eds.), *Medieval Studies Conference Aachen 1983: Language and Literature* (Frankfurt: Lang, 1984), pp. 131–41.

apRoberts, Robert, 'Love in the *Filostrato*', *Chaucer Review*, vol. 7 (1972), pp. 1–26.

apRoberts, Robert, and Seldis, Anna Bruni, (eds. and trans), *Il Filostrato* by Giovanni Boccaccio, (New York: Garland, 1986).

Arn, Mary-Jo, 'Three Ovidian women in Chaucer's *Troilus*: Medea, Helen, Oënone', *Chaucer Review*, vol. 15 (1980), pp. 1–10.

Augustine, Saint, *On Christian Doctrine*, trans. D. W. Robertson, Jr (Indianapolis, Ind.: Library of Liberal Arts, 1958).

Bal, Mieke, *Narratology: Introduction to the Theory of Narrative*, trans. Christine van Boheemen (Toronto: University of Toronto Press, 1985).

Barney, Stephen A., 'Troilus Bound', *Speculum*, vol. 47 (1972), pp. 445–58.

Barthes, Roland, 'The death of the author', in *Image-Music-Text*, trans. Stephen Heath (New York: Hill & Wang, 1977), pp. 142–8.

Bartholomew, Barbara, *Fortuna and Natura: A Reading of Three Chaucer Narratives* (The Hague: Mouton, 1966).

Baum, Paull F., *Chaucer: A Critical Appreciation* (Durham, NC: Duke University Press, 1958).

Bayley, John, *The Characters of Love* (New York: Basic Books, 1960).

Bede, *Bede's Ecclesiastical History of the English People*, ed. and trans. Bertram Colgrave and R. A. B. Mynors (Oxford: Clarendon Press, 1969).

Benoît de Sainte-Maure, *Le Roman de Troie par Benoît de Sainte-Maure*, ed. Léopold Constans, 6 vols (Paris: Firmin Didot, 1904–12).

Benson, C. David, *Chaucer's Drama of Style* (Chapel Hill, NC: University of North Carolina Press, 1986).

Benson, C. David, 'Chaucer's influence on the prose "Sege of Troy" ', *Notes and Queries*, vol. 216 (1971), pp. 127–30.

Benson, C. David, 'The *Knight's Tale* as history', *Chaucer Review*, vol. 3 (1968), pp. 107–23.

Benson, C. David, *The Medieval History of Troy in Middle English Literature* (Cambridge: Brewer, 1980).

Benson, C. David, 'True Troilus and false Cresseid: the descent from tragedy', in Piero Boitani (ed.), *The European Tragedy of Troilus* (Oxford: Clarendon Press, 1989), pp. 153–70.

Benson, C. David and Rollman David, 'Wynkyn de Worde and the ending of Chaucer's *Troilus and Criseyde*', *Modern Philology*, vol. 78 (1981), pp. 275–9.

Benson, Larry D., 'Courtly love and chivalry in the later Middle Ages', in Robert F. Yeager (ed.), *Fifteenth-Century Studies: Recent Studies* (Hamden, Conn.: Archon, 1984), pp. 237–57.

Bergin, Thomas G., *Boccaccio* (New York: Viking, 1981).

Bethurum, Dorothy, 'Chaucer's point of view as narrator in the love poems', *PMLA*, vol. 74 (1959), pp. 511–20.

Bishop, Ian, *Chaucer's 'Troilus and Criseyde': A Critical Study* (Bristol: University of Bristol Press, 1981).

Bloomfield, Morton W., 'Chaucer's sense of history', *Journal of English and Germanic Philology*, vol. 51 (1952), pp. 301–13.

Bloomfield, Morton W., 'Distance and predestination in *Troilus and Criseyde*', *PMLA*, vol. 72 (1957), pp. 14–26.

Boase, Roger, *The Origin and Meaning of Courtly Love: A Critical Study of European Scholarship* (Manchester: Manchester University Press, 1977).

Boccaccio, Giovanni, *Boccaccio on Poetry: Being the Preface and the Fourteenth and Fifteenth Books of Boccaccio's 'Genealogia Deorum Gentilium'*, trans. Charles G. Osgood (Indianapolis, Ind.: Bobbs-Merrill, 1956).

Boccaccio, Giovanni, *The Decameron*, trans. Mark Musa and Peter Bondanella (New York: Mentor, 1982).

Boccaccio, Giovanni, *Filostrato*, in Vittore Branca (ed.), *Tutte le Opere di Giovanni Boccaccio*, vol. 2 (Milan: Mondadori, 1964).

Bolton, W. F., 'Treason in *Troilus*', *Archiv*, vol. 203 (1966), pp. 255–62.

Booth, Wayne C., *The Rhetoric of Fiction* (1961; reprinted Chicago: University of Chicago Press, 1968).

Boughner, Daniel C., 'Elements of epic grandeur in the *Troilus*', *ELH* vol. 6 (1939), pp. 200–10.

Bradley, A. C., 'Hegel's theory of tragedy', *Oxford Lectures on Poetry*, 2nd edn (1909; reprinted London: Macmillan, 1950), pp. 69–95.

Branca, Vittore, *Boccaccio: The Man and His Works*, trans. Richard Monges (New York: New York University Press, 1976).

Branca, Vittore, *Il Cantare Trecentesco e il Boccaccio del Filostrato e del Teseida* (Florence: Sansoni, 1936).

Braudy, Leo, *The World in a Frame* (Garden City, NY: Doubleday, 1976).

Brewer, D. S., 'Chaucer and Chrétien and Arthurian romance', in Beryl Rowland (ed.), *Chaucer and Middle English Studies in Honour of Rossell Hope Robbins* (Kent, Ohio: Kent State University Press, 1974), pp. 255–9.

Brewer, D. S. (ed.), *Chaucer: The Critical Heritage*, 2 vols (London: Routledge, 1978).

Brewer, D. S., 'Comedy and tragedy in *Troilus and Criseyde*', in Piero Boitani (ed.), *The European Tragedy of Troilus* (Oxford: Clarendon Press, 1989), pp. 95–109.

Brewer, D. S. (ed.), *The Morte Darthur* by Thomas Malory, York Medieval Texts (Evanston, Ill.: Northwestern University Press, 1970).

Bronson, B. H., *In Search of Chaucer* (Toronto: University of Toronto Press, 1960).

Burlin, Robert B., *Chaucerian Fiction* (Princeton, NJ: Princeton University Press, 1977).

Burnley, J. D., *Chaucer's Language and the Philosophers' Tradition* (Cambridge: Brewer, 1979).

Burnley, J. D., 'Criseyde's heart and the weakness of women: an essay in lexical interpretation', *Studia Neophilologica*, vol. 54 (1982), pp. 25–38.

Burnley, J. D., *A Guide to Chaucer's Language* (Norman, Okla: University of Oklahoma Press, 1983).

Burnley, J. D., 'Proude Bayard: "Troilus and Criseyde," I.218', *Notes and Queries*, NS, vol. 23 (1976), pp. 148–52.

Burrow, John A., 'Honour and shame in *Sir Gawain and the Green Knight*', in *Essays on Medieval Literature* (Oxford: Clarendon Press, 1984), pp. 117–31.

Carton, Evan, 'Complicity and responsibility in Pandarus' bed and Chaucer's art,' *PMLA*, vol. 94 (1979), pp. 47–61.

Chatman, Seymour, *Story and Discourse* (1978; reprinted Ithaca, NY: Cornell University Press, 1986).

Chaucer, Geoffrey, *The Riverside Chaucer*, ed. Larry Benson *et al.* (Boston: Houghton Mifflin, 1987).

Chesterton, G. K., *Chaucer* (London: Faber, 1932).

Cixous, Hélène, 'The character of "character" ', *New Literary History*, vol. 5 (1974), pp. 383–402.

Clough, Andrea, 'Medieval tragedy and the genre of *Troilus and Criseyde*', *Medievalia et Humanistica*, NS, vol. 11 (1982), pp. 211–27.

Cook, Robert G., 'Chaucer's Pandarus and the medieval ideal of friendship,' *Journal of English and Germanic Philology*, vol. 69 (1970), pp. 407–24.

Conlee, John W., 'The meaning of Troilus' ascension to the Eighth Sphere', *Chaucer Review*, vol. 7 (1972), pp. 27–36.

Culler, Jonathan, *On Deconstruction: Theory and Criticism after Structuralism* (Ithaca, NY: Cornell University Press, 1982).

Cummings, Hubertis M., *The Indebtedness of Chaucer's Works to the Italian Works of Boccaccio* (1916; reprinted New York: Phaeton, 1967).

Curry, Walter C., 'Destiny in Chaucer's *Troilus*', *PMLA*, vol. 45 (1930), pp. 129–68; reprinted in *Chaucer in the Medieval Sciences*, revised edn (New York: Barnes & Noble, 1960), pp. 241–98.

Daiches, David, *A Critical History of English Literature*, vol. 1 (London: Secker & Warburg, 1961).

David, Alfred, 'Chaucerian comedy and Criseyde', in Mary Salu (ed.), *Essays on Troilus and Criseyde* (Cambridge: Brewer, 1979), pp. 90–104.

David, Alfred, 'The hero of the Troilus', *Speculum*, vol. 37 (1962), pp. 566–81.

David, Alfred, *The Strumpet Muse: Art and Morals in Chaucer's Poetry* (Bloomington, Ind.: Indiana University Press, 1976).

Dean, James, 'Chaucer's *Troilus*, Boccaccio's *Filostrato*, and the poetics of closure', *Philological Quarterly*, vol. 64 (1985), pp. 175–84.

Delany, Sheila, 'Techniques of alienation in *Troilus and Criseyde*', in A. P. Foulkes (ed.), *The Uses of Criticism* (Frankfurt: Lang, 1976), pp. 77–95.

Denomy, Alexander J., 'The two moralities of Chaucer's *Troilus and Criseyde*', *Proceedings and Transactions of the Royal Society of Canada*, 3rd ser., vol. 44 (1950), pp. 35–46.

Diamond, Arlyn, '*Troilus and Criseyde*: the politics of love', in Julian N. Wasserman and Robert J. Blanch (eds), *Chaucer in the Eighties* (Syracuse, NY: Syracuse University Press, 1986), pp. 93–103.

Dinshaw, Carolyn, 'Readers in/of *Troilus and Criseyde*', *Yale Journal of Criticism*, vol. 1 (1988), pp. 81–105.

Dodd, William George, *Courtly Love in Chaucer and Gower* (Boston, Mass.: Ginn, 1913).

Donaldson, E. Talbot, 'Chaucer in the twentieth century', *Studies in the Age of Chaucer*, vol. 2 (1980), pp. 7–13.

Donaldson, E. Talbot 'Chaucer the pilgrim', in *Speaking of Chaucer* (London: Athlone Press, 1970), pp. 1–12.

Donaldson, E. Talbot, (ed.), *Chaucer's Poetry: An Anthology for the Modern Reader* (New York: Ronald, 1958).

Donaldson, E. Talbot, 'Chaucer's Three "P's": Pandarus, Pardoner, and Poet', *Michigan Quarterly Review*, vol. 14 (1975), pp. 282–301.

Donaldson, E. Talbot, 'Cresseid false, Criseyde untrue: an ambiguity revisited', in Maynard Mack and George de Forest Lord (eds) *Poetic Traditions of the English Renaissance* (New Haven, Conn.: Yale University Press, 1982), pp. 67–83.

Donaldson, E. Talbot, 'Criseida and her narrator', in *Speaking of Chaucer* (London: Athlone Press, 1970), pp. 65–83.

Donaldson, E. Talbot, 'The ending of "Troilus" ', in *Speaking of Chaucer* (London: Athlone Press, 1970), pp. 84–101.

Donaldson, E. Talbot, 'The masculine narrator and four women of style', in *Speaking of Chaucer* (London: Athlone Press, 1970), pp. 46–64.

Donaldson, E. Talbot, 'The myth of courtly love', in *Speaking of Chaucer* (London: Athlone Press, 1970), pp. 154–63.

Donne, John, 'A Valediction: forbidding Mourning', in Helen Gardner (ed.), *The Elegies and The Songs and Sonnets* (Oxford: Clarendon Press, 1965), pp. 62-3.

Dronke, Peter, 'L'Amor che move il sole e l'altre stelle', *Studi Medievali*, vol. 6 (1965), pp. 389–422.

Dronke, Peter, 'The conclusion of *Troilus and Criseyde*', *Medium Aevum*, vol. 33 (1964), pp. 47–52.

Dunning, T. P., 'God and man in *Troilus and Criseyde*', in Norman Davis and C. L. Wrenn (eds), *English and Medieval Studies Presented to J. R. R. Tolkien on the Occasion of His Seventieth Birthday* (London: Allen & Unwin, 1962), pp. 164–82.

Durling, Robert, *The Figure of the Poet in the Renaissance Epic* (Cambridge, Mass.: Harvard University Press, 1965).

Economou, George D., 'The two Venuses and courtly love,' in Joan M. Ferrante and George D. Economou (eds), *In Pursuit of Perfection* (Port Washington, NY: Kennikat, 1975), pp. 17–50.

Elbow, Peter, 'Two Boethian speeches in *Troilus and Criseyde* and Chaucerian irony', in Phillip Damon (ed.), *Literary Criticism and Historical Understanding*, English Institute Essays 1966 (New York: Columbia University Press, 1967), pp. 85–107.

Elliott, Ralph W. V., *Chaucer's English* (London: André Deutsch, 1974).

Elyot, Thomas, *Pasquyll the Playne* (London, 1533).

Evans, Murray J., ' "Making strange": the narrator (?), the ending (?), and Chaucer's "Troilus" ', *Neuphilologische Mitteilungen*, vol. 87 (1986), pp. 218–28.

Everett, Dorothy, '*Troilus and Criseyde*', in Patricia Kean (ed.), *Essays* on *Middle English Literature* (1955; reprinted Oxford: Clarendon Press, 1959), pp. 115–38.

Farnham, Anthony, 'Chaucerian irony and the ending of the *Troilus*,' *Chaucer Review*, vol. 1 (1967), pp. 207–16.

Fish, Stanley E., *Is There a Text in This Class? The Authority of Interpretive Communities* (Cambridge, Mass.: Harvard University Press, 1980).

Fish, Stanley E., *Self-Consuming Artifacts: The Experience of Seventeenth-Century Literature* (Berkeley, Calif.: University of California Press, 1972).

Fish, Stanley E., *Surprised by Sin: The Reader in 'Paradise Lost' (London: Macmillan, 1967).*

Fish, Stanley E., 'Why no one's afraid of Wolfgang Iser', *Diacritics*, vol. 11 (1981), pp. 1–13.

Fleming, John V., 'Deiphoebus betrayed: Virgilian decorum, Chaucerian feminism', *Chaucer Review*, vol. 21 (1986), pp. 182–99.

Forster, E. M., *Aspects of the Novel* (1927; reprinted New York: Harcourt, 1973).

Frank, Robert Worth, Jr, '*Troilus and Criseyde*: the art of amplification', in Jerome Mandel and Bruce A. Rosenberg (eds), *Medieval Literature and Folklore Studies: Essays in Honor of Francis Lee Utley* (New Brunswick, NJ: Rutgers University Press, 1970), pp. 155–71.

Frankis, John, 'Paganism and pagan love in *Troilus and Criseyde*', in Mary Salu (ed.), *Essays on 'Troilus and Criseyde'* (Cambridge: Brewer, 1979), pp. 57–72.

Freiwald, Leah R., 'Swich love of frendes: Pandarus and Troilus', *Chaucer Review*, vol. 6 (1971), pp. 120–9.

Frost, Michael H., 'Narrative devices in Chaucer's *Troilus and Criseyde*', *Thoth*, vol. 14, nos 2–3 (1974), pp. 29–38.

Fyler, John M., 'The fabrications of Pandarus', *Modern Language Quarterly*, vol. 41 (1980), pp. 115–30.

Gallagher, Joseph E., 'Theology and intention in Chaucer's *Troilus*,' *Chaucer Review*, vol. 7 (1972), pp. 44–66.

Gaylord, Alan T., 'Friendship in Chaucer's *Troilus*', *Chaucer Review*, vol. 3 (1969), pp. 239–64.

Gibson, Margaret (ed.), *Boethius: His Life, Thought and Influence* (Oxford: Blackwell, 1981).

Gill, Sister Anne Barbara, *Paradoxical Patterns in Chaucer's 'Troilus': An Explanation of the Palinode* (Washington, DC: Catholic University of America Press, 1960).

Ginsberg, Warren, *The Cast of Character: The Representation of Personality in Ancient and Medieval Literature* (Toronto: University of Toronto Press, 1983).

Gleason, Mark J., 'Nicholas Trevet, Boethius, Boccaccio: contexts of cosmic love in *Troilus*, book III', *Medievalia et Humanistica*, NS, vol. 15 (1987), pp. 161–88.

Godwin, William, *Life of Geoffrey Chaucer, the Early English Poet*, 4 vols, 2nd edn (London, 1804).

Gordon, Ida L., *The Double Sorrow of Troilus: A Study of Ambiguities in 'Troilus and Criseyde'* (Oxford: Clarendon Press, 1970).

Gordon, Ida L., 'Processes of characterisation in Chaucer's *Troilus and Criseyde*', in W. Rothwell, W. R. J. Barron, D. Blamires, and L. Thorpe (eds), *Studies in Medieval Literature and Languages in Memory of Frederick Whitehead* (New York: Barnes & Noble, 1973), pp. 117–31.

Gozzi, M., 'Sulle fonti del *Filostrato*: Le narrazioni di argomento troiano', *Studi sul Boccaccio*, vol. 5 (1968), pp. 123–209.

Green, Richard F., '*Troilus* and the game of love', *Chaucer Review*, vol. 13 (1979), pp. 201–20.

Griffin, Nathaniel E., introduction to *The Filostrato of Giovanni Boccaccio*, trans Griffin and Arthur B. Myrick (Philadelphia, Pa.: University of Pennsylvania Press, 1929).

Guido delle Colonne, *Historia Destructionis Troiae*, ed. Nathaniel E. Griffin, Medieval Academy of America Publication 26 (1936; reprinted New York: Kraus, 1970); trans. Mary Elizabeth Meek (Bloomington, Ind.: Indiana University Press, 1974).

Hanning, Robert, 'Audience as co-creator of the first chivalric romances', *Yearbook of English Studies*, vol. 11 (1981), pp. 1–28.

Harvey, W. J., *Character and the Novel* (Ithaca, NY: Cornell University Press, 1965).

Havely, N. R. (ed. and trans.), *Chaucer's Boccaccio: Sources of 'Troilus' and the Knight's and Franklin's Tales* (Cambridge: Brewer, 1980).

Heidtmann, Peter, 'Sex and salvation in *Troilus and Criseyde*', *Chaucer Review*, vol. 2 (1968), pp. 246–53.

Henryson, Robert, *The Poems of Robert Henryson*, ed. Denton Fox (Oxford: Clarendon Press, 1981).

Hochman, Baruch, *Character in Literature* (Ithaca, NY: Cornell University Press, 1985).

Hollander, Robert, *Boccaccio's Two Venuses* (New York: Columbia University Press, 1977).

Howard, Donald R., 'Experience, language, and consciousness: *Troilus and Criseyde*, II, 596–931', in Jerome Mandel and Bruce A. Rosenberg (eds), *Medieval Literature and Folklore Studies: Essays in Honor of Francis Lee Utley* (New Brunswick, NJ: Rutgers University Press, 1970), pp. 173–92.

Howard, Donald R., 'Literature and sexuality: book III of Chaucer's *Troilus*', *Massachusetts Review*, vol. 8 (1967), pp. 442–56.

Howard, Donald R., *The Three Temptations: Medieval Man in Search of the World* (Princeton, NJ: Princeton University Press, 1966).

Howard, Donald R. and Dean, James (eds), *Troilus and Criseyde and Selected Short Poems* (New York: Signet, 1976).

Howell, Thomas, 'The britlenesse of thinges mortall', *New Sonets, and Pretie Pamphlets*, in Alexander B. Grosart (ed.), *Occasional Issues of Unique or Very Rare Books* (Privately printed, 1879), pp. 121–2.

Iser, Wolfgang, *The Act of Reading: A Theory of Aesthetic Response* (Baltimore, Md.: Johns Hopkins University Press, 1978).

Jauss, Hans Robert, *Toward an Aesthetic of Reception*, trans. Timothy Bahti (Minneapolis, Minn.: Minnesota University Press, 1982).

Jordan, Robert M., *Chaucer and the Shape of Creation: The Aesthetic Possibilities of Inorganic Structure* (Cambridge, Mass.: Harvard University Press, 1967).

Jordan, Robert M., 'The narrator in Chaucer's *Troilus*', *ELH*, vol. 25 (1958), pp. 237–57.

Kane, George, 'Chaucer, love poetry, and romantic love', in Mary J. Carruthers and Elizabeth D. Kirk (eds), *Acts of Interpretation: The Text in Its Contexts, 700–1600. Essays on Medieval and Renaissance Literature in Honor of E. Talbot Donaldson* (Norman, Okla.: Pilgrim Books, 1982), pp. 237–55.

Kean, P. M., *Chaucer and the Making of English Poetry*, Vol. 1: *Love Vision and Debate* (London: Routledge, 1972).

Kean, P. M., 'Chaucer's dealings with a stanza of *Il Filostrato* and the epilogue of *Troilus and Criseyde*', *Medium Aevum*, vol. 33 (1964), pp. 36–46.

Kelly, Henry Ansgar, *Love and Marriage in the Age of Chaucer* (Ithaca, NY: Cornell University Press, 1975).

Kermode, Frank, 'The use of the codes', in *The Art of Telling: Essays on Fiction* (Cambridge, Mass.: Harvard University Press, 1983), pp. 72–91.

Kirby, T. A., *Chaucer's 'Troilus': A Study in Courtly Love* (University, La: Louisiana State University Press, 1940).

Kittredge, George Lyman, *Chaucer and His Poetry* (Cambridge, Mass.: Harvard University Press, 1915).

Kittredge, George Lyman, 'Chaucer's Lollius', *Harvard Studies in Classical Philology*, vol. 28 (1917), pp. 47–133.

Knight, Stephen, *Geoffrey Chaucer* (Oxford: Blackwell, 1986).

Kolve, V. A., *Chaucer and the Imagery of Narrative: The First Five Canterbury Tales* (Stanford, Calif.: Stanford University Press, 1984).

Kynaston, Francis, 'Chaucer's *Troilus*: Sir Francis Kynaston's Latin translation, with a critical edition of his English comments and Latin annotations', by Judith M. Newton. PhD dissertation, University of Illinois, 1967.

Lambert, Mark, '*Troilus*, books I-III: a Criseydan reading', in Mary Salu (ed.), *Essays on 'Troilus and Criseyde'* (Cambridge: Brewer, 1979), pp. 105–25.

Lanham, Richard A., 'Game, play, and high seriousness in Chaucer's poetry', *English Studies*, vol. 48 (1967), pp. 1–24.

Lanham, Richard A., 'Opaque style and its uses in *Troilus and Criseyde*', *Studies in Medieval Culture*, vol. 3 (1970), pp. 169–76.

Lawlor, John, *Chaucer* (1968; reprinted New York: Harper, 1969).

Lawton, David, *Chaucer's Narrators* (Cambridge: Brewer, 1985).

Lawton, David, 'Irony and sympathy in *Troilus and Criseyde*: a reconsideration', *Leeds Studies in English*, NS, vol. 14 (1983), pp. 94–115.

Legouis, Emile, *Geoffrey Chaucer*, trans. L. Lailavoix (London: Dent, 1913).

Leitch, Thomas, *What Stories Are: Narrative Theory and Interpretation* (University Park, Pa: Pennsylvania State University Press, 1986).

Lewis, C. S., *The Allegory of Love: A Study in Medieval Tradition* (London: Oxford University Press, 1936).

Lewis, C. S., 'What Chaucer really did to *Il Filostrato*', *Essays and Studies*, vol. 17 (1932), pp. 56–75.

Leyerle, John, 'The heart and the chain', in Larry D. Benson (ed.), *The Learned and the Lewed: Studies in Chaucer and Medieval Literature*, Harvard English Studies 5 (Cambridge, Mass.: Harvard University Press, 1974), pp. 113–45.

Lounsbury, Thomas R., *Studies in Chaucer*, 3 vols (New York: Harper, 1892).

Lowes, John Livingston, *Geoffrey Chaucer* (1934; reprinted Bloomington, Ind.: Indiana University Press, 1958).

Lumiansky, Robert M., 'The story of Troilus and Briseida according to Benoit and Guido', *Speculum*, vol. 29 (1954), pp. 727–33.

McAlpine, Monica E., *The Genre of 'Troilus and Criseyde'* (Ithaca, NY: Cornell University Press, 1978).

McCall, John, *Chaucer among the Gods: The Poetics of Classical Myth* (University Park, Pa: Pennsylvania State University Press, 1979).

McCall, John, 'Five-book structure in Chaucer's *Troilus*', *Modern Language Quarterly*, vol. 23 (1962), pp. 297–308.

McCall, John, '*Troilus and Criseyde*', in Beryl Rowland (ed.), *Companion to Chaucer Studies*, revised edn (New York: Oxford University Press, 1979), pp. 446–63.

Magoun, Francis P., Jr, *A Chaucer Gazeteer* (Chicago, Ill.: University of Chicago Press, 1961).

Maguire, John B., 'The clandestine marriage of *Troilus and Criseyde*', *Chaucer Review*, vol. 8 (1974), pp. 262–78.

Malone, Kemp, *Chapters on Chaucer* (Baltimore, Md: Johns Hopkins University Press, 1951).

Mann, Jill, 'Chance and destiny in *Troilus and Criseyde* and the *Knight's Tale*', in Piero Boitani and Jill Mann (eds), *The Cambridge Chaucer Companion* (Cambridge: Cambridge University Press, 1986), pp. 75–92.

Mann, Jill, *Chaucer and Medieval Estates Satire: The Literature of Social Classes and the General Prologue to the Canterbury Tales* (Cambridge: Cambridge University Press, 1973).

Mann, Jill, 'Troilus' swoon', *Chaucer Review*, vol. 14 (1980), pp. 319–35.

Markland, Murray F., 'Pilgrims errant: the doubleness of *Troilus and Criseyde*', *Research Studies*, vol. 33 (1965), pp. 64–77.

Markland, Murray F., '*Troilus and Criseyde*: the inviolability of the ending', *Modern Language Quarterly*, vol. 31 (1970), pp. 147–59.

Mayo, Robert D., 'The Trojan background of the *Troilus*', *ELH*, vol. 9 (1942), pp. 245–56.

Meech, Sanford B., *Design in Chaucer's 'Troilus'* Syracuse, NY: Syracuse University Press, 1959).

Mehl, Dieter, 'The audience of Chaucer's *Troilus and Criseyde*', in Beryl Rowland (ed.), *Chaucer and Middle English Studies in Honor of Rossell Hope Robbins* (Kent, Ohio: Kent State University Press, 1974), pp. 173–89.

Mehl, Dieter, *Geoffrey Chaucer: An Introduction to His Narrative Poetry* (Cambridge: Cambridge University Press, 1986).

Mieszkowski, Gretchen, 'The reputation of Criseyde 1155–1500', *Transactions of the Connecticut Academy of Arts and Sciences*, vol. 43 (1971), pp. 71–153.

Miller, Ralph N., 'Pandarus and Procne', *Studies in Medieval Culture*, vol. 7 (1964), pp. 65–8.

Minnis, Alastair J., 'Aspects of the medieval French and English traditions of the *De Consolatione Philosophiae*', in Margaret Gibson (ed.), *Boethius: His Life, Thought and Influence* (Oxford: Blackwell, 1981), pp. 312–61.

Minnis, Alastair J., *Chaucer and Pagan Antiquity* (Cambridge: Brewer, 1982).

Miskimin, Alice S., *The Renaissance Chaucer* (New Haven, Conn.: Yale University Press, 1975).

Mizener, Arthur, 'Character and action in the case of Criseyde', *PMLA*, vol. 54 (1939), pp. 65–81.

Moorman, Charles, ' "Once more unto the breach": the meaning of *Troilus and Criseyde*', *Studies in the Literary Imagination*, vol. 4, no. 2 (1971), pp. 61–71.

Morgan, Gerald, 'The ending of "Troilus and Criseyde"', *Modern Language Review*, vol. 77 (1982), pp. 257–71.

Morgan, Gerald, 'The freedom of the lovers in *Troilus and Criseyde*', in John Scattergood (ed.), *Literature and Learning in Medieval and Renaissance England: Essays Presented to Fitzroy Pyle* (Blackrock, Dublin: Irish Academic Press, 1984), pp. 59–102.

Musa, Mark (trans.), *Dante's Vita Nuova* (Bloomington, Ind.: Indiana University Press, 1973).

Muscatine, Charles, *Chaucer and the French Tradition: A Study in Style and Meaning* (Berkeley, Calif.: University of California Press, 1957).

Muscatine, Charles, 'The feigned illness in Chaucer's *Troilus and Criseyde*", *Modern Language Notes,*, vol. 63 (1948), pp. 372–7.

Muscatine, Charles, *Poetry and Crisis in the Age of Chaucer* (Notre Dame, Ind.: University of Notre Dame Press, 1972).

Natali, Giulia, 'A lyrical version: Boccaccio's *Filostrato*', in Piero Boitani (ed), *The European Tragedy of Troilus* (Oxford: Clarendon Press, 1989), pp. 49–73.

Norton-Smith, John, *Geoffrey Chaucer* (London: Routledge, 1974).

Olson, Glending, *Literature as Recreation in the Later Middle Ages* (Ithaca, NY: Cornell University Press, 1982).

Ong, Walter J., 'The writer's audience is always a fiction', *PMLA*, vol. 90 (1975), pp. 9–21.

Osberg, Richard H., 'Between the motion and the act: intentions and ends in Chaucer's *Troilus*', *ELH*, vol. 48 (1981), pp. 257–70.

Owen, Charles A., Jr, 'Mimetic form in the central love scene of *Troilus and Criseyde*', *Modern Philology*, vol. 67 (1969), pp. 125–32.

Owen, Charles A., Jr, 'The significance of Chaucer's revisions of *Troilus and Criseyde*', *Modern Philology*, vol. 55 (1957), pp. 1–5.

Paris, Gaston, 'Etudes sur les romans de la Table Ronde. Lancelot du Lac.II. Le Conte de la Charette', *Romania*, vol. 12 (1883), pp. 459–534.

Patch, Howard R., *The Goddess Fortuna in Mediaeval Literature* (Cambridge, Mass.: Harvard University Press, 1927).

Patch, Howard R., *On Rereading Chaucer* (1939; reprinted Cambridge, Mass.: Harvard University Press, 1959).

Patch, Howard R., 'Troilus on determinism', *Speculum*, vol. 6 (1931), pp. 225–43.

Patch, Howard R., 'Troilus on predestination', *Journal of English and Germanic Philology*, vol. 17 (1918), pp. 399–422.

Patterson, Lee W., 'Ambiguity and interpretation: a fifteenth-century reading of *Troilus and Criseyde*', *Speculum*, vol. 54 (1979), pp. 297–330.

Payne, Robert O., *Geoffrey Chaucer*, 2nd edn (Boston, Mass.: Twayne, 1986).

Payne, Robert O., *The Key of Remembrance: A Study of Chaucer's Poetics* (1963; reprinted Westport, Conn.: Greenwood, 1973).

Pearsall, Derek, 'Criseyde's choices', *Studies in the Age of Chaucer, Proceedings*, vol. 2 (1986), pp. 17–29.

Pratt, Robert A., 'Chaucer and *Le Roman de Troyle et de Criseida*', *Studies in Philology*, vol. 53 (1956), pp. 509–39.

Pratt, Robert A., 'Chaucer's use of the *Teseida*', *PMLA*, vol. 62 (1947), pp. 598–621.

Provost, William, *The Structure of Chaucer's 'Troilus and Criseyde'*, Anglistica 20 (Copenhagen, 1974).

Reichl, Karl, 'Chaucer's *Troilus*: philosophy and language', in Piero Boitani (ed.), *The European Tragedy of Troilus* (Oxford: Clarendon Press, 1989), pp. 133–52.

Reiss, Edmund, '*Fin' amors*: its history and meaning in medieval literature', *Medieval and Renaissance Studies*, vol. 8 (1979), pp. 74–99.

Reiss, Edmund, 'Troilus and the failure of understanding', *Modern Language Quarterly*, vol. 29 (1968), pp. 131–44.

Rimmon-Kenan, Shlomith, *Narrative Fiction: Contemporary Poetics* (London: Methuen, 1983).

Robertson, Durant W., Jr, 'Chaucerian tragedy', *ELH*, vol. 19 (1952), pp. 1–37.

Robertson, Durant W., Jr, *Chaucer's London* (New York: Wiley, 1968).

Robertson, Durant W., Jr, 'Courtly love as an impediment to the understanding of medieval literary texts', in F. X. Newman (ed.), *The Meaning of Courtly Love* (Albany, NY: State University of New York Press, 1968), pp. 1–18.

Robertson, Durant W., Jr, *A Preface to Chaucer: Studies in Medieval Perspectives* (Princeton, NJ.: Princeton University Press, 1963).

Robinson, Ian, *Chaucer and the English Tradition* (Cambridge: Cambridge University Press, 1972).

Rollins, Hyder E., 'The Troilus-Cressida Story from Chaucer to Shakespeare', *PMLA*, vol. 32 (1917), pp. 383–429.

Le Roman de Troyle et de Criseida, as *Le Roman de Troilus et de Criseida* in *Nouvelles Françoises en prose du XIVe siècle*, ed. L. Moland and C. d'Héricault (Paris, 1858).

Root, Robert K. (ed.), *The Book of Troilus and Criseyde* by Geoffrey Chaucer (1926; reprinted Princeton, NJ: Princeton University Press, 1945).

Root, Robert K., *The Poetry of Chaucer*, revised edn (Boston, Mass.: Houghton Mifflin, 1922).

Rossetti, William M. (ed.), *Chaucer's 'Troylus and Criseyde' Compared with Boccaccio's 'Filostrato'*, Chaucer Society, 1st ser., vols 44 and 65 (London: 1875).

Rowe, Donald, *O Love O Charite! Contraries Harmonized in Chaucer's Troilus* (Carbondale, Ill.: Southern Illinois University Press, 1976).

Salter, Elizabeth, '*Troilus and Criseyde*: poet and narrator', in Mary J. Carruthers and Elizabeth D. Kirk (eds), *Acts of Interpretation: The Text in Its Contexts, 700–1600. Essays on Medieval and Renaissance Literature in Honor of E. Talbot Donaldson* (Norman, Okla.: Pilgrim Books, 1982), pp. 281–91.

Salter, Elizabeth, '*Troilus and Criseyde*: a reconsideration', in John Lawlor (ed.), *Patterns of Love and Courtesy: Essays in Memory of C. S. Lewis* (Evanston, Ill.: Northwestern University Press, 1966), pp. 86–106.

Schless, Howard, 'Transformations: Chaucer's use of Italian', in D. S. Brewer (ed.), *Chaucer*, Writers and Their Background (Athens, Ohio: Ohio University Press, 1975), pp. 184–223.

Scholes, Robert, *Textual Power* (New Haven, Conn.: Yale University Press, 1985).

Scholes, Robert and Kellogg, Robert, *The Nature of Narrative* (1966; reprinted London: Oxford University Press, 1975).

Schweickart, Patrocinio, 'Reading ourselves: toward a feminist theory of reading', in Robert Con Davis and Ronald Schliefer (eds), *Contemporary Literary Criticism: Literary and Cultural Studies*, 2nd edn (New York/London: Longman, 1988).

Shanley, James L., 'The *Troilus* and Christian love', *ELH*, vol. 6 (1939), pp. 271–81.

Shepherd, Geoffrey T., 'Religion and philosophy in Chaucer', in D. S. Brewer (ed.), Chaucer, Writers and Their Background (Athens, Ohio: Ohio University Press, 1975), pp. 262–89.

Shepherd, Geoffrey T., '*Troilus and Criseyde*', in D. S. Brewer (ed.), *Chaucer and Chaucerians* (University, Ala: University of Alabama Press, 1966), pp. 65–87.

Shoaf, R. A. (ed.), *Troilus and Criseyde* by Geoffrey Chaucer (East Lansing, Mich.: Colleagues Press, 1989).

Slaughter, Eugene E., 'Love and grace in Chaucer's *Troilus*', in *Essays in Honor of Walter Clyde Curry*, Vanderbilt Studies in the Humanities 2 (Nashville, Tenn.: Vanderbilt University Press, 1955), pp. 61–76.

Smalley, Beryl, *The Study of the Bible in the Middle Ages* (Oxford: Blackwell, 1952).

Smarr, Janet L., *Boccaccio and Fiammetta: The Narrator as Lover* (Urbana, Ill.: University of Illinois Press, 1986).

Smyser, H. M., 'The domestic background of *Troilus and Criseyde*', *Speculum*, vol. 31 (1956), pp. 297–315.

Spearing, A. C., *Chaucer: 'Troilus and Criseyde'* (London: Arnold, 1976).

Spearing, A. C., *Readings in Medieval Poetry* (Cambridge: Cambridge University Press, 1987).

Spurgeon, Caroline F. E., *Five Hundred Years of Chaucer Criticism and*

Allusion, 1357–1900, 3 vols (1925; reprinted New York: Russell & Russell, n.d.).

Stanley, E. G., 'About Troilus', *Essays and Studies*, vol. 29 (1976), pp. 84–106.

Steadman, John M., *Disembodied Laughter: 'Troilus' and the Apotheosis Tradition* (Berkeley, Calif.: University of California Press, 1972).

Steiner, George, *The Death of Tragedy* (1961; reprinted London: Faber, 1974).

Stevens, Martin, 'The winds of Fortune in the *Troilus*', *Chaucer Review*, vol. 13 (1979), pp. 285–307.

Strohm, Paul, '*Storie, spelle, geste, romaunce, tragedie*: generic distinctions in the Middle English Troy narratives', *Speculum*, vol. 46 (1971), pp. 348–59.

Suleiman, Susan R. and Crosman, Inge (eds), *The Reader in the Text: Essays on Audience and Interpretation* (Princeton, NJ: Princeton University Press, 1980).

Taine, H. A., *History of English Literature*, trans. H. van Laun, 4th edn, Vol. 1 (Edinburgh, 1873).

Tatlock, J. S. P., 'The epilog of Chaucer's *Troilus*', *Modern Philology*, vol. 18 (1921), pp. 625–59.

Tatlock, J. S. P., *The Mind and Art of Chaucer* (Syracuse, NY.: Syracuse University Press, 1950).

Tatlock, J. S. P., 'The people in Chaucer's *Troilus*', *PMLA*, vol. 56 (1941), pp. 85–104.

Taylor, Karla, *Chaucer Reads 'The Divine Comedy'* (Stanford, Calif.: Stanford University Press, 1989).

Tompkins, Jane P. (ed.), *Reader Response Criticism: From Formalism to Post-Structuralism* (Baltimore, Md.: Johns Hopkins University Press, 1980).

Toole, William B., III, 'The imagery of fortune and religion in *Troilus and Criseyde*', in Jack D. Durant and M. Thomas Hester (eds), *A Fair Day in the Affections: Literary Essays in Honor of Robert B. White, Jr* (Raleigh, NC: Winston Press, 1980), pp. 25–35.

Travis, Peter W., 'Affective criticism, the pilgrimage of reading, and medieval English literature', in Laurie A. Finke and Martin B. Shichtman (eds), *Medieval Texts and Contemporary Readers* (Ithaca, NY: Cornell University Press, 1987), pp. 201–15.

Tyrwhitt, Thomas (ed.), *The Canterbury Tales of Chaucer*, 4 vols (London: Payne, 1775).

Wack, Mary F, 'Lovesickness in *Troilus*', *Pacific Coast Philology*, vol. 19 (1984), pp. 55–61.

Walker, Ian C., 'Chaucer and "Il Filostrato" ', *English Studies*, vol. 49 (1968), pp. 318–26.

Wallace, David, 'Chaucer and Boccaccio's early writings', in Piero

Boitani (ed.), *Chaucer and the Italian Trecento* (Cambridge: Cambridge University Press, 1983), pp. 141–62.

Wallace, David, *Chaucer and the Early Writings of Boccaccio* (Cambridge: Brewer, 1985).

Wenzel, Siegfried, 'Chaucer's Troilus of book IV', *PMLA*, vol. 79 (1964), pp. 542–7.

West, Michael D., 'Dramatic time, setting, and motivation in Chaucer', *Chaucer Review*, vol. 2 (1968), pp. 172–87.

Wetherbee, Winthrop, *Chaucer and the Poets: An Essay on Troilus and Criseyde* (Ithaca, NY: Cornell University Press, 1984).

Wheeler, Bonnie, 'Dante, Chaucer, and the ending of *Troilus and Criseyde*', *Philological Quarterly*, vol. 61 (1982), pp. 105–23.

Wilson, Rawdon, 'On character: a reply to Martin Price', *Critical Inquiry*, vol. 2 (1975), pp. 191–8.

Wimsatt, James I., 'Guillaume de Machaut and Chaucer's *Troilus and Criseyde*', *Medium Aevum*, vol. 45 (1976), pp. 277–93.

Wimsatt, James I., 'Medieval and modern in Chaucer's *Troilus and Criseyde*', *PMLA*, vol. 92 (1977), pp. 203–16.

Windeatt, Barry A., 'Chaucer and the *Filostrato*', in Piero Boitani *(ed.)*, *Chaucer and the Italian Trecento* (Cambridge: Cambridge University Press, 1983), pp. 163–83.

Windeatt, Barry A., 'The text of the *Troilus*', in Mary Salu (ed.), *Essays on Troilus and Criseyde* (Cambridge: Brewer, 1979), pp. 1–22.

Windeatt, Barry A. (ed.), *Troilus and Criseyde* by Geoffrey Chaucer (London: Longman, 1984).

Wood, Chauncey, 'Affective stylistics and the study of Chaucer', *Studies in the Age of Chaucer*, vol. 6 (1984), pp. 21–40.

Wood, Chauncey, *The Elements of Chaucer's Troilus* (Durham, NC:. Duke University Press, 1984).

Young, Karl, 'Chaucer's *Troilus and Criseyde* as romance', *PMLA*, vol. 53 (1938), pp. 38–63.

Young, Karl, *The Origin and Development of the Story of Troilus and Criseyde* (1908; reprinted New York: Gordian, 1968).

Index